The Oblate Life

The Oblate Life

Edited by
Gervase Holdaway OSB

LITURGICAL PRESS
Collegeville, Minnesota
www.litpress.org

© The Contributors 2008

First published in 2008 by the Canterbury Press Norwich
(a publishing imprint of Hymns Ancient & Modern Limited,
a registered charity)
13–17 Long Lane, London EC1A 9PN

Published in the United States of America and Canada
by Liturgical Press, Collegeville, Minnesota 56321

British Library Cataloguing in Publication data

A catalogue record for this book is available
from the British Library

ISBN 978-0-8146-3176-8

Printed in the United States of America.

Contents

Foreword

In recent years all over the world, in countries where there are Benedictine monks and nuns, laypeople are showing a growing interest in the spirituality of St Benedict. This spirituality, anchored in the Scriptures, and the communites that live according to it are attractive to many people. For this reason we are very grateful for a handbook that deals with every aspect of the life of a Benedictine secular oblate.

Oblates are women and men who through association with a specific monastic community place their lives at the service of God while remaining at home in the world, fulfilling their obligations to their families and in their working lives. At the same time they have a particular vocation to be in places where God is present in the world. A Benedictine community has a life of its own, devoted first and foremost to the praise of God. It is the function of the secular oblate to carry this message to the wider world outside the monastery. It is a real vocation which is described and explained in this handbook. Here we are dealing with family life but also with giving witness to the merciful love of God in our day.

I am convinced that our oblates play an important role in the task of evangelization, both in countries where the Christian message is gradually being forgotten and in countries that are looking for new values on which to build individual lives and society as a whole. Christ is our origin, Christ is our goal, Christ is our anchor.

My wish is that through the witness of our oblates as many people as possible will come to hear of Christ, will come to know

him and make him the centre of their lives. This is the great task
that faces us.

† Notker Wolf OSB
Abbot Primate
Rome
Feast of St Monica 2008

Introduction

GERVASE HOLDAWAY

At the time of the first Oblates' World Congress in 2005, it was estimated that there were over 25,000 Benedictine oblates worldwide. It was considered a conservative estimate then and the number is certainly greater now. Although there have been oblates for many centuries, it seems to have been only since about 1980 that the number has increased exponentially, and this increase appears to be almost in adverse proportion to the decrease in the number of professed monastics. The number of oblates now greatly exceeds that of monks and nuns.

Also present at the Congress were Cistercian 'oblates'. For historical reasons the Cistercians (O CIST.) have not had an oblate tradition, but in the last few decades there have been so-called 'lay Cistercians', and 'today there are 48 Abbeys in the worldwide Cistercian family with around 900 lay Cistercians or Cistercian Oblates in 19 countries'.[1] The Cistercians of the Strict Observance, the Trappists (OCSO) also have oblates or lay associates.

In his closing speech at the first World Congress of Benedictine Oblates, the Abbot Primate, Notker Wolf OSB, emphasized 'communion', the theme of the congress, and he added 'naturally we need to be linked, to share and to communicate'. It is opportune, therefore, that to help facilitate this 'communication', a handbook for English-speaking oblates should appear at this time, before the second Oblates' World Congress in 2009. The majority of essays in this collection are the work of oblates or monastics of various monasteries.

St Benedict did not found an order. There is no such thing as a

Benedictine order; each monastery is independent and autonomous. For mutual support, monasteries are gathered into congregations, and the congregations, since 1887, have belonged to the Benedictine Confederation, whose leader is the Abbot Primate. There are some Benedictine congregations, mostly of more recent date and which undertake particular work, that are more akin to an order, such, for example, as the Sisters of Grace and Compassion, a congregation which entered into full association with the Benedictine Confederation in 1992, and which is ruled by a Prioress General, but these are the exception.

Since each monastery is independent, it follows that each has its own character and customs, its own personality. As oblates belong to a particular monastery, they will share in the personality of their community, as well as having the benefit of life 'outside the walls'. The particular character of a monastery is an important factor when an aspiring oblate is searching for a community to join, and often someone interested in becoming an oblate will visit several monasteries before deciding to make a commitment to a particular community.

In a symposium of this nature, there will be expressed a diversity of views, which are not necessarily those of the editor. St Benedict's Rule begins with the word *obsculta*, 'listen'. Listening is essential to being Benedictine, so it behoves us to listen to others speaking, especially when they come from a tradition different from our own, that we may be enriched by something that they may have to offer. Inevitably in a book such as this there is bound to be some repetition of ideas, since each writer has worked independently; to have edited out every overlap would not only have been a well nigh impossible task, but would often have emasculated an author's work.

As oblates have increased in number in recent years, so they have changed somewhat from their forebears. In a paper presented at the North American Oblate Directors' meeting in July 1999 and reproduced among the pre-Convention papers for the American Benedictine Academy Convention 2000, Norvene Vest explained this change. While the older idea was that the oblates were a task force for the monasteries, helping in the shop or the office, raising funds, repairing equipment, painting, cooking and so on, in return for which they attended periodic meetings at the monastery where 'Father' gave a presentation, contemporary oblates share in the spiritual and prayer life of the community, living the Rule as far as their situation in the world allows.

> I am suggesting that monastics and oblates can be mutual bless-ings, not just to provide mutual support and encouragement, though that is certainly important. But the mutual blessing may also be a shared vocation to help one another in the crucial task which God gives to Benedictines in this time: that together, monastics and oblates are to be a witness and a challenge to our society as a whole.[2]

No longer are oblates merely passive recipients of formation and teaching offered by the monastics; now oblates themselves are well able to share in this ministry of formation and teaching, as many of the essays in this symposium bear witness. Moreover, one has only to glance at the bibliography at the end of this volume[3] to see how many books are written by oblates, and from various Christian traditions.

'A witness and challenge to our society as a whole': the follower of St Benedict is called upon to exercise a prophetic role, to demonstrate an alternative cultural ethos to the prevailing one. Historically St Benedict has been thought of as exercising a prophetic function in the church and society.[4] As Marcelo Barros OSB said in a paper presented to the 2005 Oblates' Congress, 'In the course of history, for a certain time, monasteries represented a prophetic instance that helped the Churches to remember their evangelical vocation.'[5] In his day St Benedict was counter-cultural; becoming disenchanted with the decadence of the city and the disintegration of society, he left for a life of solitude, but was per-suaded to set up his own community, firmly constructed on Christian principles. 'Your way of acting should be different from the world's way' (*RB* 4.20) is among the teachings he gave his monks. Thus St Benedict was able to give the world witness of an alternative way of living, one which is solidly rooted in the gospel.

There are many similarities between the Rome of Benedict's time and our own age. We live in an age of individualism, where we are encouraged to achieve personal fulfilment as our aim in life, and to become the centre of our own universe. The oblate formed by St Benedict's Rule will challenge this assumption; seeking one's own fulfilment would never find a place as a maxim in St Benedict's thinking; rather, 'no one is to pursue what he judges better for himself, but instead, what he judges better for someone else' (*RB* 72.7).

We live in a world of great instability and rapid change. St Benedict shows us how to live out the gospel in the midst of such a world. The principle of stability is basic to Benedict's thought, and this is not to be limited to those living within the monastery; it is a principle to be practised by oblates.

The abbot in a monastery has to be a person who listens. This an important quality, to be cherished especially by those oblates who find themselves in leadership positions, whether in civil society or in the church. In his address given to a general audience in St Peter's Square on 9 April 2008, Pope Benedict XVI said:

In order to be capable of making responsible decisions, the abbot must also be someone who listens to 'the advice of his brothers' (*RB* 3.2), because 'God often reveals the most apt solution to the youngest person' (*RB* 3.3). This attitude makes the Rule, written almost fifteen centuries ago very current! A man with public responsibility, even in small circles, must always be a man who knows how to listen and to learn from what he hears.[6]

St Benedict has a chapter devoted to the cellarer of the monastery. Oblates, living in their own homes and running their own households, have to be their own cellarers, so the attributes of the cellarer as listed by Benedict have to apply to every oblate. All should endeavour to become people who are 'wise, mature in conduct, temperate, not excessive eaters, not proud, excitable, offensive, dilatory or wasteful, but God-fearing, and like a father to the whole community' (*RB* 31.1–2). The cellarer is required to be sober and not a great eater. These counsels must extend beyond the narrow confines of food and drink; it is not just a question of avoiding drunkenness and gluttony, but of not filling oneself with unnecessary things that are purely material or ephemeral, seeking instant personal gratification whether through food, drugs, sex or entertainment. Oblates, like the abbot, 'must not show too great concern for the fleeting and temporal things of this world' (*RB* 2.33), but should look for deeper values than mere instant gratification.

We live in a 'throw-away' society but St Benedict teaches us to practise the very opposite. To be wasteful shows a lack of respect for creation and for good management, but being Benedictine means respecting all of creation and caring for it. Wherever possible we should recycle things when we have no further need of them. To throw something away as rubbish, when it can still serve someone else, or can be transformed into something else useful, is quite contrary to the spirit of St Benedict's teaching. The oblate should be a model for our contemporary society in showing how created things are to be valued. If they are broken or damaged they should, if possible, be repaired.

Another area where oblates can show an alternative witness is regarding property and possessions. For monastics in the monastery the Rule is quite definite: 'No one may presume to give, accept or keep anything as personal property' (*RB* 33.2). Everyone needs to remember that there is really no such thing as absolute ownership; everything has been created by God and all belongs to him, we are but stewards of whatever is in our care. 'Outside the walls' we must be careful not to strive for a bigger house, a more prosperous business, more luxurious gadgets. We should avoid the materialistic spiral. 'Do we actually need more?' is a question that should be constantly asked, since contemporary human beings, goaded on by the advertising industry, seem to have an inordinate desire always to acquire bigger and better. We should value whatever we have, and never take things for granted, even the commonest such as water, remembering how many people in the world today lack even such basics as clean water. It is a consumerist society that we see around us, but when faced with the chance of

acquiring something we must always ask ourselves, 'Do we really
need it?' Are we obsessed with gain to the extent that we sin against
our needy brothers and sisters? Sharing is a way to detachment and
real joy. How true it is that it is better to give than to receive. In the
use of material, created things the Benedictine approach should be
to seek only what is necessary, and not to acquire more than is
needed; superfluity should be avoided at all costs.

Another, related, area for giving witness is conservation;
Benedict invites us to care about everyday things. 'On Saturday the
brother who is completing his work will do the washing. He is to
wash the towels which the brothers use to wipe their hands and
feet' (*RB* 35.7–8). 'The utensils required for the kitchen service are
to be washed and returned intact to the cellarer, who in turn issues
them to the one beginning his week. In this way the cellarer will
know what he hands out and what he receives back' (*RB*
35.10–11). 'All utensils and goods of the monastery are to be
regarded as if they were the sacred vessels of the altar' (*RB* 31.10).
'Whoever fails to keep the things belonging to the monastery clean
or treats them carelessly should be reproved' (*RB* 32.4). Benedict is
saying that all the things that we touch or use are to be handled
reverently and looked after, kept in good condition. Oblates
should take care of whatever articles they use, clean them after use
and put them away carefully, since whatever we have for our use is
only on loan, and should, if needful, be available to others who
come after us. A grave danger in the modern world is built-in
obsolescence. The Benedictine should, wherever possible, look for
objects that are fit for purpose, able to do the job for which they are
intended, which are designed for a long life of service, and which
can be repaired should they break. This is something foreign to
contemporary thinking and is where the oblate can show that there
are viable alternative values by which to live.

When we come to seek an explanation as to why so many people
have become oblates in the last few decades, although the immediate answer is that there are as many answers as there are individuals concerned, there are nevertheless discernable overall reasons. It
seems that many Christians, like St Benedict, find the modern
secular materialist environment unsatisfactory; there is a need to

seek a deeper meaning to life, and this can be found in the Rule of Benedict, since it can be adapted to situations outside the walls of a monastery. Not all are called to the vowed life of a monastic, but many feel called to take on the principles developed by St Benedict. The framework of regular times of prayer, work, reading give people a structure in which to live their Christian vocation. The counter-cultural features of the Rule present a strong invitation to live an evangelical life in the midst of a world which promotes other values with increasing clamour. The Holy Spirit is at work here. Each one has to discern where the Spirit is calling and leading.

The fundamental question for all oblates as for vowed monastics is the basic question St Benedict poses regarding admittance to the monastery: 'the concern must be whether the novice truly seeks God' (*RB* 58.7). The oblate must never lose sight of that question, which is posed in the rite of admittance of novices. In this secular age, which is indifferent or even antagonistic to Christianity, the expectation is that those who do have religious beliefs keep them private, restricted to an hour one day a week. Faith must not be allowed to affect behaviour during the rest of the week. However, for anyone living by St Benedict's Rule there can be no demarcation between the spiritual and the secular; all life is holy, and oblates will show this by the way in which they live, thereby giving hope and encouragement to those people they come across who are searching for God, even though these may be unable to articulate that desire. Benedict does not expect anyone to be other than themselves as they try to live by the Rule. As Benedictines, oblates aim to be sensible people, living simple and balanced lives, who find time for play as well as prayer, who believe and live by the standards of the Christian church and whose lives are reasonable and balanced.

In the address mentioned above, Pope Benedict XVI said that the Rule of St Benedict

> offers useful advice not only to monks, but to anyone looking for guidance on the path to God. Through his capacity, his humanity, and his sober ability to discern between what is essential and what is secondary in the spiritual life, he is still a

guiding light today . . . In the search for true progress, let us listen to the Rule of St Benedict and see it as a guiding light for our journey. The great monk is still a true teacher in whose school we can learn the act of living a true humanism.[7]

How do people find the good news that Benedict offers? More and more are doing so through the Internet, by visiting the many oblate websites, others through coming across the growing literature available, while still others through a casual visit to a monastery or a meeting with a monastic or another oblate. Oblates have a quality in their lives, which others seek to emulate. Many now make their first approach to an oblate director by email, and are invited to come and see.

Once someone embarks on becoming an oblate, formation in the spirituality of the Rule is essential. Traditionally this was done through talks at periodic meetings, but now in the spirit of Benedictine adaptability, for those who live too far from a monastery to visit with any frequency, or for whom time or other constraints prevent visiting, there exists the possibility of formation through cyberspace, due to the good work and forward thinking of the Benedictine sisters of Sacred Heart Monastery, Yankton, South Dakota.[8]

This handbook endeavours to help oblates live by the Rule of St Benedict, discover how that rule can help them to live fully the life to which Christ calls them, and how they can be mutual blessings for the vowed monastics living by the same rule within monastery walls.

Notes

1 Franziska Haitfeld-Panther OBL OCist., '*Lay Cistercians and Cistercian Oblates – People who seek that which is best, namely Christ*', in First International Meeting of Benedictine Oblates, Lay Cistercians and Cistercian Oblates, Zisterzienserkloster Stiepel Bochum Germany 29 March – 2 April 2007, p. 55.

2 *Reading the Signs of the Times: The Good News of Monastic Life*. The

Introduction

Proceedings of the American Benedictine Academy Convention, 10–13 August 2000. Book II Pre-Convention 2000 Papers. Norvene Vest, 'Monastics and Oblates: Mutual Blessings', *The Oblate*, vol. 3, no. 4, 1999.

3 Appendix 3.

4 See for instance the sequence *Laeta dies*, which uses the metaphor of Elijah and Elisha in reference to St Benedict.

5 Marcelo Barros OSB, Prior of Mosteiro da Anunciação do Senhor, Brazil, 'To Descend to the Encounter with God', http://www.benedictine-oblates.org/2005/txt-marcelo-en.pdf

6 Pope Benedict XVI, 'On St Benedict of Norcia: "The Great Monk is still a True Teacher"', 9 April 2008, http://www.zenit.org/rssenglish-22248

7 Pope Benedict XVI, 'On St Benedict of Norcia'.

8 Benedictine Oblates Online Chapter: http://www.yanktonbenedictines.org/oblates_booc_intro.html

Part One The Benedictine World

I THE BENEDICTINE FAMILY

1. The Life of St Benedict

ROBERT ATWELL

Scholars sometimes call the fourth and fifth centuries in European history an 'Age of Anxiety'. The gradual disintegration of the Roman Empire generated widespread feelings of insecurity in society. Things just fell apart. The road system, which had guaranteed the swift and safe transportation of food, troops and commerce, began to deteriorate. People became increasingly reluctant to travel because they no longer felt safe. The empire was dependent on mercenaries for its survival and there was a loss of confidence in civic life. Families began to move out of the towns and cities, which were becoming lawless, to seek refuge on country estates. These in turn gradually took on the dimensions of fortified enclosures. Rumours of barbarian incursions could easily generate panic in a populace: the forces of chaos were at Rome's very gates; civilization itself was under threat.

Parallels with our own age are not hard to draw. Many people today feel anxious and insecure. There is a collapse of trust in some sections of society. This is strange given that we are far more protected and safe than any previous generation of human history, at least in the West. We have better medicine, safer transport and better social security. International terrorism, however, has undermined public confidence, with dark forces threatening to unleash havoc in our cities. Western civilization itself is said to be under threat. Many claim to be frightened about the future, not simply for themselves but for their children. This pervasive anxiety may explain, at least in part, why we instinctively respond to the priorities of Benedictine spirituality. We find in Benedict's life and teaching not simply wisdom but reassurance.

Benedict was born in Nursia, in central Italy, around the year 480. The date is significant because only four years earlier, in 476, the line of the western emperors ended with the deposition of the boy emperor, Romulus Augustulus. As a result control of the western empire passed to Odoacer, a barbarian king, and 17 years later, following his defeat in battle, to another barbarian, Theodoric the Ostrogoth. Under Theodoric Italy enjoyed a number of years of strong government and peace. With his death in 526, however, a period of turmoil and war erupted, far worse than anything that had preceded it. The emperor of the East, Justinian, seeing his chance, resolved to recover Italy, and for the next 20 years the so-called Gothic War raged across the Italian peninsula, causing untold havoc and destruction.

Benedict was thus born at a turning-point in history. Unknown to him, he was living through one of the great periods of transition in which the face of the world changes. During his lifetime he witnessed political instability, widespread famine, violence and war, and it is against this dark backcloth that his Rule should be set with its call to stability and 'to prefer nothing to the love of Christ'. Where others had been idealistic in their vision of the monastic life or just plain verbose, Benedict succeeded in distilling accurately the essence of communal monastic life. His Rule gradually supplanted other monastic codes or gained a foothold alongside them by reason of its excellence, moderation and realism. While it is doubtful that Benedict ever thought of himself as 'founding an order', in the providence of God his teaching fostered a monastic culture that was to civilize Western Europe.

Benedict in context

Benedict was not the first Christian monk. Monasticism, considered as an ascetic way of life distinct from that of the clergy or devout Christian individuals, had emerged in Egypt, Syria and Asia Minor almost 200 years before his birth. In part it was a spontaneous expression of fervent discipleship resulting from the newly won freedom of the church. In part it was a rebellion at the moral decadence of late imperial society. The Desert Fathers and Mothers, as these early monastics are known, filled the place in the Christian imagination that the martyrs of the first three centuries had occupied. They became the new heroes of the church. Following the cessation of the persecutions, the front line of the battle had moved: the monks went into the desert to confront the forces of evil that inhabited the human heart. Their witness caught the Christian imagination and thousands followed them. Their Aramaic titles – *abba* and *amma* – meaning 'father' and 'mother', highlight the spiritual parenting given by these extraordinary individuals to other Christians, younger in the faith.

In a little over a century Egypt and Asia Minor spawned a variety of expressions of monastic living, ranging from the remote life of the hermit in his or her desert cell (typified by that of St Antony the Great) to an essentially urban phenomenon of a highly organized community dedicated to prayer and charitable work. This latter model was favoured by St Basil the Great and became popular in what is now known as Turkey. His great question 'Whose feet do you wash?' echoed across the Christian world.

The monastic ideal in its various forms was exported and mediated to the West largely through the writings of John Cassian (*c.*360–435), who had travelled extensively in Egypt and shared in the life of various monastic settlements. During the fifth century the number of monks and hermits of one kind or another in Italy grew rapidly. Regarded as a whole, however, the monastic movement was disorganized and highly individualistic. It was also economically unstable. One of Benedict's achievements that is often overlooked relates to his advice that a monastery, if at all possible, should be so constructed 'that within it all necessities, such as water, mill, and garden are contained, and the various crafts practised' (*RB 66*). This regulation, he suggested, would remove the need for monks to travel outside, for this was not 'good for their souls'. But Benedict's advice proved to be materially as well spiritually advantageous. The chaos into which Italy and Gaul (France) were falling threatened the life of all Christian institutions. As self-supporting units, Benedictine-style monasteries were well suited to the new economic order.

Robert Atwell

Thus for the next five centuries monasteries of the Benedictine type predominated and formed reservoirs of literature, learning and spirituality. In a fragile and insecure world these communities embodied stability and continuity. For a thousand years the life of Europe was shaped by its monastic culture and by the religious orders that were offshoots of, or reversions to, Benedict's ideal.

Sources for his life

Aside from the Rule itself, the main source of information we have about Benedict comes from his life, which was written by Pope Gregory the Great. This is found in the second book of the *Dialogues*,[1] which Pope Gregory composed between 593 and 594, some 40 years after Benedict's death. Pope Gregory was concerned to advance his belief that the church in Italy was as capable of nurturing holy people, worthy of emulation, as other parts of the church. Just as Egypt had heroes like Antony the Great, so Italy had Benedict. Gregory calls Benedict *vir dei*, 'the man of God'. His work proved enormously popular and in the centuries that followed, just as Athanasius' *Life of Antony* had promoted the monastic ideal, so there can be no doubt that the high regard in which Pope Gregory was held contributed to the fame and influence of Benedict and his Rule.

Reading Gregory's *The Life and Miracles of Saint Benedict* today is a somewhat bizarre experience. Unlike St Augustine who, like most late antique men, could be credulous without being necessarily superstitious, this was not true of Pope Gregory and his contemporaries. They lived and breathed a different air from that of earlier generations of Christians, a supernatural air in a world where visions and miracles were commonplace, and where demonic intervention was a fact of life to be contended with. Thus we are presented not so much with history as hagiography, a selection of stories and miraculous episodes chosen to illustrate Benedict's sanctity, and from which we have to construct the story of his life. We can do so, however, with a high degree of confidence. Pope Gregory names four of his sources, two of them successors of Benedict as abbot of Monte Cassino, a third the abbot of Subiaco,

16

and the fourth a disciple of Benedict who became abbot of a monastery in or near Rome. So even if Gregory has embellished some of the facts that he records for his own purposes, we can be confident that the broad outline of Benedict's life is accurate.

Benedict's early years

According to Gregory, Benedict was sent by his parents to study in Rome. Gregory does not give us the names of his parents, but tells us only of a sister, Scholastica – later to become a nun – and of a devoted nurse or governess who accompanied Benedict to Rome. We do not know how long he remained there, but we do know that at some point he abruptly broke off his studies, disenchanted by the decadence of the city. Gregory observes that Benedict withdrew 'knowingly ignorant and wisely uninstructed' (*Dialogues* 2, prologue). We know that he travelled with his nurse some 40 miles north-east of the city to Affile. It was here that Gregory tells us that Benedict first attracted attention.

His nurse had borrowed an earthenware sieve and accidentally broke it. She appealed to Benedict for help, who promptly mended it, apparently miraculously. Not surprisingly, the incident was widely reported. Finding himself at the centre of local interest, he left the town (and this time his nurse as well) as abruptly as he had left Rome, and sought complete solitude some five miles further north at Subiaco.

Subiaco

For the next three years Benedict settled in a cave in the valley of the river Anio and lived the life of a hermit. At some juncture he made the acquaintance of a local monk called Romanus who cared for him, providing him with bread and clothing. Benedict was probably about 20 at this time. There can be no doubt that this period of intense solitude was formative of his interior life. Indeed Gregory tells us that Benedict was so fervent in his monastic observance that he completely lost track of the liturgical seasons, and was only reminded of Easter by the visit of a priest who arrived at his hermitage complete with a festal meal.

It was not long before Benedict's reputation for wisdom and holiness attracted the attention of monks at Vicovaro, a monastery 18 miles downstream, who asked him to become their abbot. Benedict consented, but the move proved to be disastrous. Maybe Benedict was inexperienced in his leadership or pushed the community too hard too quickly, but serious conflict erupted when he attempted to reform their monastic observance. In fact so acrimonious was the conflict that, according to Gregory, the monks tried to poison Benedict's wine at dinner. This is why in some statues of Benedict he is shown holding not only a copy of his Rule, but also a cup with a serpent emerging out of it. This incident may provide a biographical clue to his admonition not to elect an abbot who colludes with a community's vices (*RB* 64).

Not surprisingly, Benedict left Vicovaro and returned to his hermitage. He soon attracted more worthy disciples, and together they built a small monastery by the side of the lake which evolved into an entire monastic colony. Gregory tells us that it was at Subiaco that two patricians of Rome entrusted their sons, Maurus and Placid, to Benedict's care. The custom of giving children to monasteries in this way was well established by the sixth century. That they were children of the nobility indicates the level of influence monasticism was now exercising in Western Europe.

Benedict organized the colony into small monasteries each with 12 monks over which he set a prior, while remaining himself in overall charge. His model would seem to have been Jesus and the 12 disciples. For some 25 years Benedict presided over the Subiaco colony, and doubtless it was during this period that the substance of his Rule began to take shape in his mind. Perhaps his antipathy to the role of the prior in a monastery can also be dated from this period. Around the year 525, a disaffected faction led by a jealous priest from the neighbourhood called Florentius tried to sow dissension among the monks and even poison Benedict's bread. The plot failed, but the experience profoundly disturbed Benedict and it led him to make the painful decision to leave Subiaco for the hill top of Casinum, familiar to us as Monte Cassino.

Monte Cassino

Monte Cassino overlooked, as it still does, a small town, some 80 miles south of Rome not far from Naples. When Benedict and his band of loyal monks arrived, they took over an abandoned hill fortress complete with a temple dedicated to Apollo set in a sacred grove. On this extensive site they constructed their new monastery, turning the pagan sanctuary of Apollo into an oratory dedicated to St Martin of Tours, and later also building a second oratory dedicated to St John the Baptist.

It is from this period that the famous story about Benedict and his sister, Scholastica, comes on the occasion of her annual visit (*Dialogues* 2, 33). According to tradition, Scholastica was abbess of a neighbouring community of nuns at Plombariola. Brother and sister met each year at a house near Monte Cassino to discuss spiritual matters. As evening approached Benedict prepared to return to his monastery, but Scholastica asked him to stay so that they might carry on talking. Bound by monastic discipline, Benedict adamantly refused. In response Scholastica prayed rather than argued, and a torrential downpour suddenly ensued making it impossible for him to leave. The point of the story is not so much the power of prayer as the power of love: Scholastica's was the greater. Even the great Benedict had to learn the merit of flexibility.

According to Gregory, it was at Monte Cassino towards the end of his life that Benedict wrote his Rule. Scholars think it highly likely that he utilized the text of an existing monastic document, *The Rule of the Master*, itself probably Italian in origin, adapting and editing the text in the light of his own considerable experience. He was certainly well qualified to do so, bringing forth from his inner treasury 'things new and old'. Unlike many other monastic documents, Benedict's Rule has the virtue of being moderate, humane and short. It is only 73 chapters long, approximately a third of the length of *The Rule of the Master*. His indebtedness to the wisdom of Cassian, Basil and other monastic writers is also evident. Although modest about his 'little rule for beginners' (*RB* 73), in reality Benedict's achievement was huge.

It is sometimes said that, unlike other monastic writers, Benedict did not expect his monks to be heroes. The events of his life reveal why this was so and why in his Rule he was both realistic and compassionate. As Pope Gregory noted, Benedict 'wrote a *Rule for Monks* that is remarkable for its discretion and clarity of language. Anyone who wishes to know more about his life and character can discover exactly what he was like as an abbot from his *Rule*, for his life cannot have differed from his teaching' (*Dialogues* 2, 36).

Benedict died during the course of the Gothic War. Gregory tells us that the war brought famine and devastation to the region, but the monks ministered among the local population, feeding them from their own reserves, and intervening to prevent cruelty. Even Totila, King of the Goths, came seeking Benedict's counsel. According to Gregory, Scholastica predeceased him and was buried in the monastery in the very grave that Benedict had prepared for himself. Benedict himself did not long survive her, but died in the oratory of the monastery on 21 March, probably in the year 550. Having received holy communion, he died with his arms lifted to heaven in prayer, his weakened body supported by the hands of his brothers. Fittingly, his death was marked by a vision granted to two of his disciples. They saw a 'magnificent road covered with rich carpeting and glittering with a thousand lights' (*Dialogues* 2, 37) that reached up to heaven. 'Do you know who passed this way?' they were asked in their vision. 'No,' they answered. 'This is the road', came the reply, 'which was taken by blessed Benedict, the Lord's beloved, when he went to heaven.'

Note

1 It should be noted that the *Dialogues* attributed to Gregory the Great have been the object of much scholarly debate; some authors question their authenticity suggesting that they were written at a later date. Gregory's *Dialogues* can be read at http://www.osb.org/gen/greg/ (Ed.)

2. The Benedictine Heritage

DEREK VIDLER

One of the characteristics of Benedictine monasticism is the vow of stability to a particular monastery. The monastery today is heir to a tradition that stretches back into the past, yet holding fast to the fundamentals of the monastic life moulded by a living tradition, which is constantly adapting its life in a wide variety of ways. In becoming an oblate a person enters a community living the Rule of St Benedict as seen through the eyes of the past masters of that community. We mould our lives on the wisdom of the past, as we shape the future. In so doing we will hand on a living and a lived tradition to which we shall make our contribution.

This summary of the Benedictine heritage is necessarily short and incomplete but hopefully will give the reader some insight to Benedict's gift to the church.

St Benedict and his Rule

Benedict was born *c.* 480 at Nursia, a small walled town north of Rome, into a fairly well-off family, who were probably land-owners and involved in town administration. The Roman Empire was collapsing and all around Benedict would have seen the decay of Roman administration and military strength. Rome itself, where the young Benedict went to study, had been subjected to invasion and destruction: it had lost its former glory as capital of a great empire. In the countryside around Rome were monasteries and hermits, and in Rome itself there were monasteries serving some of the larger churches. While at Rome Benedict became dis-

21

illusioned with his studies and companions and felt a vocation to the life of a hermit. He spent three years in a cave near Subiaco. Eventually he settled at Monte Cassino where he built a monastery and wrote his Rule. The Rule envisages a community that is for the most part self-sufficient and autonomous; a community of men and women dedicated to following Christ and sharing all in common as did the first disciples (Acts 2.44–45).

The monastery at Monte Cassino was short lived after Benedict's death, for it was destroyed by Lombard invaders sometime between 568 and 593. Benedict's Rule was one among many; only very gradually did it become the one which most monasteries followed. There is no clear evidence as to how the Rule came into Gaul, the earliest attestation being in a letter from Venerandus to the bishop of Albi, written about 620, asking that the Rule of St Benedict be used in a monastery he had founded at Altaripa. It seems many of the monasteries founded by St Columbanus gradually took on the Rule of St Benedict alongside other rules, and because of its moderation it gradually became the predominant rule.

The Benedictine years

Charlemagne (768–814) sought to stem the disintegration of society and unite his empire: the monasteries were part of his plan, he wanted them to become spiritual and cultural centres and to have single rule and observance; he legislated about the duties of abbots and sought uniformity by extolling the excellence of the Rule of St Benedict. However, it was his successor, Louis the Pious, who called abbots to the two synods of Aachen in 816 and 817, presided over by St Benedict of Aniane (750–821). In preparation for these synods Benedict of Aniane had compiled the *Concordia Regularum*, in which he places all the monastic rules he could get hold of, 26 in all, alongside the Rule of St Benedict. The synod legislated that the Rule of St Benedict should be the sole monastic rule within the empire. Smaragdus of Saint-Mihiel, an abbot and colleague of Benedict of Aniane produced the first known commentary on the Rule of St Benedict[1] to enable the requirements of the Synod, that every abbot and his monks should study the Rule and put it into practice, to be easily carried out.

St Benedict of Aniane did much to reform monastic life but he introduced an element of standardization and centralization among monasteries, something foreign to St Benedict's idea. His reforms did have a permanent effect on Benedictine life by stressing its liturgical character. St Benedict had envisaged only one or two priests in a monastery for the sacramental needs of the community, Mass being celebrated only on Sundays and feasts, although communion may have been distributed daily. Under the influence of St Benedict of Aniane the daily conventual Mass developed, and additions were made to the office, partly to meet the demands of benefactors, so the time spent on singing the office increased and the chant became more specialized. As more monks became priests, study, teaching and writing tended to replace manual work.

However, due to political instability, invasions by Vikings and others, and lay ownership of monasteries whereby abbots could be appointed by laymen for political ends, funds could be confiscated and nobility boarded in monasteries, monasticism suffered a decline and was frequently in need of reform. The attempts by Charlemagne and Benedict of Aniane to stem this tide had been only temporally successful, but there was a lasting result. The monastery of Aniane aided other houses in their spiritual renewal, including Saint Savin-sur-Gartempe nears Poitiers, which helped St-Martin at Autun; this in turn helped the monastery at Baume in Burgundy. It was a monk of Baume, Berno, whom William of Aquitaine invited to found a monastery at Cluny in 909. Berno, trained in the tradition of Benedict of Aniane, saw that the weakness for monasteries was lay interference and so decided that any monastery he founded should be directly dependant on the Pope. This, together with a strong element of centralization, and also a succession of strong holy abbots, St Odo, abbot 927–942, St Maieul, 942–994, St Odilo, 994–1049, St Hugh, 1049–1109 and Blessed Peter the Venerable, 1126–1156, ensured the success of the Cluniac movement.

England

It is not certain when the Rule was introduced into England, but it seems likely that it was by St Wilfrid (633–709) at Ripon. He said 'Did I not bring monastic life into line with the Rule of St Benedict, never before introduced into these parts?'[2] The oldest extant manuscript of the Rule of St Benedict, now in the Bodleian Library at Oxford, was copied in England, probably at Worcester in the eighth century. Wilfrid had spent his formative years on the Continent and he brought artists and singers to his churches at Ripon and Hexham, which were unrivalled this side of the Alps for their splendour. Love of art was to become part of the Benedictine inheritance. It is likely that, as on the Continent, in some monasteries the Rule of St Benedict was only one among others that was followed and this may have been the case at Ely under St Ethelreda (*c.* 640–79) and Monkwearmouth and Jarrow under St Benet Biscop (628–89). St Boniface (*c.* 675–754) was certainly a Benedictine at Exeter and Nursling and became the great apostle of Germany, spreading the Rule of St Benedict there. Boniface invited his relative, St Leoba (+782), and St Walburga (+779) from the monastery at Wimborne to join this great Benedictine mission field, the former becoming abbess of Bischofsheim and the latter abbess of Heidenheim. Walburga's remains were reburied at Eichstatt in 870, beside those of her brother, St Willibald (+676/7) who had been a monk at Bishop's Waltham before becoming bishop of Eichstatt.

In England the Viking invasions almost destroyed monastic life, but at least the nuns' monastery at Wimborne survived. King Alfred the Great began the restoration by founding Athelney for monks, brought from mainland Europe, and Shaftesbury for nuns, who were natives, and whose abbess was his daughter, Aethelgifu. Three men, however, were responsible for the major reforms, St Dunstan (909–98), St Ethelwold (912–84) and St Oswald (+ 992). St Dunstan reintroduced St Benedict's Rule at Glastonbury in 940. Later he came under the influence of Cluny at Ghent. Ethelwold was his disciple, and Oswald studied at Fleury, which had also been reformed by Cluny. Importantly, these three monks all became bishops, Dunstan at Worcester, London and Canterbury, Ethelwold at Winchester, and Oswald at Worcester and York. They were thus in positions to reform the monasteries and through them the whole church in England. One of the means was the establishment of Cathedral Priories at Canterbury, Winchester, Worcester and Sherborne, where a Benedictine community sang the office in the Cathedral and served as the diocesan chapter.[3] In 970 at a council at Winchester, attended by the abbots and abbesses[4] as well as monks from Ghent and Fleury, they drew up a customary and guide to the Rule of St Benedict, the *Regularis Concordia*. As at Cluny there was great stress upon the liturgy, especially the conventual Mass and, unique to England, all were enjoined to communicate daily at the early or 'morrow' Mass. Also peculiar to England was provision for a calefactory, the pealing of bells, monastic processions outside the abbey grounds and the assumption that laypeople would assist at Mass on Sundays and festivals. The monasteries continued to flourish after the Norman invasion (1066). The tradition of appointing monks as bishops continued and these included Lanfranc (1070–89) and St Anselm (1093–1109) at Canterbury. Also six more Cathedral Priories were established. When, in 1215 at the reforming Fourth Lateran Council, Pope Innocent III ordered all Benedictine monasteries to organize themselves into provinces and to hold regular General Chapters, the English were the first so to do in 1216, and the English Congregation today remains the oldest in existence.

Reform movements

Besides Cluny there were other reforming movements. The Cistercians were established at Citeaux in 1098 by seven monks from Molesmes. They too were highly centralized, and theirs was a highly austere expression of monastic life. It was based on the division into choir monks who were concerned with the liturgy and *lectio divina*, and lay brothers who did the manual work. The Cistercians spread rapidly through the mainland of Europe and the British Isles. Other reforming monastic movements, which still exist, were the Camaldodese, founded *c.* 1024 by St Romuald

(950–1027), who combined the eremitical life with the cenobitic, and the Olivetans, founded by Blessed Bernard Tolomei (1272–1348), who are also highly centralized, their charism being the spirit of communion, all belonging to one body.

Late medieval period

The spirit of reform that characterized the period from the second half of the tenth century began to peter out by the thirteenth. Gradually a more comfortable lifestyle developed in monasteries. They became increasingly wealthy landowners. Lay brothers and sisters and paid servants became part of the monastic community. The common dormitory gave way to individual rooms, the abbot had his own lodging, often with his private chapel and chaplains, and more and more laymen were employed. The Great Universities were set up, to which monks were drawn to study and gain degrees, and children lived in the monasteries for education. Moreover, the Black Death reduced numbers to an extent from which they never recovered.

The Reformation and its aftermath

The Reformation brought an end to monastic life in the British Isles and in much of Northern Europe. All the English monasteries were suppressed between 1536 and 1541, most of the monks receiving pensions or preferment in the church, although some like Blessed Hugh Faringdon, abbot of Reading, Blessed Richard Whiting, abbot of Glastonbury, and Blessed John Beche, abbot of Colchester, went to martyrdom. There was a brief restoration of Westminster Abbey during the reign of Mary;[5] most importantly the last monk of that restoration aggregated two Englishmen, who had become monks on the Continent, to Westminster, so that the English Congregation, restored in exile in 1619, had a direct continuity with the medieval congregation. A number of English monasteries were established in Europe, whence they sent monk missionaries to England, several of whom, like St Ambrose Barlow and St Alban Roe, were martyred. Expelled from France, three of the monasteries, Downside, Ampleforth and Douai, continue to exist today back in England.

The nuns, too, flourished, the first community of English nuns being established in Brussels in 1599, followed by Cambrai in 1625 (now at Stanbrook) and Paris in 1651 (now at Colwich). A French reformed monastery, inspired by the statutes of the English nuns of Brussels, was established at Douai in 1604, and was known as Paix Nôtre-Dame; foundations quickly followed in Arras, Namur and Liège, from which the present Abbey at Ryde on the Isle of Wight is descended and which in turn has made foundations in India.

Meanwhile a number of Congregations had been established in continental Europe, including the Bursfeld Union in 1446, which lasted until the beginning of the nineteenth century, the Congregation of St Justina of Padua in 1421, that of St Vanne in 1604 and that of St Maur in 1621. These congregations all represented reform movements and were fruitful in many ways; the Maurists, in particular were noted for their scholarship, but it all ended with the French Revolution, 40 Maurists dying on the scaffold.

After the French Revolution

Congregations that survived the French Revolution were to face many political threats during the nineteenth century; these include the Swiss congregation dating from 1602, the Austrian from 1625 and the Bavarian from 1684. The Bavarian and Swiss made foundations in the United States where the monks ministered to the German-speaking immigrants in parishes and schools. The American Cassinese Congregation dates back to 1846, when Boniface Rimmer came from Metten to Pennsylvania where he established what was to become St Vincent's Archabbey, and the Swiss American developed from the foundation Einsiedeln made at St Meinrad in Indiana in 1854. The nuns came too. Three nuns led by Benedicta Riepp came from St Walburga's Abbey, Eichstatt, in 1852 (itself founded in 1035) and began monastic life for women at St Mary's Pennsylvania, whence they spread rapidly. In 1874 a group came from Maria Rickenbach in Switzerland to Maryville, later at Clyde, Missouri, and in 1882 others came from Sarnen in Switzerland to found the monastery that would become Cotton-wood.

After the French Revolution there was a new monastic move-ment which began with the monastery of Solesmes in 1837, Beuron in 1863 and Subiaco in 1851. These three monasteries became the leaders of the Congregations bearing their names. Besides the new monasteries of men, those for women were also established, Ste-Cécile at Solesmes in 1866, and St Gabriel in Prague in 1889 (not in Germany because of *Kulturkampf*). The twentieth century has seen many foundations made for men and women in every continent, stemming both from these new monasteries as well as from those of the older traditions.

Anglican Benedictines

During Victorian times a number of efforts were made to restore religious life in the Church of England. Among them, one of the most notable was by Aelred Carlyle, who knew little or nothing about the inner life of a Benedictine monastery, but who had a vivid imagination and a somewhat romantic view of medieval monasticism. He founded Caldey Abbey, off the Welsh coast. This community soon split, many of its monks being received into the Catholic Church and establishing Prinknash Abbey. Those who remained Anglican moved to Nashdom and then to Elmore where they are today. A foundation was made in the United States at Three Rivers in Michigan. Alton Abbey in Hampshire had observed the Benedictine Rule since 1893. Among the nuns, Edgware Abbey had been founded at Shoreditch in 1866, and another community which had been founded in North London in 1891 for an active apostolate, was encouraged by Aelred Carlyle to become more contemplative and take on the Rule of St Benedict. It moved to Malling Abbey in 1916.

There are also Lutheran Benedictine Monasteries for men in the USA at Oxford, Missouri, and for women at Oestanbacks in Sweden, and there is an ecumenical monastery for women, Holy Wisdom Monastery, Madison, Wisconsin.

Today

Today Benedictine monasteries are found throughout the world, with monastics living the Rule, and engaged in multifarious works of service – running old peoples' homes, hospitals and village clinics, ministering in parishes, teaching in schools and universities, writing and publishing, farming and gardening, in short anything which is serving the church and compatible with community life, *Opus Dei* and *lectio divina*.

The Second Vatican Council in its deliberations on the religious life invited religious orders to return to the particular character and charisms of their founders. As we have seen the Rule of St Benedict has been a guiding light for nigh on fifteen hundred years. The world of the fifth and sixth centuries is not the world of today, but the wisdom of Benedict is perennial. The changing patterns of society and the church have seen his Rule modified and adapted to lead men and women to God and to seek Christ above all.

Throughout its long history Benedictine monasticism has preserved the essentials of Benedict's ideals. A Benedictine monastic takes a vow of stability to a particular monastery with its own traditions and history stretching back to the sixth century. That history has shaped and moulded the men and women who have promised to persevere in it for life. Benedictine spirituality is none other than the gospel of Christ lived out in a particular place and time, modelled on the Jerusalem community in the Acts of the Apostles where all things were held in common. The daily prayer of the *Opus Dei* and *lectio divina* are at the heart of Benedictine life.

Oblates

The oblate links her- or himself to a particular monastery with its own traditions. The Rule of St Benedict is incomparable and nothing can replace familiarity with it in its entirety. There are many excellent commentaries on Benedict's Rule and many books adapting his inspiration to oblate life: a selection will be found in the Bibliography.

Notes

1 Smaragdus of Saint-Mihiel, *Commentary on the Rule of St Benedict*, trans. David Barry OSB, Cistercian Publications, Kalamazoo MI, 2007.

2 David Farmer (ed.), *Benedict's Disciples*, Gracewing, Leominster, 1980, p. 63.

3 Dom David Knowles, 'Essays in Monastic History V, The Cathedral Monasteries', *The Downside Review*, vol. 51, no. 145, January 1933, pp. 73–96.

4 Nuns were present on equal terms at Winchester, whereas they had been totally excluded at Aachen, being required there to follow legislation laid down by men. Cf. Catherine Wybourne, 'Seafarers and Stay-at-Homes: Anglo-Saxon Nuns and Mission', *The Downside Review*, vol. 114, no. 397, October 1996, pp. 246–66.

5 Anselm Cramer, 'Siegbert Buckley, Monk of Westminster', *The Benedictine Link*, Ampleforth, 2007.

3. The Origins and History of the Oblate Movement

JUDITH SUTERA

From its beginnings, Benedictinism has touched the lives of many people beyond those who dwell in monasteries. While Benedict encouraged separation for the sake of quiet contemplation, a life ordered to spiritual practices, and control of the environment and influences, his community was not an escape from a world perceived as hopelessly evil. Rather, it was like a family that has its own customs and privacy but interacts to varying degrees with its neighbors. Benedict's Rule recognizes the presence of the monastic person in travel, in business, and in personal relationships as well as in accountability to the local church and population. It welcomes guests and suggests that there may be much to be learned from them.

It also demands that those relationships be a source of witness, of preaching by example, that will edify and transform the lives and practices of others. In the biography of St Benedict, the second book of Pope Gregory the Great's *Dialogues*, the people nearby came and 'gave him the food of the body and took back, in turn, the spiritual sustenance of life which they had received from his lips'. Other portions tell of visits by priests and kings, instruction of nuns and villagers, and works of charity to the sick, hungry, impoverished, and captive. Theoprobus, a nobleman, enjoyed Benedict's 'deep and trusting friendship' and is described as having access to Benedict's cell.

The life of a region could not help but be transformed by such a presence as that of Benedict and Scholastica. If people were converted by their teachings, they would most probably have incorporated into their lives not only the general Christian message but also the two saints' own interpretation of these values. These monastics were their neighbors, interdependent and having tangible effects on the life of the region.

There seems to have been not only a broad relationship of monastery to neighborhood but also some kind of specific relationship between the Benedictine community and particular individuals such as those mentioned above. While the word 'oblate' originally referred to a child offered by parents for religious life, some children apparently were educated in a monastery or elsewhere by monastic tutors but did not remain in religious life. They were a temporary offering, to be formed in their intellectual and spiritual life before taking their place as adults in the world. This was true of members of royalty, such as Charlemagne and Louis the Pious. This early influence would have affected perceptions of the world and, at least in these two cases, resulted in special concern for the preservation and promulgation of Benedict's Rule. These laypeople themselves became preachers and witnesses to the spirituality they had received.

Another noteworthy example is Duke Henry II of Bavaria, Holy Roman Emperor and saint of the early eleventh century, now honored as a special patron of Benedictine oblates. He is described as having supported the monastic life and participating devoutly in liturgy whenever possible. When made emperor in 1002, he sent his jeweled insignia to Cluny. He longed to live the monastic life and finally succeeded in getting a monastery to accept him. However, rather than permitting him to withdraw from the world, the abbot commanded him in obedience to continue ruling.

Even earlier, there is mention in various sources of persons or families living in communities near monasteries. It is difficult in these early examples of lay participation to identify just what the relationship to the monastery was. Feudal monasteries would have necessarily had associated settlements, where attachment may not have been voluntary or for wholly spiritual reasons. Many people depended on the monastery for their safety, employment, and material needs in addition to their pastoral care. This relationship would have influenced the life and spirituality of the area.

Apparently, some people were enrolled specifically as *confratres* as early as the ninth century. These people gave part or all of their assets to a monastery and offered their obedience in return for a guaranteed pension. For some, it may have been an economic necessity; for others, the monastery was the only 'family' with whom they identified. For some, however, the motive was that they truly wanted to be a part of something that they deeply valued, even if they were unable to be lifelong professed members of a monastic community.

This attachment expanded to include persons described as members of the faithful, both poor and rich, who requested association with the monastery. They did not renounce their own assets or lifestyle, but they sought to bring Benedictine values into the world in which they lived. In return, they were considered to share spiritually in the prayer, almsgiving, or other good works of the monastery. The community made special prayer for these associates in their lifetimes and after death. Eventually, the word 'oblate' came to be identified with such individuals who enter into a permanent relationship with a particular group of monastic men or women.

In the mid-eleventh century, William, abbot of Hirschau (d. 1091), established rules for two types of oblates, those living in a monastery without vows and those living in the world but affiliated with a monastery. Shortly thereafter, in 1098, Pope Urban II recognized the practice and praised it as being in keeping with the spirit of the ideal Christian community of the Acts of the Apostles. The Lateran Council of 1215 offers an official definition of oblate as either resident in a monastery or 'those who continue to live in the world if they have abandoned all their property to the monastery, reserving for themselves its usufruct'. In other words, they lived as laity but in obedience to the monastery and with the monastery as heir.

By the time of Frances of Rome (1384–1440), also honored as a special patron of oblates, oblation was apparently a well-established practice. It no longer required total financial obligation as much as spiritual association. Frances was a wife and mother, a wealthy matron who organized a group of women to engage in prayer and service to the needy. The women incorporated Benedictine spirituality into their lives and associated themselves as oblates with a local Olivetan Benedictine monastery. While some chose to take up life in common, others remained with their families and fulfilled their other social obligations while devoting themselves to prayer and charity.

By 1590, Abbot Tortorici is said to have gathered what was already in use when he made his rules for the reception of oblates. Further details of the period are found in the life of Elena Piscopia who, at Padua in 1678, became the first woman to receive a university degree as doctor of philosophy. Because of her fame, her biography has provided information on some of the aspects of oblation as practiced at that time. From these, it is evident that much of the current custom and understanding was already well established hundreds of years ago. The tradition has continued in many forms and places, attracting a vast array of persons. Martyrs of the English Reformation, such as St Thomas More and St Oliver Plunkett, were deeply affected by the Benedictine influence on the very foundations of English society and religion, and in their personal lives as well.

From the late Middle Ages, as other religious orders were founded, many pious laypeople associated themselves in one way or another with a community. While these later orders have had their own lay associations and 'tertiaries' (third orders), the vocation of Benedictine oblate remains unique. Oblates are not just persons who want to incorporate a certain spirituality into their lives in a general way but people who commit themselves to being associated with a particular community in its unique lived experience. They do not see themselves merely as participating in the works of the community, or supporting it financially, but as being united to it and being a part of it through their rite of oblation. Conversely, the Benedictine community has established a personal relationship with the person and has chosen to accept him or her in a mutual covenant that is direct and personal.

In the turmoil of the post-Reformation world, Benedictine

monasteries lost much of their influence, but those that survived continued to welcome spiritual seekers into association with their communities. Even in the years when monasteries were mostly isolated by cloister and social marginalization, they continued to offer spiritual direction and inspiration to many from outside their walls. In the late nineteenth and early twentieth centuries, noted individuals like Jacques and Raissa Maritain, Rumer Godden, and Dorothy Day joined countless lesser-known persons in committing themselves to being a Benedictine presence in the world.

In recent years, there has been a resurgence of popularity of the oblate movement, with some communities having large numbers of persons associated with them, sharing in the prayer and work in various ways. For many communities, the number of oblates far exceeds the number of professed members.

Several factors seem to be at work. The Catholic Church, in the years around the Second Vatican Council, increased its emphasis on the vocation of all the faithful, the need for continued spiritual growth and faith development. At the same time, all religious orders were challenged to explore the original intents of their founders and their unique gift to the church. This renewal led Benedictines to clarify and celebrate their historical and cultural gifts to the world and to communicate them more clearly to the laity.

A new understanding of the oblate relationship brought many more monasteries to organize oblate chapters. Until the latter part of the twentieth century, women Benedictines had not been active in this area of ministry. The traditional understanding was that oblates must have spiritual direction and that this direction and leadership belonged almost exclusively to ordained males. Moreover, since women usually made their profession before an abbot or bishop, it was thought that oblate profession also must be received by a male cleric. In 1961, a rescript from the Sacred Congregation for Religious declared that, since prioresses (in American monasteries that were not under bishops/abbots) received the professions of their sisters, there was no reason why they could not receive oblates as well. Benedictine women began to reclaim their role as spiritual guides and to recognize the potential of the oblate movement.

Interest in ecumenism opened the teachings of St Benedict to many Christians, both Catholic and non-Catholic, who had never before heard this practical wisdom. Monasteries opened their doors to non-Catholics who wanted to share this wisdom. Workshops and retreats started to attract more people of other faith traditions, and a growing number of monastic communities, both male and female, began to offer such opportunities and expand their retreat and guesthouse ministries.

In a time when it was rare to find a Catholic who had any concept of the liturgy of the hours, the *Book of Common Prayer* was familiar to nearly every Anglican/Episcopalian congregation. The Anglican Church, thanks to writers like Esther de Waal, began to appreciate the Benedictine influence on their own faith practices and to come home to a spirituality in which their own was deeply rooted. Through the writings of other non-Catholic oblates, such as Eric Dean and Kathleen Norris, Protestants of many denominations found a spirituality to which they too could relate. Major booksellers who would not have stocked a copy of St Benedict's Rule a couple of decades earlier now had dozens of titles exploring the meaning of this spirituality for ordinary Christians, their families, congregations, and workplaces.

Variations of the monastic liturgy of the hours also abound. To pray the divine office is to be united in the common prayer of Christians, to find nothing bound by the dogmas of a single faith but to be joined to the yearning of all peoples, even the pre-Christian writers of the psalms. To commit one's self to daily prayer and contemplation, non-violence, hospitality, the sharing of resources, the dignity of work, reverence for all creation, and a sense of community is to act upon the great hungers of contemporary culture.

The tremendous surge in the numbers of oblates and books about Benedictine spirituality, especially in the past few years, is evidence of the hunger and desire of all manner of spiritual seekers to respond. In 2005, Abbot Primate Notker Wolf gathered delegates from throughout the world for a World Congress of Oblates. There in the country where Sts Benedict and Scholastica lived more than fifteen hundred years ago, people of the most diverse cultures and lifestyles from every continent celebrated the universal truth and wisdom that mark St Benedict's teachings.

Not everyone who is touched by the spirit of St Benedict and his followers will become an oblate. Some will simply want to pray some form of the monastic liturgy of the hours, engage in personal contemplation, and strive to lead a life that demonstrates the kinds of virtues that Benedict most revered. However, those who desire a more formal, permanent commitment can become part of the family of any monastery, whether of men or women, that accepts oblates. These persons make a formal commitment to Benedictine prayer and values.

In a world where commitment is often devalued or even avoided, oblates choose to make public their desire for a life of witness. They promise their stability to a group of like-minded people who will be there for them but will also challenge them to greater holiness. They are united to the prayers and works of the monastery to which they are oblates, even as they continue to carry on their lives in their own locale and lifestyle. Just as the word 'oblate' comes from a root word denoting the offering of a gift, each oblate's life is an offering to God and a gift to the Benedictine community, which is enriched by the oblate's presence and prayer.

Giving one's self to a loving relationship is the essence of oblation and, therefore, the oblate movement should have many more centuries of prosperity. As Benedict notes, the Benedictine way is not to be harsh or burdensome but is offered to those who seek God and the sweetness of God's voice. Across cultures, generations, denominations, and lifestyles, people of good faith continue to hear and respond to that voice and to be welcomed as an offering at the altars of Benedictine monasteries.

4. Being Part of the Benedictine Family

BENEDICT GAUGHAN

Some years ago I approached a small group of visitors to our Abbey and noticed the look of amazement on the face of one of the women as I came close to her. 'Oh!' she exclaimed, 'I thought you were just an ancient monument.' We both laughed! She had obviously been following her Ordnance Survey map. Yes, we are an ancient monument, our existing buildings go back to 1027 and the foundation even earlier, to 670, but we also live here as a community. By the end of the visitor's tour she was animated and grateful to find us 'alive and kicking' after so many centuries – not 'just an ancient monument'.

Having been oblate sister for some years I am very heartened to hear from our sisters and brothers just how important Benedictine life is to them. When asked to contribute to this book I decided to ask our oblates to write a few words on the subject. The responses have been deeply humbling. Our oblate community is small, with a strong sense of family and friendship. We pray for each other by name on a weekly prayer roster and keep up communications as best we can, especially during our retreats and gatherings. There is a very strong sense of the monastery being the place of unity and the focus of prayer even when that prayer is said in physical solitude. We all feel deeply united in our search for God and like any family share our joys and sorrows. Some are more private than others and they respect the other's space in a healthy balance. Some are able to come together frequently like any extended family. They love to celebrate and are good at it, as at keeping silence during retreat times. All tell me that they value the nuns not just for being here but for being sisters of prayer and hospitality. They find strength simply through knowing that we are alive, here for and with the whole of God's amazing creation. Of course we do not forget those who have gone before us in the communion of saints. Yes, we *are* more than just an ancient monument and it is together that we hope to come to life eternal.

The following are edited responses from our oblates about what it means to them to be part of the Benedictine family. They speak for themselves in all simplicity and beauty.

'My first encounter with the Benedictine family was being present when an oblate made her final promises. The words concerning "conversion of life" really spoke to me and I knew I needed the Benedictine way to achieve it. In due course I became an oblate. Being single I find that my fellow oblates and the sisters fulfil the role of sisters and brothers in many ways. The fellowship is truly supportive both in matters spiritual and secular. The office, *lectio* and Mass can be shared and studied together. All this done in love really enforces the reality of the Benedictine family.'

Jean John

'Being part of the Benedictine family means that I can benefit from the tried and tested wisdom of Benedictines over the countless generations. The Benedictine ethos transcends all boundaries of tradition; a Benedictine is a Benedictine whether Anglican or Catholic, and from whatever part of the world. Being an oblate brings structure and stability to my life and continuing journey. The Benedictine way is spiritual but human and down to earth.'

Christine Michael

'Being part of a Benedictine community is a great privilege. It enriches the soul and helps one to grow and become more aware of one's Christian calling. At Minster we have a seven-day retreat each year from which we receive many graces, which in turn enables us to go out into the world enriched and confident as Christians to help build up God's kingdom. With the continued love, strength and support we have from the sisters we are able to "step out" in today's society in confidence. Being an oblate is also participating in the prayer of the church which is part of the great "Hymn of the Universe".'

Noreen Scholastica

'Aware of the developed world's ever-increasing materialistic attitude and of the transient nature of the goals they achieve, I find myself continually drawn by the enduring spiritual values of the Benedictines. I know I am naturally a rather chaotic and impulsive person, yet I also know that I am striving desperately for inner peace and it is here in the Benedictine family where I see and admire people attempting to follow Christ's teaching and living lives after his example that I feel peace. In the Benedictine structure some of my waywardness is kept in check. I gain pleasure from the regular and continuous prayer of the divine office and the chance to pray alone. The personal presence of a superior who represents Christ requires the obedience and steadfastness of an oblate's life.'

Veronica Walburga

'My first experience of the community was marked by the feeling of peace, tranquillity and acceptance. I felt that I had come home. For the first time I began to sense the true meaning of brothers and sisters in Christ. The concept was tangible, spoken in words and actions. My continued involvement with the community on the journey of aspiring novice and full oblate has been one of discovery with support and comfort, secure in the knowledge that there is mutual support, love and assistance because we are all on the same journey.'

Ann Martha

'Being an oblate means everything to me. I can't tell you in any other way really, but knowing that the nuns are all present in the

Abbey living the true tradition of the church and being at the core of all that is good on this earth, means so much to me. Thinking of you through the day when I read my office and knowing that I am taking a silent part in the communion of the church brings everything into perspective and makes me realize just why I am here on this earth.'

Audrey Domneva

'When I first came to Minster Abbey I felt that my spiritual life seemed to be lacking as if I was on a horizontal line but without progression. As an Anglican it was a great privilege to be welcomed in a Roman Catholic community. There was great warmth and acceptance regardless of my denomination: the acceptance that God has for us. Soon I asked to become an oblate. I was accepted and as I struggle to follow the Benedictine life, I know that God directed me to Minster. I pray that I will be able to share with others the love and peace I have found, which shines from our dear sisters and which I hope will shine from me. Then I pray others will want to know where it's from and come closer to our Lord.'

Brenda Mildred-Luke

'During my time as an oblate I have enjoyed the fellowship and friendship of both my fellow oblates and the sisters of the community. It is not always easy trying to live the Christian life in the twenty-first century and we need to support each other as much as we can. I have found that the Rule of St Benedict together with the fellowship of the oblates provides a foundation upon which to build. I hope and pray I can use this to support others on their journey.'

Nicola Mary

'Due to a domestic upheaval in my life I was invited to join an oblate retreat weekend at Minster. Being upset, I didn't actually get too involved in the group, but listened. This led to my eventually becoming an oblate novice. Since then my life has changed in many ways. My oblate family is there for me at any time. Having spiritual direction from the community of St Mildred and regular meetings have helped me to move forward in my life. Our annual retreat and silent times help us all to gain more knowledge of the Benedictine life and our statutes, which are essential to the calling. I am privileged to belong to the oblate family and thank God for his direction. I am so glad that I did "just listen" on my first visit.'

Moira Benedict

'I feel it is such a privilege and honour being part of the Benedictine family. It has made a big difference to my life, for which I am so grateful.'

Mary Hildegard

5. To Go to Rome

Perspectives from an Anglican on the
First Benedictine Oblates' World Congress

ALAN HODGETTS

After Mass one morning, Fr Abbot Giles approached me in the cloister of the abbey community of which I have been an oblate since 1982, the year I was ordained deacon in the Church of England. He asked me if I would be willing to represent the oblates of our community at the first Benedictine Oblates' World Congress in Rome. It took a process of discernment which lasted about five seconds before I answered in the affirmative, and so I travelled to Rome in September 2005, with two other Anglican oblates from Malling and Elmore Benedictine communities.

During the lead-up to the Congress, a few of the English oblates met in London to discuss the itinerary and select a representative and secretary. It was at these briefing and planning meetings that I first began to appreciate the value in oblates from other communities meeting together because the diversity we represented gave a richness of experience that I was going to deepen later. I was chosen as the secretary of the English-speaking oblates and it is in this capacity that I was asked to write this article.

The theme of the Congress was 'Communion with God, Communion with the world', inspired by the vision of St Benedict in which, according to his own description, the whole world was gathered up before his eyes 'in what appeared to be a single ray of light'. The 300 delegates represented the 5 continents and came from 35 countries. We were managed by a staff of 56 from different countries. There were instantaneous translations of the talks given by the main speakers in Italian, English, French, German and Spanish. The liturgies, however, included more languages: Portuguese, Russian, Korean, Croatian, Polish, Czech, some African languages, not to mention Latin.

The Congress was the vision of the Abbot Primate, Notker Wolf; in his inspiring closing address he said:

> We are not a wealthy or highly organised movement. My vision is of Benedictine Oblates being a spiritual movement within the Church. Our power is in the Cross and, while some co-ordination is required, this should be in the context of Benedictine freedom. We will always depend on individual spiritual fires blazing up in many places, rather than on a strong organisation.[1]

This emphasis on 'individual spiritual fires' is significant because the distinctive and individual 'charisms' of each of the communities we represented as oblates was vital to each particular expression of what it means to be an oblate. As the Congress evolved, any hint of a desire for communities of oblates independent of the community that had nurtured our vocation ran contrary to the spirit of what it means to be a Benedictine oblate. However, the experience of being together in our own *koinonia* at the Congress, did inform, nourish and nurture the realism of our vital significance as Benedictine oblates in the world.

The overarching theme of communion was developed through the week with keynote addresses and discussion groups under three headings.

Communion with God

The metaphors of fish and ocean seemed to link the three discussion group topics we explored. Thus the first of our seminar discussions, '*Communion with God*', revealed the shared experience that without this we are like fish out of water. This suggested to me the parable that, as oblates, we are part of a shoal whose life is in the ocean of God's love, '*preferring nothing whatever to Christ*'

(*RB* 72.11). However, our monasteries are perhaps like the seas of our planet, each with their own idiosyncrasies and characteristics. Our monasteries might also be compared with 'the cushion of the sea' – a place well known to submariners as that place of calm, deep water in which the storms above cannot reach. This led to the unanimous conclusion: 'No monastery – No oblate!' However, we also acknowledged that as oblates we live in the world and not in the cloister, therefore in another sense the world is our monastery too, rough seas and all! We may therefore inhabit choppy waters and have a lot to share with other oblates in coping with this, but our life is nourished and sustained by the family and fountain source of our monastery.

Communion with the family and others

The second of our discussions, '*Communion with the family and each other*', revealed a significant insight not reflected in the congress summaries synthesized from the reports of all the group discussions. For many of our English speakers had an understanding of what might be called 'impaired communion'. We acknowledged that the spirituality which might nurture our life in faith is not always shared and can even be misunderstood by our families and friends. This was seen as an advantage, however, in that it helped us live out a central charism of the Benedictine life – welcome and hospitality (*RB* 53) to those who may not thrive in our spiritual waters. In other words, we in ourselves are called to be a welcoming door.

World communion

The third and last of our discussions, '*World communion*', revealed to us how important it is for our abbeys to explore ways to extend their ministry of hospitality and welcome to 'other fish'! This conclusion was reached when we heard examples of the work of the various monasteries we represented. We acknowledged that all members of humanity swim in the ocean of God's love and so we can learn much from those of other faiths or expressions of our own faith, and our abbeys can learn from one another in ways that encourage this Benedictine spirit. In our personal lives as oblates we learned the important gift of humility in not suggesting any superiority towards others. We heard testimonies of bridge-building between others in the aftermath of horror and in hostile environments, which taught us how bridge-building in hospitality can be arduous and painful. We also discovered how, when we cross bridges, we may often have to break step with those around us if the bridge is to remain sound (conversion of life, *RB* 58), revealing a prophetic ministry for the oblate in society.

There is a tendency to believe monastics are so heavenly minded they are not of this earth. However on the Wednesday night we were treated to a wonderful concert of music by the Abbot Primate and other monastics from different parts of the world. On the Friday we enjoyed fellowship together in Rome and on our pen-ultimate day visited Monte Cassino. The abbot and his community made us most welcome and we had the abbey to ourselves for a couple of hours, enjoying uplifiting liturgy, lunch in the gargantu-an refectory and guided tours. Our final day consisted of a visit to Castel Gondolfo when, during his address, the Pope praised the oblates of St Benedict.

Personal reflections

First, I felt profoundly privileged to have been chosen to represent my monastery; and delighted to have been made to feel, together with my Anglican brothers and sisters, that I was truly a member of the worldwide Benedictine family. The worldwide Benedictine family is predominantly Catholic and I have to confess to some trepidation as an Anglican upon landing in Rome. However, my fears soon dissipated as I was made welcome and I realized that my monastic family is an authentic part of the international family of our holy father, St Benedict. I not only felt at home with my fellow oblates, I felt at home in the liturgies we celebrated together.

   The depth of sharing in our groups was both intimate and pro-found. We discovered how we swim together in the same waters of the 'river of Life' flowing from Jesus' heart. We felt so much in communion with each other that we shared the desire to create opportunities to swim together when we got to our home waters.

Implications

The Congress was the realization of the Abbot Primate's dream and his proposal for a further Congress in 2009 in Rome was warmly welcomed. His final 'charge' to the oblates at the conclusion of the Congress was inspiring. He observed how the Congress had been an opportunity for encounter – but reminded us that we are not a movement of power like so many associated with the strong and the rich. Like our monasteries, which also have no power or money, we cannot have a big show. The monasteries are like a fountain where we may be refreshed, but of course if we are to maintain links with one another we will need some limited organization, networking and co-operation. Networking was positively encouraged by the Abbot Primate who saw the Benedictine oblate as having a vital role in the life of his or her monastery and also a vital ministry in the world. Networking was something which enriched the monasteries from which the oblates came and not something which would diminish their importance. However, Abbot Notker did emphasize that we do not want centralization – this would put things into our hands, and to be a spiritual movement means we are to be in the hands of God.

He reflected how Benedictines are bound by the holy Rule based on scripture and that *lectio divina* is our daily food. 'Our spirituality has no method, we simply chew God's word until our bones and flesh are transformed by the work of the Spirit.'

He reminded us how we had experienced the universality of Benedictine life and our week had been a marvellous experience of a returning to our roots in a deeper sense. Thus we learned of the importance of being in solidarity with the needs of our world, especially in places of poverty, as we get more in tune with the heart of Jesus in *lectio divina*.

Perhaps the most lasting image of our purpose as oblates came when the Abbot Primate said that leadership in the monastery was not unlike that of Moses who went together with the people through the wilderness. He reminded us that we are looking for a way through the desert, a place which, when watered, can burgeon with flowers; a place which also has the most wonderful scenery of sky and mountains; 'the most beautiful thing', however, 'is going together!'

In conclusion

On many occasions we were reminded of the Benedictine stress on *ora, labora et lectio.*

Ora is the one aspect in the life of an oblate that is most likely to suffer, even for a priest like myself. The effect of the liturgies at the Congress once more established the centrality of this aspect of Benedictine life, and because the liturgies featured so many nationalities I was forcibly reminded that my prayer is part of that, of a much bigger family than I could ever have imagined.

Labora can so often dominate in one's life as an oblate, but the Congress enabled me to realize how, for those of us whose monastery is the world, the opportunity to reflect with fellow oblates can be a great source of support and strength to our ministry.

Lectio has similarly become more central in my life. At Lauds on the Monday of my return to England I was struck by the short reading, 'Your words were found, and I ate them, and your words became to me a joy in the delight of my heart' (Jer. 15.16). It brought Fr Luigi's[2] parting words forcibly to mind: 'I no longer believe *lectio divina* is important – I believe it is crucial!'

I entitled this article with the opening line of the Celtic prayer:

To go to Rome
is much of trouble, little of profit:
the King whom you seek there,
unless you bring him with you,
you will not find.

We all travelled to Rome and we found the Lord in our *koinonia* and fellowship. However, we also found that the Congress helped us to deepen the experience of the Lord we had first encountered in the *koinonia* of our monasteries and we found that we met with the same Lord we had brought with us!

Notes

1 Marcus Wakely, from his report to his community as an oblate of Ealing Abbey. Marcus was also acting co-ordinator for the Congress for oblates from England, Scotland and Wales.

2 Fr Luigi Bertocchi OSB, monk of St John's Abbey, Collegeville MN, who was co-ordinator of the Congress.

6. To Assemble an Oblate Collage

RACHEL SRUBAS

When I was a girl certain topics were as 'off limits' as the basement workroom where my dad stored his dangerous power tools. God, like sex, was a big taboo, so in secret I gave both God and sex a good deal of consideration. In my toy chest, underneath the Barbie dolls and Lincoln Logs, I hid two documents: a gold-inked copy of the Lord's Prayer that I had clipped from an old Christmas card, and a musty book my grandparents had owned, called *The Facts of Life and Love*. I also liked to think about the future, when I would be a glamorous, liberated grown-up. It was hard to imagine living long enough to reach the year 2000, but if I did, I would be 36.

In the year 2000, the same year I was ordained as a Presbyterian minister of Word and Sacrament, I made my Benedictine oblation. This was not quite the future I had imagined as a child. But looking back, remembering the girl with the clandestine prayer life and surreptitious reading of the facts of life and love, I see the beginnings of a Benedictine oblate who is also a happily married clergy-woman.

I am an oblate, a Christian follower of St Benedict, because I need a teacher, a tradition, and a community to help me live with prayerfulness and balance as I practice pastoral ministry and strive for personal faithfulness in a society where both contemplation and lasting relationships are challenging to sustain. But I am only one oblate. My experience of Benedictine spirituality has been more blessedly stable than varied. The best way I know, then, to present varied expressions of oblate life today is to reflect on

Benedictine monastics and oblates I have encountered, including not only those who, like me, are affiliated with the Benedictine Sisters of Perpetual Adoration in Tucson, Arizona, but also people I met in 2005 as a delegate to the World Congress of Benedictine Oblates in Rome.

My purpose in this essay is to assemble an oblate collage, informed by the Benedictine principles of hospitality, community, and good zeal. May my reflections help the reader to see that while all oblates share a commitment to living by Benedict's manifold Christian wisdom, oblate life today is varied indeed.

Benvenuto; Bienvenu; Wilkommen; Welcome

Were it not for Benedictines welcoming me as if I were Christ, I would not be an oblate today. I first experienced Benedictine hospitality – albeit with an unusual twist – at a monastery in a remote region of the American Southwest. Having driven at a creeping pace for ten miles down an unimproved mountain road, my husband Ken and I were received in the monastery's cramped gift shop by a surprisingly gregarious monk. He kept calling us 'you guys', which had a pleasantly familiar ring.

'Where're you guys from? You guys ever been to a monastery before? Hey, you guys? You know those roast beef sandwiches they make down at the general store?' We knew the sandwiches he meant: glorious strata of marbled rye bread, dill pickle slices, and savory, folded meat. 'You guys think you could bring me one of those? We don't get to eat stuff like that around here.'

To this day I feel guilty pleasure about our having smuggled a roast beef sandwich into the monastery the next day. In gratitude for this offering (which, in its plain brown wrapper, we discreetly handed to the monk in the gift shop), he let us into the monastery's library, which was off limits to the public. The room's tall, rather dimly lit shelves smelled of ancient ideas and brittle binding glue. Ken and I took great care with the books, opening them gingerly. Their spines crackled softly, and we knew we must not linger in this learned and hallowed place, where we would have loved to spend hours reading.

Later, in the monastery chapel, we attended a smoky, Gregorian liturgy where God's dominant feature was mystery. Afterward, as the brothers filed out silently to return to their duties, I watched Brother You Guys, to see if some glint in his eye would say how delicious the roast beef sandwich had tasted. But like all the other brothers, he avoided the gaze of the retreatants and guests, and through the haze of incense disappeared into the cloister.

Benedictine hospitality is neither fussy nor forgettable. It keeps you coming back. More than once Ken and I have returned to that Southwestern monastery to experience its potent combination of human spontaneity and ordered reverence. We live in Tucson, Arizona, two miles from a community of Benedictine sisters who receive visitors with a clear, uncomplicated look into the eyes and an easy embrace. The sisters welcome the public to attend their sunlit, soprano liturgies, and their hospitality helps to heal the loneliness of many who must make their way in an isolating, individualistic culture.

Roughly 100 oblates are affiliated with Tucson's monastery. We are men and women, old and young, Anglo, Hispanic, Asian, Native American and African American, straight and gay, Roman Catholic and Protestant. With other oblates I am made whole in Christ because my Benedictine hosts take me and love me as I am. Like their monastic kin worldwide, Tucson's Benedictines treat their visitors as if each of us were Christ, to be respected and cared for as well as relied on. Part of my oblation is to offer Tucson's sisters my assistance as I am able – with their fundraising projects, their bimonthly magazine, or the fruit-laden trees in their orange grove. In gratitude for the sisters' prayerful presence at the heart of Tucson, some oblates give much more than I do of their time, energy and money. Yet, like other oblates, I seek to practice Benedictine receptivity and generosity so that throughout my life, including my marital and ministerial commitments with no obvious Benedictine component, people I encounter will know I see them as Christ.

It was the Benedictine Sisters of Perpetual Adoration and their oblates who in 2005 made it possible for me to travel to Rome as one of 27 North American delegates to the World Congress of

Benedictine Oblates. Haggard from 16 hours of international transit, dragging my luggage through Fiumicino Airport, I was relieved to spot two young black-robed monks holding signs that announced *Benvenuto; Bienvenu; Wilkommen; Welcome*. They handed me a multilingual brochure someone had worked hard to desktop-publish. 'Honour due to all give,' it said in a peculiar but endearing translation of a line from the fifty-third chapter of Benedict's Rule, 'especially to brothers on belief and pilgrims.' Gradually, other travel-weary oblates from France, Poland, Indiana, and Ghana assembled around the monks in the airport, and gratefully we shared in a welcome unmistakably Benedictine in its practicality and kindness. While a Swiss monk helped some of us decipher our international phone cards, Bridget, a tall, soft-spoken oblate from Manchester, England, passed around a sleeve of ginger biscuits. Soon we boarded a bus for a conference center where over 300 oblates from around the world would live and learn together for the next week.

The creation of community

'The first result of the coming of the Holy Spirit was the creation of community – *koinonia*.' So proclaimed the visibly joyful Notker Wolff, Abbot Primate of the Order of St Benedict, in the welcoming address he presented in five languages to the World Congress of Benedictine Oblates, thus establishing community as the conference's theme. 'There are so many ways of Benedictine life,' he added. 'For example, in South Korea alone there are 600 oblates!' Two of those 600 South Koreans were present at the Congress, an extraordinarily international gathering that in fact exceeded the conference center's 300-person capacity. This overflow illustrated a point that US oblate and author Norvene Vest would later make in her address to the Congress. She cited a 1984 letter in which Benedictine abbots affirmed oblates, noting that the abbots could hardly have anticipated the great growth in the global oblate population, which by some estimates now numbers approximately 25,000.

Morning and night about 30 overflow delegates, including me, had to be shuttled to and from a perfectly serviceable hotel near the full-to-capacity conference center. It was a minor inconvenience, but the indignation it evoked from a few North American oblates would have made you think they had been asked to sleep in a cave. The situation struck me as an ideal opportunity to practice Benedictine humility and make the most of our unexpected *koinonia*. But as Benedict knew so well, the temptation to murmur under imperfect circumstances is virtually impossible even for people of faith to resist. In my emails to my husband I murmured about The Inconvenienced Americans, and some of my compatriots murmured to one another as we bumped down narrow Roman roads in our shuttle bus.

Our driver always delivered us to the conference center on schedule, and there, in an auditorium equipped with professional interpreters and hundreds of headsets through which to hear international, ecumenical presenters' translated talks, we joined a community that was downright Pentecostal in its multilingual unity. Coffee breaks and mealtimes were as important to the oblates' global *koinonia* as were the keynote addresses on this theme. I met a Nigerian painter who had made his oblation eight years earlier and asked me to take his picture beside a portrait of his hero, Pope John Paul II. A couple of married Belgian oblates proudly displayed a photo album of the ancient abbey with which they were affiliated. I introduced myself to a Lithuanian sister who hugged me upon noticing the Lithuanian surname on my nametag. Italian twin sisters and I laughed as we searched for a common language. One of them finally said to me in French, 'Il n'y a pas de division entre nous. Notre spiritualité est la même' ('There is no division between us. Our spirituality is the same'). This comment reminded me of a remark made earlier by Abbot Alcuin Nyirenda, the Tanzanian-born chaplain of Rome's San Anselmo Monastery. He told the gathered oblates, 'God did not will division. Unity is part of God's dream for the world.'

As in Eden, where an apple symbolized the disruption of God's dream, so in the conference center's dining hall were the oblates divided over fruit. Whereas servers delivered entrees directly to our dining tables, they deposited dessert – big bowls of oranges, bananas, plums, and yes, apples – on a few central serving tables from which all oblates were invited to help themselves. What a fascinating study in greed this became, as fleet-footed oblates heaped bright fruits onto their plates (apparently forgetting Benedict's teaching in Chapter 34 of the Rule on fair provision for the needs of all, not to mention Chapter 39, in which he cautions against excessive eating). Slower, less fortunate oblates were left to murmur at the fruit tables as they picked over a few bruised remainders.

I am just as capable of hoarding navel oranges (and wishing they were dark chocolate) as the next oblate. Making my oblation did not make a saint of me or any other oblate. But practicing oblation – praying the liturgy with monastics, learning from Benedict's Rule and its followers, engaging in *lectio divina* whereby, in the words of Notker Wolff, we 'chew the words of God until they soak in and our bones and flesh are transformed' – makes it harder to resist Jesus' summons to participate in the community of love and hope that is God's kingdom on earth. Wolff pointed out to the gathered international oblates that, according to St Gregory's account, at the end of his life Benedict envisioned the whole world as a globe enlightened by God. 'Europe', the Abbot Primate added, 'is no longer the navel of the world. The urge to centralize is every-where, but oblates are a movement, and God is the center.'

At every level of the World Congress the global character of the oblate community could be felt, joyfully and painfully. An Australian oblate, speaking on behalf of a smaller discussion group, affirmed that through interreligious, intercultural encoun-ters oblates express Benedictine hospitality. But several US oblates lamented their own monolinguality as preventing cross-cultural dialogue. In his Portuguese-language address to the Congress, Prior Marcelo Barros de Souza of Brazil criticized what he per-ceived as US Christians' reluctance to speak out in any language, saying, 'If American Christians had spoken out against the war on Iraq, it would have been harder to justify to the American people.'

Deceptively soft-spoken, Prioress Iona Misquitta of India deliv-ered the Congress's most prophetic call to community, saying, 'Christianity can either consider itself the one true religion or join in interreligious dialogue. The second alternative is now necessary. God's self-communication is not limited by the boundaries of Christianity.'

The diversity of God's self-communication even within Christianity became increasingly apparent throughout the World Congress of Benedictine Oblates, as previously unacquainted delegates from many countries shared stories, fortified the international oblate community by building friendships, and manifested the virtue that Benedict calls 'good zeal which separates from vices and leads to God and to life everlasting' (*RB* 72).

Global good zeal

'An oblate is a witness, through works and words,' said Angela Fiorillo, National Coordinator of Italian Oblates, in her presentation to the World Congress. 'We are called to announce the gospel with joy, strengthened by the Rule.' In other words, oblates are called to practice good zeal, fervent love, and great patience, preferring Christ above all else (*RB* 72). The particular ways in which oblates fulfill this calling are as varied as our cultures and local congregations. With the other contributors to this anthology on the oblate life, I write my Benedictine oblation. I also practise my faith through my pastoral ministry and personal life. Whether oblates write essays or care for the ill, till the soil or make art, we strive to embody Benedictine values and close-to-home practicality. As oblate Norvene Vest told the World Congress, 'The Benedictine way is not self-serving or apocalyptic. It is not noisy or extreme, but embodies Jesus' dailiness and nearness to God.'

Thus the good zeal of oblates is humble and contemplative yet transformational, and wonderfully exemplified by a Filipina follower of Benedict I met in Rome. I failed to note her name, but her words stayed with me and will make a fitting conclusion to this collage of reflections on the varied expressions of oblate life throughout the world today:

> God is present in everything oblates do. We can flee to the monastery to rest and listen with the ear of the heart, and this

energizes us for the struggles of daily living. Oblation not only influences prayer, but also deepens *koinonia*. Even when people hurt us, peace reigns in our hearts because of Benedictine values. We may be marginalized, but we advocate for peace and justice. We fight guns and tear gas with prayer.

II DISCERNING YOUR CALL

7. Life Choices

SUSAN SINK

It took ten years from the time I first went to Mass at a Benedictine monastery in 1997 until I made my promises as an oblate in 2007. It took me that long, basically, to figure out what the promises meant and how one can be a Benedictine in an authentic way without moving into a monastery. Making these promises means making one large life choice, but it is a choice to be a certain way in the world, to privilege certain things over others in a way that we hope will inform all the other choices in life.

When I observe the monks and nuns of monasteries I am always reminded of Jesus' instruction to the disciples: leave all you have and follow me. The sight of them in robes, many of them having even exchanged their names, in some way always speaks to me of relinquishing, of what one must give up to live differently. To see monastics at prayer or working elsewhere in the community makes me think of Elisha who, when called to take over for Elijah, burned his oxen and plow right there in the field and took up the call. Let the dead bury their dead. Indeed.

What exactly was being asked of me? There was that comforting part of the definition I kept hearing: oblates follow Benedict's Rule, *as much as they are able* in their particular station in life. It was the loophole of all loopholes. However, even if it was not primarily about relinquishment, a call to live by the Rule is at least a call to radical transformation. So, in fact, is the call to be Christian. It is also a call to obedience, something I do not think I am very good at, and even more a call to stability. Stay here and change.

I did not have to be told that Benedictines are about stability. It is written all over them. They are as solid as their stone churches, rooted in their places, which they spend a great deal of prayer, meditation, and hard labor to maintain. The space of a Benedictine monastery is permeated by prayer and silence, is built out of the very lives of the people living there. I felt that keenly on a visit to Blue Cloud Monastery in Marvin, South Dakota. After seeing the town (population 28), a post office and a bar, my friend and I went on to the monastery, where just over a dozen monks live in a sprawling place that looks a bit like a Catholic school and once provided cells for a large community. That weekend many of the rooms were occupied by people attending a Narcotics Anonymous retreat. The wonderful monk who took us on a tour, however, opened doors to kitchens where bread was made, and up to a tailor's shop where rich vestments in various stages were laid out on tables and hanging on racks, and through the carefully maintained greenhouse. There was a lot of life in that place, ordered and constructed by the hands and prayer, silence and community, of the men who lived there. To be an oblate would mean to somehow contribute to the life of those spaces, to find a way to bring that life into my own home. What it would require would be stability, to be sure.

An oblate I knew at a monastery in Chicago, a woman wholly committed to prayer, would only take a job that allowed her to be at the monastery for prayer five times a day. This meant basically the Catholic bookstore in the neighborhood. I couldn't change my life that dramatically, but I knew there had to be other ways to be an oblate that would be authentic. I wanted to make a promise to a way of life. I wanted to find a way to be stripped down enough and to be part of whatever it was that the monks created in their own spaces, to know that I was indeed living as a Benedictine.

More and more for me this focused on simplicity and stability, and though I never had any trouble with simplicity, I didn't feel myself to be particularly stable. I had moved every two to four years of my adult life, often across the country. I always had a good reason: love, a job, school, a fellowship, family. I didn't see myself as a person who was able to stay put very well. And staying put seemed a large part of stability.

I could of course say the prayers, if not in community then alone. I bought books to help me do this, with morning and evening prayers. Reading psalms alone when I woke and before I went to bed always made me drowsy, however, and I found myself cutting down the number. Finally I dropped the psalms altogether and just said the simple prayers and went on with my day. Then I forgot to do that. I am very serious about prayer. I don't have trouble quieting myself to pray, and I have a pretty intense prayer life. I am not good, however, at routine. I can't think of anything, certainly not flossing or taking vitamins or even eating breakfast, that I am able to get myself to do every day. I was going to have to lean heavily on 'as far as you are able' when I made those promises. The prologue to the Rule also offered this bit of encouragement to me: 'What is not possible to us by nature, let us ask the Lord to supply by the help of his grace' (Prologue 41).

Ultimately, however, it was letting go of the idea that I would have to become what I was not that cleared the way to oblation. Something about the words 'Rule', 'obedience', 'stability', and the rigorous picture of monastic life (and the challenges of Chapter 4 of the Rule) made me think this was something I was going to have to work very hard at and change myself to be able to do. Then I spent a year writing in residence at the Collegeville Institute for Ecumenical and Cultural Research at St John's University, and observed more closely the monks at St John's Abbey. It was the same experience I'd had at other monasteries, but more intense. After a semester I realized how many of the monks I knew by name, and in fact how much I knew of their personalities and life stories. It is a great paradox of monastic life that in all that silence and prayer one's personality comes out more completely and more openly than I've experienced with people in everyday life. I felt known, too, and embraced by the community I prayed with (almost) every day. This may seem like an obvious statement, but it surprised me that of course they were not all the same, and were not at all muted in their personalities and presence. Becoming an oblate would not mean becoming what I was not, but in fact becoming more truly what I am. It was not a commitment to reshape myself into some picture of a monastic I held onto. It was a commitment to express myself, as someone who loved God and loved others, more fully in my community, which is not a monastery. It had not occurred to me that I had been drawn to Benedictine spirituality from the beginning because of who I am.

When the year was up I made the more radical life choice to quit my tenured teaching position and go to work for a Catholic press, which allowed me to stay in Minnesota. As with all the other major life choices and moves I had made, it seemed the only thing to do at the time. And also, even in the midst of another major life decision and a giant move, I felt surprisingly, shockingly, stable. Nine months later I made my promises as an oblate.

Sister Kathleen Hughes RSCJ, who had been with me at the Institute and was at my oblation ceremony, fixed on a particular phrase in the promises. While I was still busy holding onto 'as far as you are able in your station in life', she pushed me to consider something more important. Whenever she saw me at noon prayer she would ask, 'How is your stability of heart?' Those were the words of the promise I had made – not stability of place, but stability of heart.

And, in fact, life choices too are much more about who you are than where you are. I remembered the feeling of wholeness, of not being shaken to the core, during a difficult divorce. Hadn't that been stability? I had made choices and taken steps always to keep loving my family through very dark times. Surely that is a kind of stability of heart? I worked to make my home a place of prayer and hospitality, and to keep my heart open to all whom I encounter as my neighbor. I had not always obeyed my mother, it was true, but I cannot think of a time I had disobeyed God or had not been grateful for God's faithfulness to me. The fact is, I had clung to God. Sometimes the only place I had been able to find God was in the depths of my own heart. In pursuing oblation I discovered that I am a person committed to stability, and it is this stability of heart that allowed me the freedom of movement I needed to make the choices I have made and pursue goals in my life.

To be an oblate is to wake up every morning and say: 'Here I am, Lord,' then to walk through the day with stability of heart and focus on the values of the Rule. There are many things about life that are beyond our control. Even the things that are in our control sometimes feel as if they are not! I find it comforting to choose to make primary in my life these things: maintaining a home that is welcoming to others and in which there is room for silence, prayer, and reading the Word. Greeting others as Christ, with an eye to meeting their needs and a desire to share in their joys and sorrows. And as for moving, well, I truly hope not to do that again for quite a while.

8. The House of the Lord

KATHLEEN NORRIS

I was glad when they said to me,
Let us go to the house of the Lord
And now our feet are standing
within your gates, O Jerusalem.

Psalm 122

Taproot

I first went to a monastery to hear a reading by the Minnesota writer Carol Bly. I had long admired her work, and as literary events are rare in the western Dakotas, I regarded the event as a true Godsend. Little did I know. I barely knew what an 'abbey' was, except as an historical term from the medieval era, and I did not know what to make of the stern-looking men in their black habits. Discovering that warm and hospitable people lurked beneath that intimidating appearance was both a surprise and a joy. I am an early riser, and when I happened to wander into the church during morning prayer a monk showed me to a seat and guided me through the books: hymnal, psalter, responsories, the Benedictus. Only later did I learn that all of this was a part of my own Christian tradition; at the time I felt as if I had strayed into an alien landscape.

I was at a spiritual crossroads in my life, just beginning to reconnect with my Christian faith after years away, and I was gladdened to discover that what the monks were doing in their daily office was in fact a significant part of my own religious inheritance. I was immediately attracted to the psalms as poetry, to be sure, but on a deeper level I was grateful to have found a taproot of prayer that I could claim as my own, as it predated all of the schisms in Christendom. The liturgy of the hours was neither Protestant nor Catholic; if anything, it was Hebraic, dating back thousands of years to the time of King David. Reciting these ancient poems was not a matter of boring repetitions and stifled yawns, although at times I was bored and I yawned as effectively as any monk. I could not deny that the psalms, resonant with poetry, history, and theology, held a profound, personal, and emotional meaning for me.

I was moved to realize that the words we were praying and singing had been uttered by monks for nearly seventeen hundred years, dating back to the fourth-century Egyptian desert. In the American West, where towns such as my own were not yet 100 years old, this continuity was inspiring. It also became a true consolation for me, as my own life at that time was marked by a great deal of turmoil and confusion. Although I had been raised in the Christian faith, and willingly attended church all through my teenaged years, by the time I was in my twenties I had come to believe that religion was something I had left behind and had of necessity outgrown. I was at a loss to explain why, as I approached my forties, religion had again assumed such importance in my life.

The monks were far less interested in what I considered my imposing and fierce religious doubts than in my desire and willingness to come to the divine office. And the calm persistence of the monks in prayer taught me not to fret unduly over the larger religious issues that troubled me, but to practice more patience as I waited for God's answers. It seemed that I would discover who I was, and what I needed to do, if I kept returning to the monastery and the liturgy of the hours. I soon found excuses to drop by the monastery whenever I was in the area, for noon prayer or vespers. Eventually I spent the night, and then a long weekend, and then a full week. By the time someone asked me if I would consider becoming an oblate I was staying in the abbey guest rooms for several days a month. In the dead of winter I was sometimes the only guest. None of this made any outward sense: I was a nominal Protestant of uncertain faith. But something significant was happening, and conversion is probably the best word for it.

The body of Christ

As a freelance writer who had long worked professionally with words, I found it a challenge to learn to be still and listen for God's word for me. When I first considered what being an oblate would mean, that 'word' came loud and clear: it would not be wise to become an oblate without first putting down roots in a church congregation. This was not a welcome thought, as it demanded that I take a good, hard look at myself and my situation. I was living a vowed life as a married woman, so joining a monastic community was out of the question. And I did not want to become 'a monklet', as one brother saucily and cheerfully put it. I realized that for all the good things that were happening as my relationship with the monastic community developed, there was also the danger of it becoming a shipboard romance. The grass might look greener in a monastery because I was always a guest there, but God was asking me to be something more.

I felt that God was directing me toward a serious question: to what extent was my attraction to monastic life and practice based on its exotic quality and the fact that it was not part of my ordinary, everyday existence? As a guest in the monastery I was deferred to and treated with a nourishing hospitality. Could I conceive of being just an ordinary member of a church, which would mean being cast into the rough rock tumbler of community life, and being called to offer hospitality rather than always receive it? Paradoxically, I was guided in my deliberations by the fact that I genuinely felt at home in the monastery. The hospitality of the Benedictine men and women who had come into my life was essential to my growth in faith, and I absolutely needed that sense of belonging to reach the next stage of my development as a Christian. Without the monastic connection I doubt that I would ever have seen the necessity of joining a church. For a whole host of reasons I didn't fully understand, I had found the monastic com-

Kathleen Norris

munity approachable in ways that a church congregation was not. But the monastery was not and could not be my community in the fullest sense. I had not undergone formation there, I had not made life vows there, and the abbot was not 'my' abbot in the way he is for a professed monk.

Gradually a conviction took hold: I needed my own place to stand in the body of Christ, my own worshiping community. I needed to take part in ordinary congregational life and resist the temptation to believe that the monastery could fulfill that basic requirement of the Christian faith. My options were not all that appealing: the hometown church I'd been attending sporadically was in the process of dismissing its pastors in a spectacularly dysfunctional manner, and I much preferred the quiet dignity of Benedictine liturgy to wordy Presbyterian worship. But, given where I was living at the time, this small, struggling congregation was what God had provided. In a consumer culture we are often encouraged to idolize choice, and to identify freedom as having many options available to us. But God's ways are not our own, and in my journey toward becoming an oblate I was learning that God sometimes chooses to attract our full attention by narrowing our options. A biblical metaphor for this process might be found in Isaiah, in the image of the highway on which even fools do not go astray. Once you set out on that road there can be no other path to your destination.

So, on a bitterly cold January day, I joined the Presbyterian church in Lemmon, South Dakota, a church my maternal grand-parents had belonged to for some 60 years, and the church where I had attended Sunday school during childhood summers. This prospect was not nearly as pleasant as enjoying the privileges of being a guest who is 'welcomed as Christ'. I could still go the monastery for spiritual renewal, and because it was a good place for me to write, but my own ascetic practice would have to be grounded in the nitty-gritty, incarnational reality of congrega-tional life. Just as the Benedictine must pray that the other lunatics in the asylum are the very people God has provided as companions in the journey, I had to regard these other Christians as God's gift to me. We were all in the boat, together, attempting to navigate on

66

stormy seas, and hoping against hope that Jesus was still with us, still able to calm the waters and guide us to shore.

Such lofty thoughts were all to the good, but on the day I joined the church I still felt miserable as I stood in a vestibule with the pastor and members of the 'session', the elected and ordained church elders. The head elder, a man not given to theological speech, cleared his throat. Visibly uncomfortable, he looked at his shoes, which were freshly shined, and said, 'I would like to welcome you to the body of Christ.' Oh dear, I thought. This was someone I had never liked much, but I had just been commanded to love him. Oh dear, I thought: what have I gotten myself into? The body of Christ, indeed.

Practices

Early on I found that my participation in the church was greatly enhanced by some of the practices I had learned in the monastery, such as 'sleeping on the gospel', taking some time on Saturday night to read and meditate on Sunday's gospel and letting its words sink into my unconscious overnight. And when I was asked by the church worship committee to take on preaching duties, as we were between pastors, the practice of *lectio divina* served very well. I would look up the lectionary readings well in advance so that I could brood on them in odd moments: while waiting in a doctor's office or washing dishes. I would scribble just a few things in my notebook, and consult a commentary or two to avoid making too many amateurish mistakes. But mostly I tried to simply live with those Bible texts, inviting them to live inside me, as it were, until some thought occurred that seemed appropriate for a sermon. It was having learned the practice of *lectio divina* from the Benedictines that gave me the confidence to serve my church congregation in this way. As it happened, I preached two sermons or more a month for nine months, until a new pastor came. Both *lectio divina* and the working on sermons brought me closer to the Bible, which was a great gift.

Another thing I had gained from my experiences with the Benedictines was a renewed sense of holy ground, and in particular the idea that any church, like a monastery, is a place apart – a place where, as the psalm says, our feet are already standing within Jerusalem's gates. When we pray together and sing our hymns, whether it is in a monastery choir or a church congregation, we are not only on pilgrimage to the city of God, we are in some sense already there.

The non-negotiables

This thought was a great consolation to me when my husband became seriously ill, and it became clear that we could no longer travel back and forth between my family's home in Honolulu and the small town on our beloved Plains where we had made our home for 25 years. Over the years I had come to value the Benedictine 'non-negotiables' of prayer, stability, and conversion of life. But I was thrown into confusion when my settled life was suddenly 'converted' in such a drastic way. We still had our community of two, a stable and happy marriage. And I still had prayer, and was deeply grateful to know that even when the duties of caregiving exhausted me so that I was unable to pray, the Benedictines were still praying, expressing the stability of God's love. But my duties as a caregiver meant that I could no longer go on long retreats, and the monastery in North Dakota to which I had made my oblation over 20 years before was now thousands of miles away. But what are miles when we are speaking of Jerusalem, and the 'house of the Lord'? It is prayer that led me to the monastery, and prayer that still unites me to it. In less exalted and more temporal terms, I found that I could keep in touch through the abbey and oblate newsletters, which include some of the conferences and homilies offered by the abbot to the monks. I also employed email, snail mail, and the occasional phone call to my monastic family. At times I would run into community members at monastic conferences and enthusiastically embrace them as my 'homeboys'.

I knew that I needed to seek out a new church home in Hawaii, and the love of liturgy that originally had been fired up by the Benedictines landed me in a lively Episcopal congregation that strikes what is for me a happy balance between liberal activism and a largely traditional liturgical observance. As it happened I joined this church at a critical time in my life. I had been helping to teach a confirmation class of teenagers and decided to become confirmed along with my students. I came home happy that Sunday, my confirmation certificate in hand, and wearing beautiful and fragrant flower leis that people had given me. My husband was happy for me as well. But early on Tuesday morning he suddenly suffered a recurrence of the respiratory distress that had plagued him since his chemotherapy for lung cancer. He often joked that the treatments that had saved his life were also killing him, but it was literally true, and we had grown accustomed to medical emergencies. I kept a 'hospital bag' packed in our bedroom. In the pre-dawn hours of that Tuesday we went by ambulance to the hospital emergency room, and he was admitted to the ICU. On Wednesday he rallied, but he began to fail on Thursday, and on Friday morning he died.

When I went to church on the following Sunday it was difficult for me to believe that this was the church I had officially joined just a week before. My world had changed so much in those few days. The gospel reading that morning told of Jesus asking a blind man, 'What do you want me to do for you?' The man replies, 'Let me see again.' As I attempted to apply Jesus' question to myself: 'What do you want me to do for you?' I knew that I could not ask for my husband back, because he had suffered enough over the past five years. For him there would be no more ambulances, emergency rooms, or ICUs, and I could be glad about that. But as for myself, I was numb, and lost, and did not know what to ask for. Lines from Psalm 27 came to mind:

> There is one thing I ask of the Lord,
> for this I long,
> to live in the house of the Lord,
> all the days of my life,
> to savor the sweetness of the Lord,
> to behold his temple.

In another translation that I like the last line reads: 'and to inquire in his temple'.

Where may 'the house of the Lord' be found? Is it enough to say 'where two or three are gathered in Jesus' name'? We are speaking of a place that may be found in the human heart, and anywhere that people gather to glorify and worship God. And we are also speaking of cosmic time, in which the dead and the living coexist, and the Sanctus we sing on Sunday morning rises to the heavenly host. Here and now, in this cruel and imperfect world, we must begin our journey on the pilgrim way. Here and now we sing as we approach God's holy city and find ourselves already standing within Jerusalem's gates.

9. *Suscipe Me, Domine*! Uphold Me, Lord! Abba, Daddy, Pick Me Up!

A Meditation on Final Oblation

PAUL F. FORD

How many of my fellow oblates have struggled to understand the first degree of humility (*RB* 7)? I first encountered what I thought to be St Benedict's teaching on humility as a 22-year-old in 1969. Long did I wrestle with the questions: How was I to relate to the God pictured in Chapter 7? How was I to 'keep the fear of God before [my] eyes and beware of ever forgetting it', to 'let [my] thoughts constantly recur to the hell-fire which will burn for their sins those who despise God', to 'keep [my]self at every moment from sins and vices . . . ' and to 'check also the desires of the flesh'? How could I live with a 'God [who] is always looking at [me] from heaven'? How could I live where '[my] actions are everywhere visible to the divine eyes and are constantly being reported to God by the Angels'? How could I live under such surveillance, in such a police state?

Clearly, I had some healing to undergo. I made my final oblation as a naked intent directed to God[1] and the healing followed later, in at least two insights. The first of these came when Father Simon O'Donnell taught me the meaning of the *Suscipe*, the highpoint of monastic profession and of oblation. With arms outstretched, the finally professed sings: *Suscipe me, Domine, secundum eloquium tuum et vivam. Et non confundas me ab expectatione mea* ('Uphold me, Lord, according to your word and I shall live; let not my hope be put to shame', Ps. 119.116). As you will read below in

71

'The heart of the rite: the *Suscipe*', this is the equivalent of saying, 'Abba, Daddy, pick me up!'

The second insight came when I observed a radiantly well-loved little boy ask, to his father's near-exhaustion, 'Daddy, did you see me do that? Did you? Did you?' All of a sudden I saw how the deepest part of us wants to be seen and exulted in. So much of what I was attracted to in Chesterton's chapter 'The Ethics of Elfland' (*Orthodoxy*, IV), in C. S. Lewis's sermon 'The Weight of Glory', and in George MacDonald, who greatly influenced Chesterton and Lewis, all came together. The final ingredient I found in Maria Boulding's meditation on Psalm 139, 'O Lord, you search me and you know me':

As Julian of Norwich said, creation 'would fall to naught for littleness' (*Revelations*, 5). To me this truth is sheer joy. His creation of you is not something that happened once, *x* many years ago; he is still at it. His healing, creative hands are upon your body, upon your mind, upon that fine point of your spirit where his likeness is stamped on you – not a static likeness but an evolving reality. The whole strength of his loving will is in that creative act by which he wants you, loves you, rejoices in your being; and you can let yourself go in joyful agreement with his creative will, saying with Jesus, 'Father, into your hands I commit my spirit.' When I was a child my father's hands meant a great deal to me. They were the most beautiful hands I have ever seen: large, beautifully shaped, strong, very sensitive and kind. I have many memories of clinging to them, but one recurrent joy stands out, that of being bathed by him as a small child. He used to run plenty of water into the bath, and make it very soapy and then put his child in. He scorned flannels, sponges and other impediments and did the whole job with his hands, caressing the child all over. At the time I simply enjoyed it with a mixture of sensuous delight and love; since then the memory of it has become for me a kind of sacrament of resting in the loving, cleansing, healing, creative hands of God.[2]

Together, then, let us look *at* and *through* the signs of final profession – the significant gestures, postures, words, songs, touches and sights – for what they say about being an oblate of St Benedict. (A few of these ceremonies differ in some monasteries in both their number and their arrangement.)

Final oblation is not a sacrament but a sacramental

Christ instituted the seven sacraments; and even if their *fruitfulness* depends on our faith, their *power* comes from Christ's activity on our behalf through the Spirit to the Father. The church instituted sacramentals to reinforce the sacraments; in the case of oblation, the sacraments of baptism/confirmation. The power of sacramentals depends on the quality of our faith-filled prayer. This is why every gesture, posture, word, song, touch, and sight of the sacramental of final oblation is chosen to excite powerful faith in us.

Every time we hear the presider or superior ask 'Let us pray' during a final oblation, he or she is not just being polite, but is inviting us to exercise the priesthood given us in our baptism (and confirmation) by praying for the persons making final oblations and for our intentions and those of the whole world. It is just a little exaggeration to say that this final oblation will not be able to go forward if we do not pray every time we are invited to pray.

For what are we all praying at a final oblation? For the gifts of the Holy Spirit to descend in a new way on the oblates so that they can offer themselves totally to God, who is eager to receive them.

The rite of final oblation often takes place at the community's conventual Mass. To emphasize what unites us as Christians, the rite of final oblation of non-Catholics may be celebrated at evening prayer or at another hour of the divine office. The following feasts are the most fitting times for a final oblation (and for renewing one's oblation privately or even publicly): 2 February, Presentation of our Lord; 21 November, Presentation of the Blessed Virgin Mary; 21 March and 11 July, feasts of St Benedict; 10 February, feast of St Scholastica; 9 March, feast of St Frances of Rome; and 13 July, feast of St Henry.

The basic shape of the rite of final oblation

Liturgy of the Word (or the Psalmody of the Hour)	*Preparatory rites* • Invocation of the Holy Spirit • Address and interrogation	**The heart of the rite:** • **Reading and signing of the oblation chart** (• the *Suscipe*) • **Acceptance and the prayer**	*Explanatory rites* (• Presentation of the medallion) • Kiss of peace	Liturgy of the Eucharist (or the recitation of the Lord's Prayer)

Liturgy of the Word (or the Psalmody of the Hour)

To build on an image of St Ephraem, the readings at every Mass are the oven and the cask in which the offerings are 'baked and fermented' by the fire of the Holy Spirit and transformed into the communion sacrifice of Jesus' body and blood. In the rite of Christian initiation of adults, the Sunday liturgy of the word and the celebrations of the word especially for catechumens are the oven and the cask in which the catechumen is transformed into an adult Christian. At a final oblation the readings chosen are the oven and the cask in which the oblate is transformed into an offering to God.

If the table of liturgical days permits, the community and the oblate to be finally professed may be able to select a suite of readings from the ritual section of the lectionary for the Mass in which the final oblation will take place. If such complete substitution cannot be done, perhaps one reading from this ritual or another part of the scriptures may be substituted; if not, appropriate hymns, psalms or songs could be sung. At the liturgy of the hours an appropriate psalm (such as Psalm 63, 'O God, you are my God, for you I long', with its passionate verse 9: 'my soul clings to you; your right hand *holds me fast* [*suscepit*]'; or Psalm 139, 'O Lord, you search me and you know me') may be substituted. If at evening prayer, listen for this line in Mary's canticle: 'God *has helped* (*suscepit*) child Israel, remembering mercy.' God is about to remember mercy and help you.

Preparatory rites: the invocation of the Holy Spirit

The presider or superior's invocation of the Holy Spirit begins the rite proper. The first part of the invocation, 'Come Holy Spirit, fill the hearts of your faithful, and enkindle in them the fire of your love', is part of the antiphon for Mary's canticle from evening prayer for the solemnity of Pentecost. The versicle and response, 'Send forth your Spirit and they shall be created. And you shall renew the face of the earth,' are from Psalm 103.30 (Vulgate).

The collect is from the votive Mass of the Holy Spirit. Its first petition, 'grant us by the same Spirit to know what is right', asks that we might not only intellectually know the right things but also that the Spirit may help us *recta sapere*, to savor or relish the right things, the correct (and often narrow) ways of God. Its second petition asks the Holy Spirit to give us the ability to rejoice always (1 Thess. 5.16) in the consolations that the Spirit gives us.

The third petition focuses on asking for a renewal of the special gifts the Holy Spirit gave to St Benedict: 'Raise up, O Lord, in your church, the Spirit which animated our holy father Benedict, so that, filled with that same Spirit, we may strive to love what he loved, and to practice what he taught.' Throughout an oblate's novitiate the novice has striven to love what St Benedict loved and to practise his teachings.

'What did St Benedict love?' might better be asked, 'Whom did he love?' He loved God and God's Son, and he loved the brothers and his sister and the guests. He loved the work of God and obedience and humility and heaven with all the passion of his being.

Preparatory rites: the address and interrogation

As the presider asked at your baptism, 'What do you ask of God's church?' the presider or superior may now ask, 'What do you seek?' You are free to say or adapt the formulaic response: 'The mercy of God and fellowship with you as an oblate of our holy father Benedict.' Your oblate director may be asked about your discernment and your practice and experience of the Rule you have gone through to get to this day. Based on what he or she has heard, the presider or superior affirms you and permits you to make your final oblation.

At your baptism (and at your confirmation) you renounced sin and professed faith. At your final oblation you again reject sin and renounce the glamour of evil so as to live in the freedom of God's children. You both promise the ongoing reformation of your life and also dedicate your life to the service of God and humankind, all according to the spirit of the Rule. Finally, you pledge to strive to be faithful and persevere in your holy resolution until death: all of these with the help of God and never without!

In response to your answers the presider or superior may now exclaim: 'Thanks be to God!' If it is the custom of your monastery, all may now applaud, as they may do at professions and ordinations. It is time for you to breathe in their affirmation, to soak up their love. All are praising God and the work God has done and is doing and will do in your life.

The heart of the rite: the reading and signing of the oblation chart

At baptisms, professions and ordinations now would be the time when all the angels and saints, our ancestors and beloved dead, are asked to help the earthly church accomplish what it proposes to accomplish. Perhaps your monastery sings the litany of the saints at this time; even so, it would be appropriate for you to have prayed a litany of the saints in preparation for this day, invoking in a special way the saint by whose name you have chosen to be called as an oblate. In most oblation formulas you invoke the Blessed Virgin Mary and all the saints (especially those whose relics are buried below the altar in the monastery's church) as witnesses and allies.

It is now time for you to read aloud the oblation chart you so carefully wrote out on fine paper. Your feelings may overwhelm you or they may desert you – don't worry: 'Your feelings are the last things to be converted,' as C. S. Lewis said. You call yourself by your baptismal name(s) and then by the name of the saint whose life has spoken to you especially during the time of your oblate novitiate. You name the place (town, parish, diocese, state) in which you are now attempting to live your life as an oblate. Naming the place may seem so prosaic and temporary, but it is in the everyday that all of us are called to live, and the oblate *lives* where she or he is now living. All of our lives are on loan to us, and we are asked to be and make something beautiful for God with the time we have been given.

There is only one 'condition' in your chart: 'insofar as my state in life permits'. St Benedict was so real and practical, and this clause reflects his discretion. By including it you are giving the strong part of you something to strive after and not dismaying the weak part of you (*RB* 64.19). You are facing the future and welcoming the good times and the hard times.

When you have read out your chart, you sign it on the altar and the superior or presider signs it as well. You leave your chart on the altar as a sign that you are offering yourself as a living sacrifice (Rom. 12.1). Although the physical chart is later filed away, the person it stands for – you – remains on the altar until your death.

The heart of the rite: the *Suscipe* (an option in some monasteries)

The climactic moment has arrived. In most (but not all) final oblations you now open your arms to God (as you might when praying the Lord's Prayer) and say or even sing, 'Uphold me, Lord, according to your word and I shall live, let not my hope be put to shame.' Your sisters and brothers say or sing the *Suscipe* again with you and all bow low with you to praise the Triune God who aches to receive and foster all.

What does the drama of the *Suscipe* mean? In pagan Rome the *paterfamilias*, the head of the household, was the one before whose feet every newborn child in the household, freeborn or slave, was placed. If he decided to be the *susceptor* by picking up the child to hand it to its mother, then the child could be nursed and brought up. If he chose not to lift up the child, the child was left to die.

Christians who spoke Latin immediately gave to the Abba of Jesus and our Abba the title of *Susceptor*. By singing the *Suscipe* you are begging your heavenly Father to pick you up, to sustain you, to confirm the incredible act of hope that final oblation is. No wonder St Benedict says that the humble brother or sister 'has . . . acted . . . as a weaned child on its mother's breast [because] . . . You solace my soul' (*RB* 7). God has proved to be the perfect parent.

The heart of the rite: the acceptance of the oblation and the prayer over the newly professed

The superior now acts as God's representative and receives your oblation and grants you the privileges of being a child of St Benedict and oblate of your monastery. (If your oblation is celebrated during the liturgy of the hours, a flavor of the eucharistic liturgy is preserved by the singing or saying of the Lord's Prayer, the first part of the communion rite. If you were baptized as an infant, a similar recitation took place as a down payment on your first holy communion.)

Then the superior prays two prayers, the first to invoke the Holy Spirit for the gift of your perseverance, and the second to ask the intercession of the Blessed Virgin Mary that you may become worthy to be presented in the temple of [God's] heavenly glory. Why this latter prayer? The mystery of the presentation – of the Lord and of Mary (the latter is not canonical but spiritually true) – is the one the church has long associated with vow-taking, so much so that for the Presentation of the Lord the church has reserved until just recently the gorgeous introit: *Suscepimus, Deus, misericordiam tuam in medio templi tui; secundum nomen tuum, Deus, ita et laus tua in fines terrae; iustitia repleta est dextera tua* ('We have received your mercy, God, in the heart of your temple; even as your name, so also your praise reaches to the ends of the earth; your right hand is filled with justice'.) In the *Suscipe* you asked God to receive you; at every liturgy we all have been and are *being* received. And at night prayer we renew the gift of ourselves by entrusting ourselves into the hands of God. In this way night prayer can be a daily oblation.

Explanatory rite(s): the kiss of peace (and the presentation of the oblate medallion – optional) and the blessing

Some communities have a special medallion for oblates; if so, it is given now. It is a sign of the special fellowship you now have with your monastic sisters and brothers.

The sign of fellowship is the kiss of peace. The superior now bestows this kiss on you. If it is your community's custom, you may also receive it from the community members and from your fellow oblates present. This is not just a friendly greeting. It completes the circle of care and also widens it. The kiss of peace reminds you of your vocation as an oblate: the service of God and humankind. St Paul concludes and sums up the encouragement he gives the Roman community begun in Romans 12.1 ('Therefore, out of the mercy of God, I encourage you to offer your bodies as a living sacrifice . . .') with Romans 15.7: 'Welcome (*suscipite*) one another, therefore, as Christ has welcomed (*suscipit*) you to the honor of God.'

If the oblation is celebrated at the liturgy of the hours, the superior or presider now gives the blessing; if it is at the Eucharist, the liturgy continues with the preparation of the gifts. You may be asked to bring the gifts in procession, yet another sign of your giving of yourself. Again, your feelings may overwhelm you or they may desert you. But your life has changed: 'You have died, and your real life is hidden with Christ in God. When Christ your life appears, then for the first time you too will appear with him in glory' (cf. Col. 3.3–4). How happy we are to have an Abba who never tires of looking at us with love, who has taken us up with 'loving, cleansing, healing, creative hands' and will never let us go.

Notes

1 *The Cloud of Unknowing*, 24.
2 'A Tapestry, from the Wrong Side', in Maria Boulding OSB (ed.), *A Touch of God: Eight Monastic Journeys*, Triangle, London, 1988, p. 39.

III THE FOUNDATIONS OF AN OBLATE'S LIFE

10. *Opus Dei*

SIMON JONES

The priority of the *Opus Dei*

There are two places in the Rule where Benedict urges his monks to hurry to the oratory to celebrate the divine office, the *Opus Dei*, the Work of God. To the contemporary reader, Chapter 22 conjures up a rather comic picture of monks leaping from their dormitory beds, trying to outdo each other to be the first to arrive for the night-time office of Vigils. Indeed, so that nothing whatsoever may hinder their journey, they are instructed to sleep fully clothed. 'But', says Benedict, with a characteristically practical note of caution, 'they should remove their knives, lest they accidentally cut themselves in their sleep' (*RB* 22.5[1])!

In Chapter 43 he is equally insistent of the need to hurry to the other offices:

> On hearing the signal for an hour of the divine office, the monk will immediately set aside what he has in hand and go with utmost speed, yet with gravity and without giving occasion for frivolity. Indeed, nothing is to be preferred to the Work of God. (*RB* 43.1–3)

As Benedict suggests, these injunctions are not given to cause amusement – far from it. For Benedict, nothing should delay, obstruct or take priority over the celebration of the Work of God. With its night-time vigil and sevenfold punctuation of the day, the divine office beats at the very heart of the community's life. At least four hours of every day are devoted to the *Opus Dei*, which provides a balanced framework into which the monks' other occupations are woven, so that the daily life of the monastery is held together by these carefully regulated times of prayer.

The fact that it is the abbot's responsibility (either personally, or by delegating it to a 'conscientious brother') to signal the times of the offices (Chapter 47), and that those who make mistakes during them (Chapter 45) or who arrive late for them (Chapter 43) are required to make public satisfaction for their shortcomings, attest to the centrality of their performance. Since 'nothing is to be preferred to the Work of God', the offices are not only the cement which binds the community together, they are also its primary vocation, its source and inspiration. The Work of God constitutes a group of individuals into a community, a 'school for the Lord's service' (*RB* Prologue 45), whose common and sole purpose is to give glory to God.

In this chapter we will explore how such a priority might be translated into the life of the Benedictine oblate. Those of us who have offered our lives in spiritual union with a community which is formed and directed by Benedict's Rule need to ask ourselves frequently what it might mean to share in its primary vocation, the *Opus Dei*. It goes without saying that Benedict's 'little rule for beginners' (*RB* 73.8) was never written with twenty-first-century oblates in mind, and the challenge to interpret the Rule's injunctions concerning the divine office into a variety of contemporary postmodern contexts is a no less demanding task than to interpret any other aspect of the Rule's teaching. And yet, few Christians would disagree that to hurry to make the Work of God a priority in our lives is as necessary and as urgent for us as it was for those sixth-century monks for whom the Rule was written.

Before looking in more detail at what Benedict has to say about the Work of God, let us consider for a moment where these forms of prayer came from and how they relate to the worship of Benedictine communities today.

Origins and development

There is a sense in which the Benedictine office is not particularly Benedictine at all. Although the pattern of daily prayer described in the Rule contains some innovations to what we know about the Roman liturgical tradition of the sixth century, such as the use of hymnody at the beginning of each of the hours, its origins lie, not so much in the mind of Benedict, but in two principal external sources: the Roman office which Benedict himself would have known and prayed, and the *Rule of the Master*, an anonymous sixth-century collection of monastic instructions, which Benedict adapted.

That said, although there may be nothing particularly Benedict-ine about the Rule's liturgical roots, thanks to Benedictinism, its subsequent liturgical influence cannot be underestimated. In west-ern Christendom, as the Rule was adopted by more and more mon-astic communities, they very naturally also revised their (Roman) office in accordance with its instructions. As Robert Taft points out, by the second millennium Benedict's office had become *the* office of western monasticism,[2] a situation that remained unchanged until the reforms of the Second Vatican Council in the last century.

Since then, there has been no official monastic breviary in the Roman Catholic Church. Rather, individual monastic communi-ties have been encouraged to create their own forms of daily prayer, based on the Rule and in accordance with various authori-tative norms. It is of particular interest to oblates that, within these guidelines, the Roman Catholic Church has made a particular point to emphasize the unique relationship between the com-munity and its prayer: 'The Work of God and the celebrating community . . . should correspond so closely to each other that each community can be said to require its own proper liturgy.'[3] Such close correspondence is not at all foreign to the spirit of the Rule, nor is local variation. For example, in Chapter 18, having spent some time outlining his scheme for the recitation of the psalter, Benedict goes on to say that: 'Above all else we urge that if anyone finds this distribution of the psalms unsatisfactory, he should arrange what ever he judges better' (*RB* 18.22).

For the purposes of this handbook, we need to acknowledge this variety; we need to be realistic about the fact that, when we worship with the communities to which we belong, or use their office book as our office book, very few of us will be following Benedict's liturgical guidelines to the letter. Nevertheless, we can assume that, wherever the Work of God is offered, it will reflect something of the uniqueness of the community which is celebrating it as well as of the Rule which inspires it and unites us. This we do in the hope that, through our common offering of a life of liturgical prayer, every member of the family of Benedictine communities is being transformed, is experiencing spiritual conversion, so that 'as we progress in this way of life and in faith, we shall run on the path of God's commandments, our hearts overflowing with the inexpressible delights of love' (*RB* Prologue 49).

Praying in community

As oblates, one of the main questions which confronts us when thinking about liturgical prayer is how the way in which we pray should reflect and relate to the way in which the community with which we are united is praying. The community where we have made our oblation is, in a sense, our spiritual home, and its form and pattern of prayer must obviously be taken into account when considering how and when we should pray. Chapter 50 from the Rule offers some advice here, when it describes what should happen when one of the brethren is away from the monastery:

> Brothers who work so far away that they cannot return to the oratory at the proper time . . . are to perform the Work of God where they are, and kneel out of reverence for God.
>
> So too, those who have been sent on a journey are not to omit the prescribed hours but to observe them as best they can, not neglecting their measure of service (*RB* 50.1–4).

This raises a couple of interesting points for those of us who are more often absent than present. First, how often should we celebrate the Work of God? And second, what form should that prayer take?

To follow the full pattern of monastic liturgical prayer, outlined by Benedict in Chapter 16 of the Rule, would be an indigestible and, for most oblates, an unhealthy daily diet. Benedict uses Psalm 118[119].164, 'Seven times a day have I praised you', and Psalm 118[119].62, 'At midnight I arose to give you praise', as a scriptural warrant for the daily celebration of Vigils, Lauds, Prime, Terce, Sext, None, Vespers and Compline.

If we are ever tempted to feel guilty that we cannot live up to Benedict's liturgical ideal, we should remember that, in the Prologue to the Rule, Benedict himself says that 'we hope to set down nothing harsh, nothing burdensome' (*RB* Prologue 46). In Chapter 50 we see that even the monks themselves are only required to observe the hours 'as best they can' when they are unable to be present. A generous degree of practical flexibility and realism is built into the Rule, just as it should be built into the rule of life of any oblate. It is as true for us as it is for our monastic communities that we each require our own proper liturgies which take account of our individual lifestyles, work patterns and responsibilities.

For all oblates, the monastic community will not be the only religious community to which we belong. In addition to local church communities, we may also belong to a study group or cell group, be involved in supporting the religious life of a local school, prison, hospital or homeless shelter; we will have our own denominational allegiances and, not least, our commitment to family and those with whom we share our lives. If there is to be a close correspondence between the Work of God and those who are celebrating it, then it is obvious that our belonging to any one of these or countless other communities will have an effect on our celebration of the *Opus Dei*, and must not be overlooked when considering what form it might take. In resolving possible tensions between these and our monastic community, we must not lose sight of the words of the psalmist, which Benedict quotes in the prologue to the Rule: 'They praise the Lord working in them, and say with the Prophet: Not to us, Lord, not to us give the glory, but to your name alone' (*RB* Prologue 30).

For many oblates it may only be realistic to attempt to pray one office a day, at whatever time suits our own timetable, perhaps first thing in the morning, or during a break at work, or once the children have gone to school, or in the stillness of the night. For some, it may be possible for this time of liturgical prayer to be offered with other Christians. For others, it may be a case of disentangling ourselves from the lives of those around us to retreat to a quiet space which we have set aside for this purpose. But however and wherever the Work of God is celebrated, a point to which we shall return, Chapter 50 encourages us to punctuate the day with other opportunities to pray.

Benedict's absent monk would not have had an office book to carry with him when he was working outside the monastery or travelling. His observation of the prescribed hours would have required the use of his memory to recall the appointed psalms for a particular office. Committing the psalter to memory is a practice which Benedict encourages in Chapter 8 of the Rule when he directs that, during the winter months, 'in the time remaining after Vigils, those who need to learn some of the psalter or readings should study them' (*RB* 8.3). Today, it is unfortunate that the prevailing liturgical culture seems to insist that an office is not an office without a book to read it from. Despite the fact that there are many excellent pocket-sized breviaries available, the discipline of punctuating the day with self-generated excerpts from our liturgical memories is a wonderfully liberating experience. On a train or standing in a queue at a supermarket checkout, in front of a computer screen or walking the dog, sitting in a doctor's waiting room or cooking a meal, we can use our memories to fulfil Benedict's injunction to 'perform the Work of God' wherever we are. What matters here is frequency rather than form. There will be very few oblates who do not have a liturgical memory, and cannot offer an uncomplicated form of prayer: an opening response with the Gloria, a short portion of psalmody, a couple of verses from scripture, some brief biddings, the Lord's Prayer and a simple ending. We would not want this to be the only source of nourishment in our liturgical diet, but as a brief and frequently repeated act of liturgical prayer, offered in addition to at least one more substantial meal, it helps us to live out our vocation to make the

Work of God the priority in our varied and complicated lives, dipping beneath the surface of our daily routine to be fed by the divine presence which is everywhere, 'but beyond the least doubt we should believe this to be especially true when we celebrate the divine office' (*RB* 19.2).

But, if that goes some way to answering the question about how often we should pray, what about the relationship between the form of our prayer and that of our monastic community? Despite what I've just said about praying from memory to enable us to pray more frequently, in the liturgical tradition inspired by the Rule, Benedict's emphasis on obedience and stability leaves no room for individual choice. The Work of God is a given to be observed by all, and is not subject to the whims or preferences of individual members of the community.

For some Christians, the repeated use of structured liturgical forms of prayer, with psalms recited and readings chosen according to a predetermined scheme, stifles the activity of the Holy Spirit, who seeks to breathe spontaneity and variety into the worshipping life of the church. But to interpret Benedict's instructions in this way is to misunderstand one of the fundamental principles of his Rule. Benedict does not provide his monks with a liturgical straightjacket; rather, he enables his community to deepen their relationship with God by being immersed in an unceasing offering of praise and prayer, through the recitation of psalmody, the singing of hymns, and the proclamation of scripture. The Holy Spirit is not silenced by this; rather, he is freed to articulate his own voice beneath the surface of the community's liturgical voice, praying through the heart of the community as the community prays by heart. As Joan Chittister has observed, 'The function of prayer is not to establish a routine; it is to establish a relationship with God who is in relationship with us always.'[4] The *Directory for the Celebration of the Work of God* makes a similar point by describing the office as a dialogue with God:

Care should be taken to ensure that the formal elements of the Office preserve their value as a means to establish a dialogue that grows ever more and more intense: namely, listening and responding to the Word of God, now in psalmody, now in prayer, either communal or silent.[5]

Spiritual depth is one reason why Benedict's patterns of prayer should be valued and cherished. Another is that the Work of God is liturgy, literally (from the Greek) the 'work of the people', not the work of an individual. It is a celebration of the whole community, presided over by the abbot, who represents Christ. As oblates, we belong to that community, and so must retain some liturgical connection with those with whom we are spiritually united by attempting to make part of their community prayer our prayer each day.

For some oblates, this may be possible by using the same form of office as the monastic community to which we belong, or at least following the same liturgical calendar. For others, our daily routine may be such that it is possible to say at least one office at the same time as it is being celebrated in the oratory. For all oblates, we should try to pray for our communities each day, just as they are praying for us, and to keep a list of the names of the professed and their daily timetable in our office books. Some communities also produce their own prayer diaries or cycles of intercession, which provide another way of expressing our spiritual union and supporting each other in prayer.

Benedict devotes one chapter of his Rule to the oratory, stating very clearly that 'the oratory ought to be what it is called, and nothing else is to be done or stored there' (*RB* 52.1). Although the sort of liturgical prayer from memory which I have encouraged makes a virtue of the freedom to pray anywhere, when it comes to our daily offering of the monastic community's prayer, the praying environment is important and should not be overlooked.

Very few oblates will be able to devote a whole room to the *Opus Dei*, but to set aside some space for this purpose unites us with the spirit of the Rule. Even those whose daily prayer takes place in a church or chapel will do well to consider the arrangement of the space they are using. Wherever we pray, a visual focal point is often helpful, whether a cross or crucifix, an open Bible, or a candle, and may be varied according to the season. An icon of St

Benedict can also provide a powerful visual reminder of our spiritual identity and of our membership of a community which seeks to model its life in accordance with his Rule.

Having spent some time considering how the oblate's celebration of the *Opus Dei* relates to that of the monastic community, in terms of frequency, form and location, the rest of this chapter will be devoted to the importance of praise and silence within the Benedictine tradition, as well as the place of psalmody within the Work of God.

Praise

Set reminder in Outlook?

You do not have to worship with a Benedictine community for very long to appreciate that praise permeates the whole of the *Opus Dei*. In the five short verses of Chapter 16 of the Rule, which, as we have seen, give a biblical warrant for the eightfold pattern of daily prayer, the word 'praise' appears no less than five times. The previous chapter concerns the liturgical use of 'Alleluia', whose literal translation is 'praise the Lord'. Here we find one of Benedict's few liturgical innovations, as the use of this Hebrew acclamation of praise is extended to the whole of the Christian year, with the exception of Lent. The use of the Gloria and the singing of hymns, mentioned already, strengthen this emphasis, as does the use of the Laudate psalms (Ps. 148–150) at Lauds (*RB* 13.11). In the threefold repetition of Psalm 50[51].17 *Ps 51* at the beginning of Vigils, 'Lord, open my lips and my mouth shall proclaim your praise' (*RB* 9.1), the community greets the source of its life and the goal of its longing with words which make clear that it has embarked afresh upon the Work of God whose single-minded purpose is the praise of God. But this is only possible because God has taken the initiative; he himself has opened the lips of his people so that he may be at work in this celebration of praise and prayer. In the words of Esther de Waal, 'I pray not only because I am seeking God but because God is also seeking me.'[6]

For the Benedictine oblate as much as for the monastic community, praise must be at the heart of our prayer. It is praise which rebalances the relationship between God and the community and puts the author of life at the very centre of our being. Most forms of the office contain substantial elements of praise, particularly at Morning Prayer. Oblates may wish to strengthen this by making sure that one of the Laudate psalms is always included (which need not be limited to the last three psalms, but may include Ps. 145[146]-147 as well as Ps. 116[117]). A threefold repetition of Psalm 50[51].17 at the beginning of the daily celebration of the *Opus Dei* would also be suitable, particularly when praying alone. Indeed, even if a full form of monastic prayer is offered in the morning, a threefold repetition of this verse would be appropriate for any oblate at the start of the day.

Silence

The Prologue to Benedict's Rule begins with an exhortation to listen: 'Listen carefully, my son, to the master's instructions, and attend to them with the ear of your heart' (*RB* Prologue 1). At the beginning of Vigils, having asked God to open the lips of the community that they might proclaim his praise, the office moves on quite quickly, within the second of the appointed psalms, to emphasize the importance of listening to the voice of God: 'O that today you would listen to his voice. Harden not your hearts' (Ps. 94[95].8).

It goes without saying that listening with an open heart requires stillness and silence. In several places the Rule emphasizes the importance of silence, but not explicitly with respect to the Work of God. In Chapter 6, Benedict makes clear that 'Speaking and teaching are the master's task; the disciple is to be silent and listen' (*RB* 6.6). The following chapter lists silence as the ninth step of humility (*RB* 7.56) and Chapter 42 makes clear that those who speak during the greater silence after Compline should be severely punished (*RB* 42.9). This is not silence for silence's sake, but rather silence to listen with the heart.

Some oblates may have the opportunity to find time during the day to keep an extended period of silence to quieten the soul and open the ear of the heart. But for the majority for whom this is not possible, it is important that the *Opus Dei* should include some opportunity for silence, even though it is not one of Benedict's liturgical instructions. For oblates, with our wordy offices, there's always a danger that our faith can become little more than 'poor little talkative Christianity', which was Mrs Moore's experience in E. M. Forster's *A Passage to India*. Silence is an important counter-balance to this. Many contemporary Christians find liturgical silence an awkward experience. It is often perceived as a gap in the service, something to be stood, knelt or sat through, rather than used for any useful purpose.

Whenever possible, we should prepare for the office in silence: 'On God alone my soul in stillness waits; from him comes my salvation', sings the psalmist (Ps. 61[62].1). Silence can also be used after the psalmody, to develop the spiritual emotion which has been expressed through them, be it praise, lament, thanksgiving or intercession. Equally, if our form of the office contains long passages of scripture, a period of silence for absorption, as much as for reflection, is often helpful, and can help turn the proclamation of God's word into a springboard for intercession for the needs of God's world.

Even though we may, more often than not, say the office on our own, silence should not be neglected. It doesn't just give space for the prayers of individual members of a community during a corporate liturgical celebration. More importantly, it gives space for God to speak: 'O that today we would listen to his voice.'

Psalmody

No consideration of Benedict and the daily office would be complete without some attention being given to the importance of psalmody. Benedict's Rule is littered with quotations from the Psalms, to the extent that the psalter is quoted more often than the New Testament. Liturgically, more time is given over to the recitation of the psalter than any other element within the Work of God. Though showing some flexibility in the order in which the psalms might be said in the course of a week, there is no leeway when it comes to quantity:

For monks who in a week's time say less than the full psalter with the customary canticles betray extreme indolence and lack of devotion in their service. We read, after all, that our holy Fathers, energetic as they were, did all this in a single day. Let us hope that we, lukewarm as we are, can achieve it in a whole week. (*RB* 18.24–25)

Moreover, we have already seen that, not only does Benedict advocate the recitation of the whole psalter over the course of a week, he also requires that the psalms should be learnt by heart. As Esther de Waal points out, Benedict 'clearly wished that in his monastery the life of the community and the life of each individual should . . . be shaped and formed by them . . . until the words of the psalms might inform the mind and penetrate the heart'.[7]

For those of us who are oblates, if our minds and hearts are to be transformed by the psalter, then we need to make sure that psalmody plays a central part within our celebration of the *Opus Dei*. Michael Perham has observed that 'All too often nowadays psalmody can feel like one of the preliminaries, especially when it has been reduced to a snippet.'[8] When it came to the psalter, Benedict had no time for snippets, and nor should we. Whatever form of office we use, we should make sure that the recitation of the psalter is given its full and proper place. Even though most oblates will not be able to achieve the 75 psalms a week which the *Directory for the Celebration of the Work of God* requires,[9] at least one substantial portion of psalmody should be part of our daily diet.

But why give the psalter such an honoured place within the office? Commentators on the Rule give different reasons to justify its central position in Benedict's liturgical code. For me, its chief glory lies in its ability to allow us to address God, and God to address us. Christian prayer can so often lack honesty and integrity when it fails to reflect the reality of the world in which we find ourselves. The psalms earth us in this reality and enable our prayer to be real. Esther de Waal puts it like this:

Sometimes they seem like incantations lulling me into the certainty of the goodness of God. Sometimes they are battle hymns that will not let me forget the tremendous battle against the forces of evil that surround me. Sometimes God is close, sometimes he is distant. Sometimes they speak of fullness and riches, at other times of poverty and emptiness.[10]

The psalter, then, gives the community which prays it permission to be itself before God, a voice to express itself to God and, not least, an ear to hear the voice of God. This ties in with what we have already said about the Spirit speaking beneath the surface of our liturgical prayer, as well as in and through it. We know from the writings of Origen that, from as far back as the third century, in some forms of the office the community observed a period of silence after the psalmody, which was concluded by a collect. One of the purposes of the collect was to give the psalm a christological interpretation, but it also drew together the thoughts and prayers of the community which had been triggered by their engagement with the psalter. It is not by accident that Benedict refers to the psalmist as the Prophet (see *RB* 19.3, for example). As well as providing a means of honest spiritual self-expression, the psalter also speaks a prophetic word to the community which points to Christ as well as inviting a response in prayer.

We are not used to thinking of the psalter in these terms, but the use of psalm collects can help us to attune our ears to its prophetic voice. Several contemporary collections are available. Complete sets can be found in the Church of England's *Common Worship: Daily Prayer* as well as John Eaton's *The Psalms: A Historical and Spiritual Commentary*.

Conclusion

This chapter has attempted to provide some insights into what the celebration of the Work of God might mean for a Benedictine oblate, as well as what form it might take; but it cannot be too prescriptive. From the starting point of our own individual situations, it is up to each of us, guided by our communities, to discern how the Rule's teaching concerning the divine office might lead us into a deeper dialogue with God and one another. In the divine conversation, which is the life of discipleship, the *Opus Dei* is both life-giving and life-transforming. It expresses our belonging to a 'school of the Lord's service', but more importantly it opens the ear of our heart to listen to the voice of the God who calls us constantly into union with him. In the words of the Prologue: 'Clothed then with faith and the performance of good works, let us set out on this way, with the Gospel for our guide, that we may deserve to see him who has called us to his kingdom' (*RB* Prologue 21).

For oblates, living in union with a human community in order to be drawn into a divine community, 'nothing is to be preferred to the Work of God'.

Notes

1 The translation of the Rule quoted in this chapter is taken from *RB 1980: The Rule of St Benedict in English*, ed. Timothy Fry, Liturgical Press, 1982.

2 Taft, *The Liturgy of the Hours in East and West*, p. 140.

3 Field (ed.), *The Monastic Hours*, p. 43.

4 Chittister, *The Rule of Benedict: Insights for the Ages*.

5 Field (ed.), *The Monastic Hours*, p. 22.

6 de Waal, *A Life-Giving Way*.

7 de Waal, *Living with Contradiction*.

8 Perham, *Benedict and the Worship of the Church Today*, p. 9.

9 *The Monastic Hours*, p. 75.

10 Waal, *A Life-Giving Way*, p. 66.

Further reading

Joan Chittister, *The Rule of Benedict: Insights for the Ages*, Crossroad, 1992.

Common Worship: Daily Prayer, Church House Publishing, 2005.

Esther de Waal, *A Life-Giving Way: A Commentary on the Rule of St Benedict*, Mowbray, 1995.

Esther de Waal, *Living with Contradiction*, Canterbury Press, 2003.

John Eaton, *The Psalms: A Historical and Spiritual Commentary*, T&T Clark, 2003.

Anne Field (ed.), *The Monastic Hours: Directory for the Celebration of the Work of God and Directive Norms for the Celebration of the Monastic Liturgy of the Hours*, Liturgical Press, 2000.

Michael Perham, *Benedict and the Worship of the Church Today*, Alcuin Club, 2006.

Robert Taft, *The Liturgy of the Hours in East and West*, Liturgical Press, 1993.

11. The Psalms

SIMON BRYDEN-BROOK

Confusingly there are two different numbering schemes for the psalms. The first number given below is that used in our Catholic and Orthodox liturgical books. This is followed by the number used in the Hebrew text and most Bibles.

Jesus the Christ   *Jesus prayed the Psalms*

The psalms lie at the heart of the *Opus Dei*, which St Benedict insists is central (*RB* 43). But how can Christians make the Jewish prayer book the core of their daily prayer in this way? As Christians, not only do we believe in the message of Jesus, the words that he uttered and which are recorded, admittedly with elaborations and commentary, in the Christian scriptures, but we believe in Jesus as the Christ, God's anointed, the Messiah. But were not the psalms written long before Jesus was born and in ignorance of him and his message? Even so, for us Psalm 109[110] refers to the victorious Jesus:

> The Lord's [God the Father's] revelation to my Master [Jesus]:
> 'Sit on my right;
> your foes I will put beneath your feet.'

We see in Psalm 2 a reference to the future sufferings of the newly born Jesus:

> Why this tumult among nations,
> among peoples this useless murmuring?

They arise, the kings of the earth;
princes plot against the Lord [God the Father] and his
    Anointed [Jesus].

The Jews knew that humankind is the very image of God (Gen.
1.26). For Christians the full meaning of humanity is to be found
in Jesus the man, who is the Christ, the very best image of God.
This is where an understanding of the incarnation enables a
Christian to *live with reality*, or 'have life to the full' (John 10.10).
Christianity is no opium as Marx had it, no drug to dull the pain
of earthly existence, but the way to be fully human, following
Jesus, the complete person and 'God's true likeness'. Part of this
way of living in Christ involves entering into the true nature of
suffering, as Jesus did on the cross, where the psalmist often finds
suffering incomprehensible and an affront to God's omnipotence
and love. So for Christians the despair of Psalm 21[22] can only
seem to come from Jesus on the cross, and only then, from ourselves when we unite our sufferings with his:

My God, my God, why have you forsaken me?
You are far from my plea and the crying of my distress.
O my God, I call by day and you give no reply.
I call by night and find no peace.

Jewish and Christian prayer

If understanding Jesus as God's anointed is central to a Christian
use of the psalms, then so is our understanding of prayer and of
God's presence. For the Jew, God is intimately present at all times,
willing to listen to whatever God's people have to say and as a
loving parent, never being shocked or rejecting, however childish,
self-centred or even vengeful the outpourings:

O God, break the teeth in their mouths;
tear out the fangs of these wild beasts O Lord.
Let them vanish like water that runs away;
let them wither like grass that is trodden underfoot.
(Ps. 57[58].7–8)

The psalms cover the whole gamut of human emotions. But the Jews have always recognized that far more important than what they have to say to God is what God has to say to them. Listening to God, hearing God's message and responding to it by acting in accordance with God's will is central to Jewish prayer and this is the prayer of the psalms. The Christian who prays the psalms is doing no less than the Jew who does so, seeking to hear God's voice and having the strength to respond to it – precisely what Jesus prayed and did. But in fact we are doing more than the Jews, for we pray the psalms *along with* Jesus and *in* Jesus, sharing in his priestly prayer and, we hope, his priestly life and ministry.

Of course, the term 'God's word' means much more to a Christian than to a Jew. For us Jesus is God's own Word, God's last Word, as it were. Just as the Jew sees God's word as fecund (Isa. 55.11) and reviving (Ps. 18[19].8), Christians see in Jesus God's life-giving Word, God with us (Emmanuel means just that), to whom we respond 'not only with our lips but in our lives' so that we come to live 'in Christ', as St Paul teaches (Gal. 2.20), and become the very Body of Christ ourselves, the Word incarnated in our twenty-first-century world. Ezekiel prophesied:

> 'I will put my sanctuary among them for ever.
> My dwelling place will be with them;
> I will be their God,
> and they will be my people.
> Then the nations will know
> that I the Lord make Israel holy,
> when my sanctuary is among them for ever.' (Ezek. 37.26–28)

Christians see this prophecy as fulfilled in the Christian community, striving to be the presence of the Risen Christ in the world. So Psalm 8 seems to speak of our great vocation to share in this redemptive work of Jesus:

> When I see the heavens, the work of your hands
> The moon and the stars which you arranged,
> what are we that you should keep us in mind,
> men and women that you care for us?

You have made us little less than gods
and crowned us with glory and honour,
gave us power over the works of your hands,
put all things under our feet.

Our relationship with God

Central for the Christian using the psalms is an understanding of
our relationship with God. The Jewish scriptures tell us how from
the very beginning God sought intimacy with humankind. Unlike
the pagans who believed their gods present in idols, the Jewish
people rejected any image of God. They learnt of God present in a
burning bush, in the 'still small voice of the storm' (1 Kings 19.12),
present in the Ark carried through the desert, present in the Holy
of Holies in the Temple on Mount Zion, and present indeed in his
name YHWH, which must never be uttered. All of these figure in the
psalms. For Christians, God is still with us but now pre-eminently
made present in the person of Jesus, the Risen Christ, present
sacramentally in the Eucharist, celebrated in the liturgy of the
hours and incarnated in us his people, the Church.

O where can I go from your spirit,
Or where can I flee from your face?
If I climb the heavens you are there.
If I lie in the grave you are there.

If I take the wings of the dawn
and dwell at the sea's furtherst end,
even there your hand would lead me,
your right hand would hold me fast. (Ps. 138[139].7–10)

We hear the whole story of God's relationship with his people
every Holy Saturday in the readings prescribed for the liturgy of
the Easter Vigil. God loves humankind and is totally committed to
it; for the Jewish people of course, this means that God is committed to the Jews as God's people. The psalms delight to rehearse
God's dealings with his people:

They forgot the things he had done,
the marvellous deeds he had shown them.
He did wonders in the sight of their forebears,
in Egypt, in the plains of Zoan.

He divided the sea and led them through
and made the waters stand up like a wall.
By day he led them with a cloud,
by night, with a light of fire.

He split the rocks in the desert.
He gave them plentiful drink as from the deep.
He made streams flow out from the rock
and made waters run down like rivers. (Ps. 77[78].11–16)

Even so, the scriptures make plain that in fact the covenant relationship is between God and the whole of creation, of which we
are the custodians.

How many are your works, O Lord!
In wisdom you have made them all.
The earth is full of your riches.

There is the sea, vast and wide,
with its moving swarms past counting,
living things great and small.
The ships are moving there
and the monsters you made to play with.

All of these look to you
to give them their food in due season.
You give it; they gather it up.
You open your hand; they have their fill. (Ps. 103[104].24–28)

The later prophets insisted that God was not in fact exclusive in his
favours and that God's love extends to the rest of the world, to
those whom the Jews referred to as 'the nations'. God's love, we

know as Christians, extends to *all humankind* not just to those who do God's will, the virtuous, or those who belong to the chosen race, to the elect, or even just to the household of faith.

> All the nations shall come to adore you
> and glorify your name, O Lord.
> For you are great and do marvellous deeds,
> you who alone are God. (Ps. 85[86].9–10)

God's rule

Perhaps even more important for the Christian using the psalms is our understanding of God's rule, that is, the values which God wishes to prevail among humankind.

> Yours is an everlasting kingdom;
> your rule lasts from age to age. (Ps. 144[145].13)

What is this 'rule'? For the Jews it is a world where justice and peace reign, where God's will is venerated and observed.

> It is God who gives bread to the hungry,
> the Lord who sets prisoners free,
>
> the Lord who gives sight to the blind,
> who raises up those who are bowed down,
> the Lord who protects the stranger
> and upholds the widow and orphan. (Ps. 145[146].7–9)

Here is an echo of the prophecy of Isaiah that God would make his people 'a light for the gentiles, to open eyes that are blind, to free captives from prison and to release from the dungeon those who sit in darkness'. (Isa. 42.6–7).

How can a Christian hear these words without immediately recalling our Lord's parable of the last judgement, the separation of the sheep from the goats?

When did we see you see you hungry and feed you,
or thirsty and give you something to drink?
When did we see you a stranger and invite you in,
or needing clothes and clothe you?
When did we see you sick
or in prison and go to visit you? (Matt. 25.37–39)

Surely too we also recall the words of the Mother of God as recorded in Luke's Gospel:

You have put down the mighty from their seat
and have lifted up the powerless.
You have filled the hungry with good things
and have sent the rich away empty . . .

You, remembering your mercy,
have helped your people . . . (Luke 1.52–54)

Isaiah's promise of a light blazing forth on the people that walk in darkness (Isa. 9.1) also reminds us of Simeon, who took the infant Jesus into his arms when he was presented in the Temple and said:

Now my eyes have seen your salvation . . .
a light for revelation to the gentiles
and for glory to your people Israel. (Luke 2.29–32)

Similarly, we can hardly forget the words of John the Baptist's father Zechariah, who said of his newly born son:

You, my child, shall be called a prophet of the Most High . . .
you will go . . . to prepare the way for him . . .
the rising sun will come to us . . .
to shine on those living in darkness
and guide our feet into the path of peace. (Luke 1.76–79)

With the Jews, we join with the psalmist in proclaiming:

The Lord has made known his salvation;
has shown his justice to the nations.
He has remembered his truth and love
for the house of Israel.

All the ends of the earth have seen
the salvation of our God. (Ps. 97[98].2–3)

But of course we understand this differently. 'I will give you a new heart and put a new spirit in you', promises Ezekiel (Ezek. 36.26), and for Christians this promise is both fulfilled in Jesus and *being fulfilled in us*, his church, the Body of the Christ, for that is the essence of the Christian vocation, to be the presence of God in our world. Psalm 84[85] speaks of the coming golden age, when with our help God's will rules the cosmos:

I will hear what the Lord God has to say,
a voice that speaks of peace,
a peace for his people and his friends
and those who turn to him in their hearts . . .

Mercy and faithfulness have met;
justice and peace have embraced.
Faithfulness shall spring from the earth
and justice look down from heaven.

The Lord will make us prosper
and our earth shall yield its fruit.
Justice shall march before him
and peace shall follow his steps. (Ps. 85[86].9, 11–14)

The concept of God's rule, which Jesus proclaimed as breaking in upon us now, is therefore central to an understanding of the psalms and how they are understood by Christians. The three gospel 'canticles' quoted above, called by their opening words in Latin *Magnificat*, *Benedictus* and *Nunc Dimittis*, are but Christian psalms, using the vocabulary and concepts of the traditional

Jewish psalms but in the light of God's revelation in Jesus. In the praying of the psalms with Jesus we ask ourselves how we are going to respond to this proclamation of God's rule.

The message of the psalms

With the insights which our faith gives us, Christians must therefore continue to pray the psalms with our sisters and brothers the Jews, but with and in Jesus, the Christ. In the psalms we learn that God is ever present as transcendent Creator. Not only this, but the ever-present, all-seeing God, loves me and wants intimacy with me and yearns for my commitment in return. In my life I see that God blesses me and at times seems to withdraw and even allows me to suffer.

But in my suffering God reappears, returns to me, offering both forgiveness for actions of mine that may have taken me from God's presence (Ps. 50[51].13) and comfort in my pain. God seeks me out and revives me. For Christians of course this reviving, this new life which God gives us after raising us up from the depths, often so eloquently described in the psalms, is nothing but the new life mediated to us by the resurrection. 'I live – not me – but Christ lives in me' (Gal. 2.20).

Conclusion

Like the Jews but with the faith that comes from our understanding of Jesus as God's anointed, we stand in the presence of God. This presence is symbolized for us in church by the altar (our rock), to which we turn at the start of Morning Prayer, making the sign of the cross on our lips, to recite the *Venite*, the invitatory psalm (94[95]) with its solemn call to listen to God's voice and 'harden not your hearts'.

> Come, ring out our joy to the Lord;
> hail the rock who saves us.
> Let us come before him giving thanks;
> with songs let us hail the Lord . . .

Come in, let us kneel and bend low.
Let us kneel before the God who made us
for he is our God and we
the people who belong to his pasture
the flock that is led by his hand.

O that today you would listen to his voice!
'Harden not your hearts as at Meribah,
as on that day at Massah in the desert
when your forebears put me to the test;
when they tried me, though they saw my work.'

(Ps. 94[95].1–2, 6–9)

We hear of God's covenant love for his people down the ages, knowing that this extends not only to the Jews, his own chosen people, but to all of humankind. We yearn, with the psalmist, for the rule of God, for God's reign of justice and peace on earth, knowing that Jesus has told us that the kingdom is breaking in now and it is up to us to respond and to realize it. 'Your kingdom come; your will be done.'

Further reading

The Grail Psalms: An Inclusive Language Version, London, Collins, 1986. (Quotations above from this version.)

The Psalms: A New Translation, Singing Version, Paulist Press, New York and Mahwah, 1966. (Grail. This edition has brief but helpful notes preceding each psalm.)

Sidney Condray, *O Gracious One: 150 Psalm-Inspired Prayers*, Twenty-Third Publications, Mystic CR, 2005. (This shows how we can make the prayers of the psalms our own.)

Anne M. Field (ed.), *The Monastic Hours: Directory for the Celebration of the Work of God and the Directive Norms for the Celebration of the Monastic Liturgy of the Hours*, Liturgical Press, Collegeville MN, 2000, 2nd edn. (Technical guidelines specifically for Benedictines.)

Lynn Fraser, *Prayers from the Darkness – The Difficult Psalms*, Church Publishing, New York, 2005. (This gets to grips with some of the harsher, even un-Christian, psalms and shows how we can use them.)

Simon Bryden-Brook

Maxwell Johnson et al., *Benedictine Daily Prayer: A Short Breviary*, Columba, Dublin, 2005. (Used by many oblates for daily prayer, closely following the Rule and Benedictine tradition.)

Robert Taft, *The Liturgy of the Hours in East and West: The Divine Office and Its Meaning for Today*, Liturgical Press, Collegeville MN, 1986. (A magisterial theological and historical work.)

12. *Lectio Divina*

LUKE DYSINGER

One of the most ancient and traditional approaches to Christian contemplation is the practice of *lectio divina*, the art of inwardly repeating and praying a biblical text in such a way that the Word of God gently becomes an experience of union with God. This practice is especially prized by Benedictine monks, nuns and oblates, who accord it a privileged place in their daily rhythm of prayer and work. *Lectio divina* originated in veneration of the Torah and meditation on the sacred scriptures that characterized ancient Judaism: Philo of Alexandria, a contemporary of Jesus, described its practice among Jewish monastics in Egypt and Palestine.[1] Christian leaders such as Cyprian of Carthage, Ambrose of Milan and Jerome eagerly recommended it to the Christian faithful and thereby attest to its widespread practice in the early church.[2] But it was in early Christian monasticism that the practice of *lectio divina* reached its full flower. Faithful to the traditions of St Basil and the Egyptian monastics of the desert, St Benedict encouraged his monks to reserve the best hours of each day for *lectio divina*, a form of prayer that he, unlike some of his predecessors, regarded as a contemplative joy rather than an ascetical burden.[3]

Lectio divina is much more than a method of meditating on the Bible: it is a means of beholding the whole created order charged with God's meaning and purpose. For the monastic or oblate who practises it daily, *lectio divina* becomes a spiritual laboratory in which God is contemplated: first, in the scriptures; then, in the mysterious movements of the human heart; and, finally, refracted in the glory of a world beyond the self. Having discovered God present within and beneath the 'letter' of the scriptures, the practitioner of *lectio divina* gradually learns to look up from the sacred text into the relationships and events of daily life, and to incorporate them into a rhythm of reflection, prayer and contemplation that reveals these, too, as 'salvation history'. With the aid of *lectio divina* it becomes possible to behold God present in interpersonal relationships, daily tasks and world events, and to consecrate these experiences to God in prayer, along with the inner world of one's temptations, fears and hopes. The means by which *lectio divina* encourages this prayerful offering of text, heart and world is perceptible within the structure of the practice itself.

The theory of *lectio divina*

Underlying the art of *lectio divina* is the presumption that all human experience entails an alternating rhythm, a life-giving, energizing movement back and forth between the poles of spiritual 'activity' and 'receptivity'. The active pole includes speaking, searching and working; receptivity entails listening, perceiving and quietly being. Well-balanced spiritual practice always consists in a gentle oscillation between these two. The importance of this rhythm is obvious even in activities modern culture considers 'secular'. For example, wholesome conversation requires both listening and speaking, with appropriate intervals given over to reflecting, commenting, pondering and asking for information. Similarly, efforts in the workplace are often most productive when they are regularly punctuated by intervals of relaxation and movement, during which the solution to complex problems sometimes emerges unexpectedly. If this balanced rhythm is characteristic of all healthy human endeavors, it follows that our experience of God (who, after all, placed this rhythm within the human heart!) should also include and even celebrate this gentle oscillation. And it is precisely this that the practice of *lectio divina* seeks to do.

The practice of *lectio divina*

The goal of *lectio divina* is, quite simply, prayer. *Lectio divina* is not Bible study in the usual sense of the term, and should not be confused with it. The biblical text that is pondered in *lectio divina* is entirely secondary and instrumental: it is a means rather than an end. The primary purpose of the biblical text is to become transparent, to give way to the loving embrace of the God who originally inspired and who is present, waiting, within the text. Although it is not an exegetical method in the modern sense, *lectio divina* must always proceed from a profound respect for the literal, historical meaning of the text[4] and should therefore be grounded in the best possible modern exegesis. A trusted modern commentary is often the best place to begin the practice of *lectio divina*.[5]

Since the twelfth century, largely through the influence of Hugh of St Victor and Guigo the Carthusian, introductions to *lectio divina* customarily describe four (sometimes five) rungs or steps in a spiritual 'ladder'.[6] While this model may be helpful for beginners, it can give modern readers the false impression of a fixed technique that necessarily proceeds in a stepwise progression. In practice, the order of movement between Guigo's 'rungs' is constantly changing, more like a dance or a musical fugue than linear ascent. Rather than steps or rungs, the following four subjects could perhaps be more profitably conceived as recurring 'notes' in a changing musical phrase, or as interweaving 'colors' in a complex tapestry.

Lectio – *reading/listening*

The art of *lectio divina* requires the cultivation of inner quiet. Beginning with a few minutes of silence or monologistic prayer[7] can help prepare for a method of reading that is radically different from what is taught in modern schools. In antiquity reading, even in private, was generally done aloud. Thus the text was seen, heard, felt as vibration, and even in a sense 'tasted' as words were formed on the tongue and lips. While this may no longer be appropriate or possible, it is a reminder that in the ages when *lectio divina* flourished, reading, *lectio*, meant taking a text in, allowing it to literally become part of the self. In *lectio divina* the goal is not to master a text, to mine it for information, but rather to be touched, to be formed by it. Interior quiet facilitates an ability to read gently and attentively, inwardly listening 'with the ear of the heart'.[8] Like Elijah, who had to ignore wind, fire and earthquake in order to hear the still, small voice of God (I Kings 19.11–12), the practitioner of *lectio divina* learns to read the biblical text slowly, expectantly, listening for the 'faint murmuring sound' that represents God's invitation to take in a verse or two, then to memorize and repeat the text inwardly.

Meditatio – *meditation*

The inward gentle repetition of a text that allows it to slowly touch the heart is called *meditatio*; in Hebrew, *hagah*, in Greek, *meletē*.[9] In Christian antiquity the word *ruminatio* was often used as its equivalent: the image of a ruminant animal quietly chewing its cud became a symbol of the Christian pondering the Word of God and savoring its sweetness. But a much more popular and vivid invitation to *lectio divina* was found in the example of the Virgin Mary who 'pondered in her heart' what she saw and heard of Christ (Luke 2.19).[10] This inward pondering, *ruminatio*, on sacred text allows the Word to interact with thoughts, hopes, memories, and desires. As this interaction proceeds, additional words, images and insights often arise. In many schools of meditation these emerging thoughts and memories are condemned as 'distractions' and rejected; but in *lectio divina* the response should be very different. What arises within the heart during *meditatio* is not something alien, intruding from without: these memories and insights are part of the self and are proper matter for that act of consecration that ancient Christian writers called *oratio* – prayer.

Oratio – *prayer*

'Prayer' is often conceived primarily as dialogue with God: indeed, 'conversation with God' (*homilia pros theon*) is an ancient and traditional Christian definition of prayer.[11] In *lectio divina* this dialogue should be characterized by *parrēsia*, a biblical concept that includes frankness and honesty in speech.[12] Through an upwelling of thoughts and images the practice of *meditatio* provides a (not always welcome) glimpse of the self: this in turn should stimulate dialogue with God that is utterly frank and candid. Having seen both what is good and what needs to be changed within the self, one can engage in honest 'conversation with God' and offer straightforward petition and intercession for self and others.

While the practice of scriptural *meditatio* naturally leads into dialogue with God, it can also encourage another, deeper kind of prayer. Early Christians noted the close connection between the Greek word for prayer, *proseuchē*, and the word for vow, *euchē*.[13] Prayer can be a kind of vow, an act of self-offering in which the self and all of one's relationships, hopes and concerns are consecrated, presented to God in an act of blessing that transforms and fills what is offered with new meaning.[14] The word of consecration or blessing that effects this offering can be the same phrase that is pondered in *meditatio*. Just as the elements of bread and wine are consecrated at the Eucharist, God invites those who practise *lectio divina* to exercise their royal priesthood by consecrating everything that arises during *meditatio*, whether seemingly trivial 'distractions', valuable insights or difficult and pain-filled memories. Over all of these should be gently recited the healing word or phrase God has given in *lectio*. In this *oratio*, this consecration-prayer, the innermost self together with all of one's relationships are touched and changed by the Word of God.

Contemplatio – *contemplation*

Contemplatio has traditionally been understood as an act of 'gazing' that entails participation in and communion with the object of contemplation.[15] In the context of *lectio divina* this refers to receptive, wordless prayer, silent gazing and rest in the embrace of the God who has offered his Word through *lectio* and *meditatio*. In contemplation the practitioner of *lectio divina* ceases from interior spiritual *doing* and learns simply to *be*, to rest in the presence of a loving Father. Although deeply enjoyable and a source of spiritual refreshment, *contemplatio* should not be regarded as the principal goal or purpose of *lectio divina*. The quality or efficacy of *lectio divina* should not be judged by the amount of time spent in any of its phases. No spiritual technique can guarantee or even prolong true contemplative prayer, which is always a pure grace and often an unexpected gift.[16] Instead, the awareness that this gift is sometimes offered can prepare the practitioner of *lectio divina* to cease using words when words are unnecessary and then return joyfully to the sacred text or to *ruminatio* when the (often brief!) moment of silent *contemplatio* has passed.

Lectio divina as a laboratory of Christian contemplation

The regular practice of *lectio divina* can help liberate the practitioner from a narrow modern definition of contemplation. In early Christianity the natural oscillation, described above, between 'active' and 'receptive' modes of spiritual experience slowly came to be associated with Platonic and Aristotelian notions of the active life (*bios praktikos*) and contemplative life (*bios theoretikos*). It was not a question of choosing or specializing in one or the other: these 'lives' were presumed to interact in every person in a mutually reinforcing rhythm. The 'active life' consists chiefly of the moral work of rooting out vices and practising virtue. Contemplation entails a second balanced movement between two mutually enhancing poles: *theoria physikē*, kataphatic, image- and word-filled contemplation of God in creation; and *theologia*, apophatic, wordless apprehension of God beyond all concepts and images.[17] Both modes of contemplation were considered necessary for a well-balanced spirituality.[18] Unfortunately, some spiritual authors today so emphasize apophatic practices of imageless, wordless prayer that *theoria physikē*, the contemplation of God in text, story, history and symbol is either neglected or not regarded as 'contemplation' at all. *Lectio divina*, on the contrary, teaches the practitioner to delight in moving back and forth between active and receptive experiences of God. In *lectio* the grandeur and complexity of biblical salvation history slowly focuses down on a single biblical phrase; the ruminated phrase then evokes complex personal responses. These responses, in turn, invite prayer, sometimes in words, sometimes in a simple act of consecration. At intervals one senses an opportunity simply to rest in the presence of God; then the invitation arises to return to the sacred text. As this rhythm of *lectio divina* becomes natural and familiar, one's understanding of 'contemplation' expands. One discovers that the same rhythm of listening and praying that reveals God in the scriptures can also be applied to that portion of salvation history that is one's own journey of faith: the glory of God becomes perceptible both in the macrocosm of the universe and in the microcosm of one's own heart.

This expanded experience of contemplation learned in the laboratory of *lectio divina* offers many possibilities. Spiritual texts that would otherwise seem opaque are rendered comprehensible. When read as the record of another's *lectio divina*, patristic and medieval biblical commentaries no longer seem awkward and tangential; they become, instead, treasured gifts from distant spiritual friends. Ancient enthusiasm for symbolism, architecture, and commentaries on the liturgy begin to make sense when one recognizes in their authors kindred spirits who experienced the meeting of microcosm and macrocosm in rituals and sacred places. And finally, the wisdom distilled in the ascetical literature of early monasticism becomes vibrant with the discovery that their great art of 'discerning thoughts' consisted in '*lectio* on life', a reading of the heart that laid bare both the temptations (*logismoi*) and divine purposes (*logoi*) present in all human choices.

Concluding thoughts on matter, time and space

The question is often asked whether sacred scripture is the only proper matter for *lectio divina*. Throughout the history of Christian monasticism the Bible has always retained 'pride of place' during the time set aside for *lectio divina*. But it is also true that certain other texts can be read in the same spirit and will enhance one's practice of biblical *lectio*. Benedict particularly commended to his monks the *Institutes* and *Conferences* of John Cassian, the *Rule of Basil*, and the *Lives* and *Sayings* of the Desert Fathers and Mothers.[19] All these have in common that they can in some sense be regarded as the fruit of other Christians' *lectio divina*. They reflect the wisdom and experience of monks and nuns whose spiritual lives were formed and shaped by the regular praying of scripture, and they frequently cite the Bible or (in the case of the desert texts) regularly allude to biblical models and images. It could be said that they 'whet the appetite' for biblical *lectio*, they encourage the reader to frequently turn back to the biblical text. The same can be said of the biblical commentaries of Origen, John Chrysostom, Augustine, Gregory the Great and Bede: these were often read together with (but never replaced!) the Bible in monastic *lectio divina*. There are modern authors whose works can similarly enhance the oblates' or monastics' experience of *lectio*: perhaps a simple rule of thumb is the question, 'Does this encourage me to return to the Bible?' If the answer is 'Yes', then the text is fit matter for *lectio divina*.

It needs to be frankly admitted that oblates who are able to set aside daily time for *lectio divina* have attained a much higher level of ascetical virtue than their monastic sisters and brothers. Those who are privileged to live within monasteries experience an environment where *lectio divina* is encouraged and protected: their oblate sisters and brothers enjoy no such luxury. Life 'in the world' and the responsibilities of family guarantee that time intended for prayer and *lectio divina* will regularly have to be sacrificed. For this reason it is important for oblates to have alternative 'quick and simple' approaches to *lectio divina* for those all-too-frequent days when minor emergencies arise. One simple approach is to place the text in a prominent place where it can be glanced at, if only briefly, while one dresses in the morning. Oblates whose faith communities emphasize liturgical worship often make use of the lectionary in their *lectio divina*. It is not difficult to leave a lectionary open on a desk or a shelf and to glance at some portion of the day's texts during such mundane preparations as brushing one's teeth. It is surprising how little time it takes under such circumstances for a word or phrase to present itself for *meditatio*. Even when time for extended *meditatio* and prayer is not available, the word that was taken in can serve as a means of consecrating events and relationships throughout the day. And for those whose work involves the use of a computer, websites such as http://www. universalis.com permit the laborer periodically to glance at the day's liturgical texts throughout the workday.

Notes

1 Philo, *On the Contemplative Life*, 13–31, 75–80; *That Every Good Man Is Free*, 80–5.

2 Cyprian, *Letter to Donatus* (Letter 1), 14–15; Jerome, *Commentary on Isaiah*, Prol.; Ambrose, *De Officiis* I, 20.

3 In the *Rule of the Master* (RM), St Benedict's principal source, the practice of *lectio divina* is called 'the work of the spirit' (RM 50.16). In the Master's monastery this practice occupied the hours between None and Vespers and was evidently regarded as unpleasant work, since the monks were freed both from it and from manual labor on Saturday afternoons as part of their 'Sunday rest' (RM 75.1, 4). Benedict however, in his Rule (RB) adds to the Master's daily afternoon *lectio* a morning period between Vigils and Lauds (RB 48.2–13), an interval during which the Master's monks were permitted to return to bed (RM 33.16). Far from being dispensed as an onerous burden, *lectio divina* is an important part of Benedict's Sunday observance (RB 48.22).

4 The most eager early exponents of this ancient art, such as Origen and Jerome, spent considerable portions of their lives in biblical language study and in quests for the best available manuscripts of the scriptures.

5 An insightful and practical study of the interrelationship between modern exegesis and *lectio divina* is provided by David Stanley SJ, 'A Suggested Approach to *Lectio Divina*', *American Benedictine Review*, March 1972, vol. 23, pp. 439–55.

6 Hugh, a canon and educator, wrote first, emphasizing the intellectual aspects of *meditatio* and including a fifth step, *operatio*, 'action' or 'work' (Hugh of St Victor, *Didascalion* 5, 9). Guigo, who knew Hugh's text, adapted it for Carthusian monks by removing the step of 'action', to produce his four 'rungs' of *lectio*, *meditatio*, *oratio* and *contemplatio* (Guigo II, *Scala Claustralium* 2–3, 12).

7 Various forms of monologistic ('short phrase') prayer are widely practised in Christianity. In the early fifth century John Cassian recommended inward repetition of the phrase 'O God, come to my assistance; O

Lord, make haste to help me' (*Conference* 10). Since the thirteenth century the 'Jesus Prayer' ('Lord Jesus Christ, Son of God, have mercy on me, a sinner') has been widely used by monastics in the Christian East. Modern variants of these monologistic methods include 'Centering Prayer' and John Main's 'Christian Meditation'.

8 Benedict, *RB* Prologue, 1.

9 In the first psalm *hagah/meletē/meditatio* (in, respectively, the Hebrew, Septuagint, and Vulgate versions) is commended as the proper use of sacred scripture by the just who 'delight in the law of the Lord'.

10 In the medieval western iconographic tradition the Blessed Virgin is always portrayed as engaged in *lectio divina* at the moment of the annunciation: this symbolically depicts the belief that pondering the scriptures facilitates reception by the soul of Christ, the Word of God.

11 Clement of Alexandria, *Stromateis* 7.7.39.6; Evagrius Ponticus, *On Prayer* 3.

12 Originally used to describe the privilege of Greek citizens to speak openly at public political assemblies, St Paul and the Letter to the Hebrews recommend prayer characterized by 'confidence of access' (*parrēsian*, Eph. 3.12) and 'confidence' (*parrēsias*, Heb. 4.16).

13 Origen, *On Prayer* 4, 1–2.

14 A vivid example of this consecration-prayer is found in the revelations of St Gertrude of Helfta: 'And all these things together, completely purified of every blemish and wonderfully ennobled in her heart by the heat of her loving desire – namely that these be transformed into submission to their lover – like gold purified in the crucible, these she seemed to present to the Lord.' *The Herald of Divine Love*, 4.4, 9.

15 The Latin word *contemplatio* is the equivalent of the Greek *theoria*. Under the influence of Plato *theoria* came to mean an exalted spiritual 'seeing', an experience of 'beholding' the truer world of the Forms that lies beyond the limited, material world perceptible by the senses (Plato, *Phaedrus* 7; the 'Parable of the Cave', *Republic* 7).

16 The terms 'contemplative prayer' and 'contemplation' are sometimes loosely used by modern spiritual authors to describe states attained through techniques that encourage imageless, wordless attentiveness to God, often employing monologistic prayer formulae (see note 7 above). Such apophatic attentiveness has sometimes been described in Christian ascetical and mystical theology as 'prayer of quiet'; and it can, indeed, be spiritually beneficial. However, such states are not the equivalent of *contemplatio/theoria* as these were understood by early Christian monastic and medieval spiritual writers. An analogy with interpersonal relationships may be helpful. In committed, loving relationships moments naturally and spontaneously arise when words are unnecessary and silent communion is preferable. It becomes possible during such moments simply to be with and to

silently enjoy the presence of the beloved. However, such moments cannot be artificially induced or prolonged through any technique. Rather, what can and should be sought is awareness that such moments do occasionally arise, together with a willingness to enjoy them. It is, not surprisingly, the same in one's relationship with God. The gift of *contemplatio* cannot be summoned or induced through spiritual practices: it can only be gratefully enjoyed when God offers it.

17 Evagrius Ponticus, *Praktikos* 1–3, 92; *Gnostikos* 20; *On Prayer* 57, 58, 86.

18 A good example of this balance is the sixth-century author Dionysius the Areopagite, who introduced the terms 'apophatic' and 'kataphatic' into Christian theology. He wrote *The Mystical Theology*, perhaps the most famous apophatic Christian treatise on *theologia*, as well as *The Divine Names*, *The Celestial Hierarchies* and *The Ecclesiastical Hierarchies*, which celebrate aesthetic and intellectual complexity through the splendor of God's presence in the church's sacraments, liturgical rites and the ranks of church leadership.

19 Benedict, *RB* 73.5.

Further reading

The two most important ancient texts on *lectio divina* are:

John Cassian, *Conference 14*, 'The First Conference of Abba Nesteros – On Spiritual Knowledge'. A literal Victorian translation of this text may be downloaded from the Internet in volume 11 of *The Nicene and Post-Nicene Fathers* (http://www.ccel.org) The best modern translation is by Boniface Ramsey, *John Cassian: The Conferences*, Paulist Press, 1997.

Guigo II, *The Ladder of Monks*, Cistercian Publications, 2004. The classical description of the medieval monastic practice of *lectio divina*.

Modern introductions to *Lectio divina*:

Michael Casey ocso, *Sacred Reading*, Ligouri, 1996. An excellent, complete introduction to the history and practice of *lectio divina*.

Luke Dysinger osb, *Accepting the Embrace of God, The Ancient Art of Lectio Divina*. Downloadable from the Internet, this introduction to *lectio divina* includes descriptions of private and group *lectio divina* and an exercise of 'lectio on life'. http://www.valyermo.com/ld-art.html.

David Foster osb, *Reading with God: Lectio Divina*, Continuum, International, 2005.

Thelma Hall, *Too Deep for Words*, Paulist Press, 1988. Basic introduction with many recommended passages for daily *lectio divina*.

André Louf OCSO, *Teach us to Pray*, Cowley, 1992. A rich, readable introduction to monastic spiritual practices, including *lectio divina;* praying the liturgy of the hours (the divine office); and monologistic prayer (the Jesus Prayer). Worth rereading regularly.

13. Silence

SUSIE HAYWARD

Why no! I never thought other than
That God is that great absence
In our lives, the empty silence
Within, the place where we go
Seeking, not in hope to
Arrive or find.[1]

Silence is not simply the cessation of words, or speech, or sound. It is a deeply complex and philosophical concept whereby our perceptions of a wordless space are challenged, often without encouragement. Silence is hard to attain because it has to be actively sought – even learnt – and its fruits are not always peaceful. Silence challenges us because, in its pursuit, we are simply switched into a world where we have to rely on our own inner resources – we are alone. But for those of us who actively seek relationship with God, becoming silent is a necessary part of prayer and the spiritual journey. It is not an easy path to take – it could be a risk but should we take that risk our lives can be positively transformed in surprising and extraordinary ways.

If we are to learn about silence and cultivate its art form, the monastery is the first place to visit, for it is within the ancient tradition of monasticism that we can begin to understand the relevance and the need for silence as a discipline and a way of life. It is highly relevant that the very first word of the Rule of St Benedict is 'Listen' – 'Listen, O my son, to the teachings of the master, and turn to them with the ear of your heart' (*RB* Prologue 1).

'Listen' (*obsculta*) – an imperative – is the first and most important instruction to the monk and sets the tone for the spirituality of
the entire Rule. Importantly, it suggests the adoption of an integrated attitude of humility and obedience to the one who teaches;
it is phrased in a paternalistic and loving way. To listen with the
'ear of your heart' is more than just an act of hearing; it implies
listening with your intellect and your whole emotional affectivity
and being.

In exploring these questions, this essay will have four sections:
the practice of silence; negation and silence; the value of solitude;
and the love of silence.

The practice of silence

> And the simple fact that by being attentive, by learning to listen
> (or recovering the natural capacity to listen which cannot be
> learned any more than breathing), we can find ourself engulfed
> in such happiness that it cannot be explained: the happiness of
> being at one with everything in that hidden ground of Love for
> which there can be no explanations.[2]

The world is crowded. In contemporary society noise and sound
emanate from every nook and cranny of our lives; we cannot get
away from it, even if we wanted to. Silence has become rare and
unaccustomed – unfashionable even. We are simply not used to it.
Indeed we may feel uncomfortable in the absence of noise. But we
actively need silence. Silence has the power to stimulate and regen-
erate our stressed minds and tired bodies – and without silence
God has no voice.

As an art form and an attitude to life silence is, largely speaking,
poorly practised and ill-attempted. Skills need to be learnt to
enable us to disappear into silence and become invisible from our
frenetic society. This reluctance to be silent leaves us vulnerable
and we may turn to every form of activity other than that actual
moment of 'switching-off'. Beginnings are always difficult. We
learn gradually to listen and to enjoy silence by reducing the noise
around us and turning down the volume. There are many ways we

can actively seek silence, for example by going on 'retreat', by taking time out to potter and be leisurely and mindful of ourselves and our surroundings. Inner resources can also be built up through hobbies that are both solo and absorbing activities, such as reading, walking and, paradoxically, listening to music. We must not feel guilty about becoming content and still. It is not difficult to take on a mantle of hyperactivity. Society encourages us to feel that being busy is a sign of success and that taking time out is a sign of weakness or failure. But the truth is that a high valuation of self-worth is dependant on building our inner resources and the only way we can do this is by stopping, reassessing and becoming still. We will begin to see the 'world' differently, our breathing will become more rhythmical, surrounding colour will intensify and brighten and our eyes will see more clearly and with greater perception. When this is achieved we will learn, gently and respectfully, how to pay attention – to become attentive and reflective to our inward workings and to the movement of God. Without becoming attentive we cannot hope to listen with the 'ear of the heart' (*RB* Prologue 1). The one leads to the other. Each attitude requires commitment, focus and a genuine desire to find God in the depths of our being and the Sacred within our relationships.

Silence can also be described as either 'interior silence' or 'exterior silence'. Interior silence relates to our inward search for knowledge and truth and integrity – for unity with God in seclusion. Exterior silence fuels our experience whereby speech and silence are in balance with each other; each attending to the other and making a harmonious whole. Without exterior silence we cannot learn both how challenging inner silence is but also how possible it is. A person who is familiar and comfortable with exterior silence – who is not fearful of their own solitude – will find inner silence and its transforming power considerably easier to attain.

Listening is basic to good communication because we cannot talk and listen at the same time. Speech drowns out silence.

If we fail to listen correctly and with full attention to what is really being said to us, misunderstandings will occur which will leave us perplexed and disengaged. Conversely, when we are not listened and attended to, there is that awful sense of saying or even revealing something important and subsequently feeling misunderstood. No matter how or what we say to justify or rectify our position the matter can't be put right. There is nothing more likely than this failure in communication to raise our levels of anxiety and anger.

In contrast, some of us will have been fortunate enough to have had the experience of feeling the total 'presence' of another person, in such a profound way that 'in that moment' we will have felt absolutely heard, totally cared for and completely understood. In some inexplicable way, we will feel healed and reconciled with ourselves and even with the world. Such experiences are truly spiritual and all too rare, but once received will never be forgotten. Listening reflectively in this attentive and empathic way allows each person to respond to the other fruitfully. As the Rule says, 'A disciple should be quiet and listen' (*RB* 6.6).

Listening attentively is the highest form of empathic response and eminently creative. And what is more, it is an entirely free commodity – it costs us nothing other than the time to become self-forgetful. If we aspire to practise this form of silence, which is active not passive, we will increasingly become more observant and intuitive. Unquestionably, our lives will hold greater depth and a gentle transformation of our personal and spiritual lives will occur in unimaginable ways.

Negation and silence

> You know, brothers, that silence is a burden for many. Quiet weighs them down. As a result, everything becomes a burden when they have to stop speaking and be quiet: their head aches, their stomach rumbles, they cannot see, their kidneys weaken . . . You may see a monk sitting in the cloister, looking this way and that, yawning frequently, stretching his arms and legs. Now he puts the book down. Now he takes it up again. Finally, as if stung by a goad, he gets up and wanders from place to place and from one parlour to another.[3]

The expectation that silence will always bring us peace and tranquility is, we all know, a false assumption. Silence and its empty spaces can make us fearful. Supposing we have chosen to be silent and there is a felt absence of God, of peace and a distaste for what we are doing. We feel restless and out of sorts or possibly depressed and our thoughts move distractedly from one painful situation to another. Our imaginations run wild and any value that we may attribute to ourselves or to our status becomes meaningless. Stark reality is challenging.

We all have issues that need to be addressed and it is often in silence that our sadness and anger, resentment and anxiety come to the fore. Wave upon wave of memories and past regrets can haunt us. This is an uncomfortable and lonely place to inhabit and we may wonder why we have invested so much of our precious free time in ways that feel so counterproductive to the real peace and sense of consolation that we all desire. Be patient – the space between painful memory and the present moment will eventually dissipate and fade. Pain need not turn to anger. This space permits us to make choices, stand back and sort our feelings out. With perseverance our self-awareness will increase and empower us to make better choices. This is a mark of our desire to find inner reconciliation.

Silence, within its many dimensions, can have personal negative connotations. We can all create situations within our everyday environment when we choose to be unresponsive to people. This will be at least hurtful and perhaps destructive to the person who is at the other end of 'our silent attack'. By staying silent, or by ignoring, we manipulate, take control and create hostility. Power games played out like this hurt and take their toll on relationships. These are two of the most psychologically cruel and damaging ways in which we can reduce another to invisibility or to becoming a non-person.

There are times, as well, when we may have to speak up for the sake of social conscience or political justice. For example, are we prepared to be inclusive, to give voice to political action? Or will we refuse and stay silent to save our social or political position? To be aware of the harm that we can cause through lack of courage and personal integrity will force us to think and give us greater insight into *caritas*.

Within such negative silence, God can feel truly absent. However, our memories of God's presence in the past can act, even in these difficult moments, as a powerful reminder that at some point there is the promise of future hope. Without a prior sense of God's presence there would not now be a sense of God's absence. And in the ever-changing seasons of the heart consolation will not be far away.

The value of solitude

> When from our better selves we have too long
> Been parted by the hurrying world, and droop,
> Sick of its business, of its pleasure tired,
> How gracious, how benign, is Solitude.[4]

When silence is well practised and familiar, when it becomes a place of life-giving need which juxtaposes challenge and peace rather than a place of fear or negativity, a gradual shift will occur in the quality and depth of relationship that we have with God within that silence. This place that we come to inhabit, this need which becomes a desire, is the heart of true solitude.

This kind of interior solitude is a place of regeneration, a place of simplicity where God alone is the centre of our existence and can be found in the ordinary and extraordinary elements of life. Solitude here is not physical aloneness but implies a deeper quality of silence that has the capacity to strip away the extraneous trappings of life, to reach the core of our being. We desire solely to be possessed by God and to possess God alone.

The particular experience of *physical* solitude in the wilderness or in desert spaces as an intense way of seeking God has attracted people yearning for wholeness through all generations. For it has been in places such as these that hermits and monks have discovered intimacy with God, intensification of prayer and ways to discern and become spiritually wise. From high mountains to arid deserts, throughout both Old and New Testament literature,

God's revelation is communicated often in startling and dramatic ways, always in space and solitude. For example, in the Old Testament Moses on Mt Sinai (Exod. 19.16–25) and Moses' song in Deuteronomy 32.10; in the New Testament, Jesus' transfiguration (Matt. 17.1–9; Mark 9.2–10; Luke 9.28–36), and Jesus' temptation in the wilderness (Matt. 4.1–11; Mark 1.12–13; Luke 4.1–13). In our own times solitary explorers of the Arctic wastes, mountaineers and round-the-world yachtspeople have sought some kind of spiritual enhancement in their isolation and in the hardest physical environments.

However, for the vast majority of us who neither have the opportunity nor perhaps even the desire or inclination to seek solitude in such extreme ways, physical solitude is as important and relevant to our lives as the air we breathe. Many of us find a sense of unity and peace through solo hobbies and activities that require focus and concentration, such as painting, music, pottery and gardening, or sports activities like golf, swimming and walking. Passionately enjoying ourselves in these ways should not make us feel guilty about finding God within our moments of leisure. Additionally, we should all seek out an empty and familiar space within our homes, whether we live on our own or not, where we can retreat safely to a place which is reserved especially for the purpose of being alone. Within this context physical solitude will teach us to love the silence that leads to the inner solitude that I have already mentioned. As the words of a Cistercian motto say, *O Beata Solitudo, O Sola Beatudo.*

In conclusion, solitude is not at all like loneliness. It is a feeling of fulfilment and contentment with being 'alone'. The sense of painful self-questioning, isolation or emptiness is requited. Time can be filled with creative thought and energy or spent in quiet reflection and contemplation. Even in a crowded city, within friendship, or in an empty space the attitude of being 'solitary' sustains, stabilizes and roots us. It is an option for us all.

The love of silence

But the silence in the mind
is when we live best, within
listening distance of the silence we call God . . .
It is a presence, then,
whose margins are our margins; that calls us out over our
own fathoms.[5]

A monk's life is spent in the 'School of the Lord's Service' (*RB*
Prologue 45), seeking God through prayer in the corporate silence
of the choir. Even out of the choir the life is lived largely in silence
and restraint of speech (*De taciturnitate, RB* 6.1–8). The Rule says
(*RB* 42.1), 'Monks ought to strive for silence (*silentium*) at all
times, but especially during the night hours.' Without growth in
the practice and love of silence the monk is unlikely to survive
the rigours and hardships which are required to fulfil the tenets of
the Rule, namely stability (*stabilitas*), fidelity to the monastic
lifestyle (*conversatio morum*) and obedience (*oboedientia*) (*RB*
58.17).

The regular and communal practice and cycle of prayer and
chant within the divine office (*Opus Dei*), along with private
prayer (*lectio divina*), must sustain and nurture the monk in his
vocation to seek God. Governed by the call of bells and sharp
timekeeping, each period of prayer seamlessly flows into the other
interspersed by manual labour, recreation and the general works
of the monastery inculcating shape, repetitiveness and pattern to
the everyday. Each day, with its familiar rituals, is lived as the last
and the monk gradually and imperceptibly becomes rooted in the
tradition.

The foundation and essence of monastic prayer is *lectio divina*,
or the ancient custom of reading, recitation, absorption and
assimilation of a text – a text that is classically sacred in origin.
Although 'holy reading' is mentioned earlier in the Rule it is not
until Chapter 48 that *lectio divina* is spoken about as an instruction to the monks in terms of practice rather than any described
form of prayer. We know little about what *lectio divina* actually

meant to the early monks, although its importance is stressed and as much as three hours given each day to this practice.

The four moments of prayer associated with *lectio divina* – reading (*lectio*), meditation (*meditatio*), prayer (*oratio*) and contemplation (*contemplatio*) – are first found in the late twelfth-century short treatise, *The Ladder of Monks (Scala Claustralium)*, written by the ninth prior of the Grand Chartreuse, Guigo II. The ladder, a connection between heaven and earth, was viewed as a symbol of ascent, or a gradual heightening or spiritual development of the self. The Cistercians and Carthusians sometimes referred to their cloisters as the *Scala Dei* – a place of spiritual development. The four steps of *lectio divina* are rungs on the ladder of prayer towards contemplation or union with God.

It occurs to me that as each stage of the cycle of *lectio divina* moves us towards a deepening of our prayer it also leads us to a different quality and level of interior silence. I am not intending here to describe a technique of prayer but simply to talk about the levels of silence that are involved with this practice.

The first level, *lectio*, is a detachment from the cacophony of life and normal activity and a move towards the concentration on a sacred text. The practice of reading the text involves a multiplicity of words, images, ideas and narrative. The head is fully engaged, the action is discursive and intellectual. From this point there is an eventual movement towards *meditatio*, with the focus on a single word, a phrase or an image which is held as a focus of concentration; the rest of the words of the text are left behind. A choice has been made and in the focused concentration the level of stillness deepens. In *oratio* we are drawn to the innermost level of the heart, a place of deep personal encounter and affective response with the Divine. The final and most complete level of silence, *contemplatio*, bears no resemblance to anything else, it is never to be expected or manipulated. We may fleetingly but not by any conscious choice be drawn into a communion that is beyond word, beyond image, beyond affectivity. It is the sublime ground of our being, for in the words of Raimundo Panikkar, 'God is silence itself.'

God is so far beyond everything that we can scarcely speak,
Thus it is also by means of your silence that you adore him.

Remain silent, beloved, silent; if you can rest completely in
silence,
Then God will give you more blessings than you would know
how to ask for.[6]

Notes

1 From 'Via Negativa', R. S. Thomas, *Later Poems*, Macmillan, London, 1983, p. 23. Permission sought.

2 Thomas Merton, *The Hidden Ground of Love: The Letters of Thomas Merton on Religious Experience and Social Concerns*, ed. William Shannon, Farrar Strauss & Giroux, New York, 1985, p. 115.

3 Aelred of Rievaulx, *Sermo in Adventu Domini* 11, cited in Michael Casey, *Sacred Reading*, p. 96, n. 15.

4 William Wordsworth, 'The Prelude' in *The Complete Works of William Wordsworth*, ed. John Morley, London, 1950, p. 26.

5 R. S. Thomas, *AD. Counterpoint*, Bloodaxe, Newcastle upon Tyne, 1999, p. 50. Permission sought.

6 Angelus Silesius, *The Cherubic Pilgrim* I.240 and II.8.

Further reading

Benedict's Rule: A Translation and Commentary, ed. Terrence Kardong OSB, Liturgical Press, Collegeville MN, 1996.

Guigo II: The Ladder of Monks and Twelve Meditations, ed. E. Colledge and J. Walsh, Mowbray, London, 1978.

Peter-Damian Belisle OSB Cam., *The Language of Silence: The Changing Face of Monastic Solitude*, Darton, Longman & Todd, London, 2003.

Enzo Bianchi, *Words of Spirituality*, SPCK, London, 2002.

Douglas Burton-Christie, *The Word in the Desert*, Oxford University Press, New York, 1993.

Michael Casey OCSO, *Sacred Reading*, Liguori Publications, Liguori MI, 1996.

Michael Casey OCSO, 'Silence', in Philip Sheldrake (ed.), *New SCM Dictionary of Christian Spirituality*, SCM Press, London, 2005.

Silence

Silence

David Jasper, *The Sacred Desert*, Blackwell Publishing, Oxford, 2004.

Patrick Leigh Fermor, *A Time to Keep Silence*, John Murray, London, 2004.

Andrew Louth, *The Wilderness of God*, Darton, Longman & Todd, London, 2003.

Thomas Merton, *Creative Silence*, University of Louisville Press, Louisville, 1968.

Jürgen Moltmann, *Experiences of God*, Fortress Press, Philadelphia, 1981.

Raimundo Panikkar, *The Experience of God*, Fortress Press, Minneapolis, 2006.

Anthony Storr, *Solitude*, Harper Collins, London, 1989.

Rowan Williams, *Silence and Honey Cakes*, Lion Publishing, Oxford, 2003.

14. Prayer

PHYLLIS TICKLE

In Christianity, prayer is the principal activity of the believer. We first receive this understanding not from the apostles and early church fathers, but from our Lord himself, who teaches us not just in example and edict, but also in holy parable.

Over and over again all the evangelists show us Jesus at prayer. Favorite gospel passages like 'in the morning, getting up long before daybreak, he went out and departed to a solitary place and there prayed' (Mark 1.35),[1] or 'and when he had sent them away, he departed to a mountain and there prayed' (Mark 6.46), are underscored by their very frequency and ordinariness. After the feeding of the five thousand, for example, Matthew says, 'and when he had sent the multitudes away, he went up onto a mountain apart to pray; and when evening came, he was there alone' (Matt. 14.23), while Luke tells us that after an afternoon of preaching to the crowds and healing their sick, 'he withdrew himself into the wilderness and prayed' (Luke 5.16). The Gospels have even left us the words of some of Jesus' prayers, the most poignant and stark of them being in the Garden as he prepares for betrayal, trial and execution. Who of us can read 'Father, the hour is come' (John 17.1) without recognition that prayer is the first and last resort of those of us who would follow this God/man?

In addition to the words of Jesus' prayers that the evangelists recorded, and beyond their many references to his prayer habits, we have also the edicts and calls to prayer that he himself gave his followers, both then and now. 'Watch therefore, and pray always, that you may be found worthy to escape . . .' (Luke 21.36). 'Pray for those who despitefully use you . . .' (Matt. 5.44). 'Take heed, watch and pray, for you do not know when the time [of my return] is' (Mark 13.33), etc. Nor can any believer ever forget the very specific instructions:

> 'When you pray, do not be like the hypocrites . . . but when you pray, enter into a hidden place, and when you have shut the door, pray to your Father . . . who also is in secret . . . and when you pray, do not use pretentious repetitions as heathen do . . . rather, pray in this manner, saying "Our Father, Who is in Heaven . . .".' (Matt. 6.5–15)

Yet the most telling of all, perhaps, is the grittiest of parables:

> He spoke a parable to them that people ought always to pray and not give up, saying, 'There was in a city a judge, who feared neither God nor man; and there was a certain widow in the same city who came to him, saying, "Give me relief from my adversary." And the judge would not for a while; but afterward he said to himself, "Though I am afraid of neither God nor man, yet this widow woman is bothersome and I must grant her relief before, by her continual coming to me, she wears me out."' (Luke 18.1–8)

The apostles, too, teach us about prayer, both by example and by edict, the most often repeated of their commandments being Paul's 'pray without ceasing,' to the Christians at Thessalonica (1 Thess. 5.17). It was the early church fathers, however, who were most vocal about prayer and the life of prayer as being at times exhausting and, at many other times, discouraging.

St Benedict has in the past been credited with the saying *'orare laborare et laborare orare est'*, 'to pray is to work, and to work is to pray', but this is not in the Rule. Nevertheless, prayer has to be given time and effort as great as that given to work, the process is demanding and difficult, and it does not exclude that other forms of human work may be pursued in such a way as to become prayer.

What, then, is prayer? Prayer is, first of all, that occupation in which the heart and the brain (or the spirit and the mind, if one prefers those terms) can speak to each other in their respective languages with comprehension and consequence. Second, prayer is that place in which what the heart and the brain each bring experientially to their gathering can be sorted before, and through, the grace and mercy of God into what is to be laid aside and what is to be realized or effected. In prayer, as in any art, the potter labors with the clay, but the clay also labors and suffers the firing. The resulting pot, then, is which of them? Is it the potter? Is it the clay? Who can say, for they can no longer be separated, one from the other. Prayer is a process, and this is the process that prayer is.

Like any process, prayer can be spoken of in terms both of the categories inherent in it and of the distinctions resident in the circumstances informing it. Theologian Scot McKnight offers what is probably the most valid and useful discussion of the second of these. He separates all Christian prayers into one of two categories: those prayed with the church and those prayed otherwise. The utility of this distinction is that it separates the daily offices and corporate prayer from the private or, to use Jesus' image, the closet prayers we all must offer if we are successfully to form as Christians. When we pray the offices each day, where we are and with whom is of no consequence. Whether we are alone in a parked car or a room in our home or walking in the woods or whether we are gathered with dozens of other pray-ers in some Gothic nave is of no moment. As soon as the appointed hour of prayer comes and as soon as we begin to speak or chant the Invitatory, just so soon are we praying with the church as it has prayed over the centuries. What each of us enters into in entering the office is the communion of the saints, the company of all believers, across past time and across the immediate time of our particular time zone where thousands of others like us also are stopped to adore, worship, thank, and praise.

Likewise, when we pray in community but with words other than those of the offices we pray with the church as it is immediately present and physically forming in the other Christians around us. Even when praying with the church in this way, we can become exquisitely aware of ourselves as being in communion with the company not only of those physically around us but also of departed Christians who, through the centuries, have prayed and who are the church with us. This is especially true when we offer the fixed prayers of the church – the Our Father or the Gloria or the Magnificat or the Songs of Miriam or Moses or Isaiah, for example.

One of the helpful things about McKnight's categories, especially for oblates in saying the offices, is that they make obsolete the old categorization of oral as opposed to silent prayer. Common sense and even minimal personal experience show us that whether alone or with others, many Christians chant the hours aloud while many others speak them softly, and still others simply offer them silently. All are praying with the church, for the delivery system does not matter; the gathering of the saints across time and space does. History, in turn, shows us something else about prayer that is pertinent here, namely that there are, for lack of a better word, 'fashions' in prayer, just as there are in everything else human.

Although the early church apparently spoke all its prayers aloud, leaving little time or emphasis for more individualistic private or silent prayer during worship, in the monastic tradition, there were periods of silence during the psalmody. Moreover, if at other times someone chooses to pray privately, he may simply go in and pray, not in a loud voice, but with tears and heartfelt devotion' (RB 52.3–4).[2]

Meditation as part of prayer is generally understood as a product of later times: individual contemplation was practiced during the Middle Ages, as can be seen from the popularity of the Rosary, especially among the unlettered. In the twentieth century, with the advent of Pentecostalism and then with the spread of Buddhism into the West, meditation has become even more fixed in popular praxis. There was, among many Christians during that time, a kind of fear of, maybe even scorn for, the orality and ecstatic prayer of the Pentecostal, just as there was a kind of cultural and envious fascination with the centeredness of the Buddhist. Distinguishing prayer into liturgical and private grants us the grace with which to embrace shifting ways of praying without questioning the integrity of another's way of doing so. Just as surely as in the offices and corporate prayer we are exercising the privilege and the duty of the church universal, just so surely in private prayer are we exercising the privilege and the duty of the smallest unit of that church, each of our selves.

Traditionally the church has spoken of prayer, whether private or corporate, as being divisible into four categories: adoration, confession, thanksgiving and supplication. To think of types or categories of prayer may be helpful in private prayer, for it reminds us first that daily prayer can be governed by each of us who prays and, second, that our daily courses should reflect a balance of sorts among all the divisions, which is not always an easy task. The disproportions that seduce most of us occur with adoration and supplication, there being too little of the first and too much of the second, unless we are watchful.

Some Christians who enjoy an active corporate prayer life with the church find it all too easy to drift over into the notion that adoration, properly offered, is oral and a category of prayer that is better done with the church than alone, although those of the Catholic tradition will be familiar with silent adoration of the Blessed Sacrament. None of us can create a majesty of words equal to that of the psalms, which are part of God's word in the scriptures, and few can equal the traditional hymns of the church. Few of us, in fact, can even render psalms and hymns, once created, with the majesty and power of either gifted lectors or of the devout in unison. As a result, subtly but steadily we assign adoration to the corporate, and not the individual, part of our prayer life. In addition, even if we are aware of the tendency to minimize adoration in closeted prayer, we still, more often than not, come to our private prayer with such urgency of need or, at times, dryness of duty as to forget to raise thankful and adoring hearts as well as our needs and our sorrows.

If more and more over the years, though, adoration has been drifting toward becoming primarily a corporate rather a private prayer form, the exact opposite has happened with confession, and in this case with great benefit. Rarely now, if ever, is confession made corporately, save in fixed prayers that are generic enough to cover all our bases while not particularized enough to embarrass any of us. That is not to scorn such prayers or to question their efficacies and/or meaning for the truly penitent. It is to say, however, that the individual self, like every other human domicile, needs a thorough cleaning from time to time, getting its debris carried away and its closets sorted.

As any householder knows, cleaning the family or public areas of one's home is often done with help and, usually, with much ado, all to good effect. Cleaning the hidden places – the basements and attics and closets – however, is a different issue. Going through the boxes and shelves and trunks of 'Did I really keep this?' and 'Who stashed this in here when I wasn't looking?' or 'Who paid good money for this thing?' is a self-exploration that masquerades as an impersonal chore. In much the same way, when confession can be made to an accountability group, the more overt part of the house-cleaning is accomplished. The self is eased of that of which it knows itself to be guilty. Like setting out intentionally to clean a room, they involve primarily the mind or intellect, that constant monitor that articulates to us so unceasingly what it is that is amiss in our unit of creation. What is needed as well for complete good housekeeping – for the closets and attics – is being alone under the direction of the Holy Spirit not only with one's intellect but also with the inventories of one's heart. 'How ever did I allow this to take up space here?' 'When did I buy this? I didn't even know I had it.' 'Oh, goodness, I wouldn't want to be caught dead owning this.' We confess, first, in order that we may learn who we are, and only second that we may be forgiven.[3]

Thanksgiving is as natural to us, however, as confession is difficult. Sometimes we are even counseled – and wisely – to monitor with at least a modicum of care what we thank God for. To the extent that all things come from God, arguably all things are therefore at least susceptible to being fit subjects for thanking God. There is danger in unmediated thanksgiving, though. It quickly becomes a habit of the mouth that, with its clatter, hides or obscures not only the care of God but also lazy or sloppy thinking about the nature of God. The classic example is the woman who, finding a parking spot, says – and means it – 'Thank you, God!' More troubling is the man who, late for a connecting flight, prays that the second flight will likewise be late and who, when that happens and his connection is made, turns and thanks God for this exercise of favor on his private behalf. The fact that 250 other people have been delayed seems never to enter the conversation. More to the point, by superficial thanksgiving both the passenger and the driver have avoided the difficult work of asking in focused prayer about the appropriateness of their thanks.

Discerning what to be thankful for is part of the work of prayer, but of far greater worth is discerning how to give thanks for the painful, the wearisome, the not-immediately gratifying things in the self's experience. Careful thanksgiving and informed thanksgiving are prayerfully constructed thanksgiving, in other words; and only prayerfully constructed thanksgiving is made acceptable to God by the efficacy and added prayer of the Spirit.

Prayer is a place and/or process of instruction in which we are shown the will of God and the affection of God for us. The work of prayers of supplication, in particular, shows us this. In the world of human affairs we evidence to ourselves and others who we are by the things we seek, ask for, spend our substance for. Our asking and wanting are, in fact, our most readable and consistently accurate self-descriptors. Since we are assured by our Lord that the Father already knows what things we have need of before we ask, we can safely assume that our asking of God serves some end other than, or in addition to, obtaining a particular purpose or fulfilling a particular desire. It would seem, then, that we should always and everywhere be alert to the inventory of what we pray for. In that way not only can the Father grant us our petitions but the Spirit can show us more of who we are, of what we should be praying to become, and of where our greatest deficiencies are. When we pray in supplication and petition, in other words, we need often to remind ourselves that we are praying to Mercy – wondrous, instructive Mercy – that in time is giving us our selves as well as our desires.

Intercession as a part of supplication has probably received more coverage and been the subject of more exegesis than any other type of prayer. Because it asks for a specific thing – more often than not, for healing – for a specific person or group, intercession has a kind of efficacy gauge built into it. Of intercession in general, it is often asked, 'Does it work?' and of a particular intercession, 'Did it work?' The result is that intercession has become a kind of prooftext for prayer, primarily to those who do not pray overmuch, but also from time to time to the devout, even the oblate, the postulant and the religious. 'Working' in the sense of eventuating in what was asked for is a temporal concept, admittedly, and many who feel called upon somehow to 'defend' prayer frequently employ that fact as a rhetorical, if not very persuasive, defence. Better to admit that we stand in a paradox. We are told, and believe, that whatever we ask in the name of Jesus will be granted us, even as we see, all around us, earnest requests that are not being granted. Which are we to believe, the teachings or the physical facts? Probably both.

The great gift of intercessory prayer – the thing that makes it unique among other forms of supplication and prayer – is that it is the one means or avenue by which one of us ever, in this life, knows another of us. In deep and earnest intercession the self slips over into the self being prayed for. What happens there is the great secret that cannot be measured or demonstrated or even definitively described. It is beyond the boundary of words and of the brain that employs them. It simply is, and those who are faith-filled intercessors attain to it. The skilled intercessors also are the ones who argue most matter-of-factly that we are granted what we ask for in Jesus' name even when we do not objectively appear to have effected anything. The forming Christian, and especially the oblate or postulant, could not better serve the kingdom of God than to enter into this realm of mystery, becoming skilled in working there.

If much is written about intercessory prayer and its overt efficacy, perhaps just as much, if not more, is written about preparing one's self and one's surroundings for closeted prayer. Many of these instructions will prove useful, of course, just as the utility of each type of preparation will vary from one pray-er to another. The only caveat is that too much attention paid to external and even bodily circumstances can distract one from the one thing necessary to all prayer that would be devoutly intentional, namely, the state of being poor in spirit.

One cannot fake being poor in spirit, any more than someone can tell another Christian how to begin to live in that state. It is not humility, though humility matters; nor is it openness or quiet, though those too are good. It comes nearest perhaps to purity in the sense that an empty cylinder, when washed clean, is pure because it contains nothing, holds nothing, is filled with nothing – nothing at all except the faint, sweet music its air-filled emptiness makes when the wind's air blows across it.

Our Lord speaks often of the poor in spirit, an injunction all too readily understood as some kind of moral observation or principle of social justice. It is just as easy to overly spiritualize as to overly physicalize any part of Holy Writ, but in this case the oblate or postulant who would learn truly to pray will attempt something nearer to actualizing Jesus' words. What he is saying, the pray-er will learn, is that to pray is, of necessity, to be empty. Those of us who carry with us in our daily lives too much of anything will never, despite all the instructions and gimmicks and exercises we may try, be able to be empty enough for the Wind to make fullest music as it plays across us. It will not happen until we are poor in spirit; and in this we all fail to some greater or lesser degree, and to this we all aspire, to some greater or lesser degree.

No discussion of prayer should end without one last word about the eroticism of prayer. The ages are filled with the words of the great mystics of the church and the great saints of the church who speak directly to this part of prayer or, barring direct mention, allude in some way to its presence in their lives. Living Christians tend to be more cautious about their comments, less public and more selective about choosing those to whom such a perception is revealed. Yet though it be place and process and state, prayer is also lovemaking – not always erotic, in the sense that daily acts of love do not always terminate in erotic consummation, but always erotic in the sense that every act between lovers has the potential for *eros* and bears the possibility ever within it. Those who do not love God ought never to pray unless they are willing to be loved by

God, for it is there in prayer that God waits for us, a suitor at the self's gate. We open it at our own risk.

Notes

1 Scriptural citations in this essay, while based on the Authorized (King James) Version, have been modernized.

2 Editor's note: see Terrence Kardong OSB, *Benedict's Rule: A Translation and Commentary*, Liturgical Press, Collegeville MN, 1996, p. 217: 'So the *oratio* discussed here must be silent prayer said by all during or after the conclusion. Cassian tells of pauses between the psalms, when all prostrate in prayer (*inst.* 2.7). Lentini, 245–247, is of the opinion that Benedict assumes a short period of silent prayer *after* the conclusion of the Office. That is what is implied in RB 52, and it was customary in traditional Benedictinism. Vogüé, however, has a different theory of prayer (see 7.139–149, among many other places) altogether. For him, *oratio* is strictly silent, private prayer and never verbal or communal. Psalmody, to his way of thinking, prepares the heart for prayer, but is not itself prayer. Therefore, it is logical that the monks paused between the psalms – to pray!'

3 Editor's note: we are not talking here of the sacrament of reconciliation.

IV THE ESSENTIALS OF BENEDICTINE SPIRITUALITY

15. The Rule and the Oblate: Formation in the School of the Lord's Service

SIMON O'DONNELL

The Rule of St Benedict presumes that there is a connection between the seeking of God and a multitude of practices. No page of the Rule is without a hint that the purpose of our life is to return to God and no page is without some details about necessary exercises to arrive at our goal. We can easily think that the shortest route to the discovery of God is a simple matter of the heart, but Benedict knows that without exercise or ascesis, a training of the body, of the mind, and of the memory, the heart will remain without its proper direction. The monastic life seeks to shape habits that promote developing a way of life that makes easy the interior pursuit of abiding in the presence of God. These are the reasons why Benedict establishes 'a school of the Lord's service' (*RB* Prologue 45). Entrance into the school is indicated in Sirach when the 'unlearned gather together in the house of learning' (Sir. 51.23). Augustine saw the church as the house of learning and stated that all are called to it (*On Christian Discipline* 1.1).

The Prologue to Benedict's Rule is a grand invitation to enter the school of the Lord's service. The scriptures issue the invitation in the language of theophanies, a divine light and a divine voice calling out to us (*RB* Prologue 9). We respond to this light and voice when we open our ears to hear, when we take on the traits of an otic personality, an ear that is attuned to God. In one sense all monastic practices are geared to creating an ear that is attentive to the divine voice. The school or monastery becomes the home of the divine word. Two things jump out in the use of *divina* in the Rule. First, 'divine' refers to God and what is divine cannot come from what is human; it comes from heaven. Second, 'divine' refers to what God wants me to know. Monasticism is a way of life that seeks to discern what God wants me to put into practice. The monastery school is the place for divine nourishment and divine delights, where we are fed with divine food. From the school the monastic peers into heaven and begins to see as God sees. Faithful to the taking of divine nourishment, the monk begins to reach out. We will reach his tent only if we run there with good works (Prologue 22). If we wish to reach eternal life we must do what frees us for eternity (Prologue 43). If we desire to reach heaven's heights, we climb by a humble life (*RB* 7.5). By climbing the steps of humility we will quickly reach perfect love of God (*RB* 7.67). We must set out on the course by which we reach the Creator (*RB* 73.4).

In the school of the Lord we are to learn to reach out for heaven and the higher summits of virtue (*RB* 73.9). To reach out is to be eager about the goal, to keep it in view, to appropriate those acts and virtues that resemble life at goal's end. The monastery school, the Rule, creates the culture of heaven. As lofty as are the goals set forth in the Rule, Benedict knows there is a this-worldly character to the school. The simplest actions constitute the bringing of heaven to earth: the kind word, the generous deed, the humble act, the prayer of the moment, the loving service of others.

Anyone who enters the school must now be formed in the monastic dispositions that open a person to the Other who is God and to all others who are neighbors. Chapters 4–7 of the Rule put before us a formation program that not only marks a beginning of new life but calls for progressive formation throughout life. Chapter 4 is a call for a radical change of preferences. The response to this call involves nothing less than a new creation, a transformation of the person. To be formed in these good works is demanding because it involves attention to others and not to self, submission to others and not to self. Chapter 5 takes us further on this path. Listening or obedience to another tolerates no delay, but demands immediacy of response. This is what is pleasing to God and to others. There is peace and tranquility (Chapter 6) and no need to speak; the one formed in silence prefers to listen. At the height of this formation is humility, the virtue in which there is total self-honesty, especially about sin and weakness, and the total readiness to respond to others, not to self, not to one's own desires or wants. It is this formation that holds the hope for monastic maturity. The mature monastic now can do the acts of this new life with ease, in non-assuming clarity, and out of preference for Christ (*RB* 7.67–70).

Just below the surface of the Rule, and on almost every page, is a portrayal of the mature monastic. This person bears certain traits that are found specifically in discussions about the cellarer and the abbot. The cellarer is a person who has charge over his inner self. He is not given to flights of fancy; he does not live in fantasies of his own production. Keeping watch over himself and his passions, he is able to meet the needs of others even when the monastery is without the specifically demanded provision, for he can always offer the best gift, a good word. The nexus between self-custody and offering the good word is very close. It stems from his desire not to sadden or annoy his confrères and his determination that nothing will be overlooked or neglected. This monk is well tuned to situations and needs and approaches everyone and everything with proper alacrity and insight, without pride and without delay. He is ever mindful not of self but of others. Everything he does is done with a measured and fitting signature.

This keeping watch over self consists in two things. The first is self-knowledge, which comes from an inner scrutiny of one's self, of God, of others. It leads not to facts but to an awareness that I live in the presence of another. This sense of presence is always kept in mind and ultimately it assures us that we are accompanied, supported, and consoled. Like breath that brings oxygen to the whole body, so memory or heart brings life to the whole self. So for the mature monastic the crucial question is: what goes into the heart or memory? Just as insufficient or bad air will diminish the life of the body, so bad mind or bad memory will diminish the life of the self. Self-knowledge in Benedict's sense is to have a constant recollection that I am in the presence of another, God and neighbor.

The second part of keeping watch over self is self-mastery. Mastery comes from control over what enters the memory, what is kept in the memory, and what issues from the memory. It is not only information that seeks entry to the heart. Information is vulnerable to emotions and passions, and these too want entrance, storage, and emission. When the matters of the heart are ruled by feelings we have bad memory or what the Rule calls *malus animus*. Self-mastery results in a good memory or what Benedict would call a *bonus animus*. Good or bad memories are important because they make their home in the heart and they want to come out of the heart. The evil person reveals the evil in his or her heart. Self-mastery allows the mature monastic to protect the good memory and to bring forth from the heart only what is good. The monk is always to possess a tranquil heart or, in the language of the Rule, is to have an *aequus animus*.

The cellarer keeps careful guard not only over his soul but over his body, its needs, and the way he answers physical needs. Control over the body is the matter of many of the good works in Chapter 4: 'Keep the body in check; do not seek after luxuries' (*RB* 4.11–12); 'Be not given to wine, nor be a glutton, nor given to sleep or sloth' (*RB* 4.35–38). 'Keep guard at all times over the actions of one's life' (*RB* 4.48). This program seems to be part of the physical discipline of the cellarer, for it forms him as moderate; he measures everything well. What is needed is accepted; what is unnecessary is abandoned. He is content; everything that is received is well received because it is sufficient and he is content with a sufficiency. The cellarer and mature monastic has become wise; nothing trivial gets to him, and he is discreet and judicious. He is temperate, even-minded, frugal, careful in his intake of food and drink, measured in his use of things. He is not indolent. In him there is no procrastination, and all is done in a timely manner so that others are well pleased, even happy, with his service. Finally, he is not neglectful. He belittles nothing and no one; he respects everything and everyone.

The abbot, too, is to exhibit the virtues of the mature monastic and be a person at rest. He is not to be turbulent or fretful, extreme or stubborn, competitive or suspicious. From his vantage point he is able to see with foresight and consideration; he becomes the model of discretion and in his wise teaching affords a challenge to the strong and a balm to the weak. Thus it is that the cellarer shares a trait with the abbot. The abbot will be ever mindful not of self but of others. In all he does he will discern whether to be the stern teacher or the gentle father. In his maturity he can, without detriment to self, conform and adapt to everyone.

The abbot's own monastic practices have fitted him with wisdom to be a teacher and master. But even if the abbot is teacher and master, the one who speaks and teaches, he still must be the one who listens (*RB* 3). In order to maintain his magisterial acumen the abbot must resort to listening. It is in the abbot's at-rest-ness that he learns to listen and through this resting heart gains the wisdom to fulfill his ministry. The abbot is to show forth maturity by virtuous living and by his treatment of the monks. There are three words in the Rule to describe the abbot's concern for the monks. They are care, mercy, and fairness. Let us look first at care.

Each person is present in the community to benefit others. A community is without strength when members seek their own advantage and see their needs as opportunities to put demands on others. To accept the self with its weaknesses is a burden each must carry. If it is carried graciously, the person becomes a genuine benefit to others. Benedict wonderfully expresses the role of the abbot in these words: 'care for the weak, not tyranny over the strong' (*RB* 27.6). Care is a constant admonition for the abbot and those who share his responsibilities. All are to show concern for one another, but only one in authority is to show care. Care is exercised by one who has been trusted to oversee and provide for another, but never because the other belongs to the caregiver. The caregiver of the Rule is very much like the curator of a museum. Curators have care of all that museums possess and they act for the good of the collection and its upkeep. But they never own it. Curators work to advance the good of others and not to push gains for themselves. The mature monastic lives to advance the good of others. The word *prodesse* used by Benedict in Chapter 64 can mean to give another the proper dosage of medication. Caring promotes the well-being and growth of another.

Mercy is another trait of monastic maturity. It is not learned in ivory towers but in generously shared living. It is not mastered in military camps but in schools of mercy. In such schools the least are important, the injured are cared for, the neglected are befriended, the weak are lifted up. In schools of mercy hearts are opened to see their own feebleness and thereby come to see the deeds of mercy shown to them. Embraced by mercy, monastic companions become bearers of mercy toward the needy in their midst. What is mercy exactly? Of course it implies tenderheartedness, kindness, consideration. But it arises in the perception of where others really are, what they really need, what will promote their good. Mercy's acme is to be able to place one's self in the shoes of another. To identify with the troubled or sorrowing, to know how they feel, to get into their pleas – this identification is most important. Free from judgment, mercy leads us to dig deeply into the real worth of the individual in need, to discern that the needy has worth beyond the moment's need. Mercy recognizes that the other is there, that the other is worthy, that the other is in need, and that the other seeks personal acceptance even more than an answer to the lacks of the moment. This mercy leads to authentic solicitude. This often-used word in the Rule is the virtue shown in response to a particular call for help. 'I need this' or 'I want that' may be what is expressed, but fulfilling such a request is not completely satisfying. Without the deeper recognition the gift is always too little. With the deeper recognition even the least gift is appreciated. To accept the whole person and to provide an answer to a particular need is the virtue of mercy.

Fairness is the third word we want to examine. There are, in fact, several words used in the Rule to describe this idea but all of them seem to say that 'the abbot is not to prefer one more than another' (*RB* 2.17). Fairness is an adaptation of the mature person to the other so that there is only a sense of presence, not of control. In fairness there is no room for tyranny. Tyranny is always an arbitrary use of authority over another, a use that is always cruel because it sweeps all into its waves and inspires fear. An abbot who acts on whim will very quickly snuff out the spirit of his monks. Fairness is an act of love that is practiced in such a way that the other is convinced that the one acting has only his or her best good in mind.

These monastics know that they are diminished in virtue by heeding their own inner voices. Therefore they are fully engaged in listening to others. They know that self-love brings a person low, making him or her less than human, and therefore they are fully engaged in unselfish brotherly love. These two engagements, listening and loving, are the prime virtues of mature monastics. Benedict cherishes these characteristics because they belong by nature to those who have come to the perfect love of God that casts out fear. They have learned to live with themselves and with others, with God and with their companions. Communal living is where many of these qualities of the mature are used. There are three marks of communal living: *consortio, participatio, colloquio.* In some way I find these marks to be the reason for many of the practices demanded in the Rule. Let us look at *consortio.*

We might translate *consortio* as shared stuff. The word describes a family situation quite exactly. Benedict would view it as a description of life in the monastery. There is a community of goods and a sympathetic connection among all the members to share what is held in common. One of the serious vices that Benedict discourages is private ownership (*RB* 33.1). In Benedict's consortium great reverence must be shown for all things held and used in common. There is to be a wholesome equanimity among the members in the use and distribution of goods. This consortium demands constant recognition of one's own limitations and a constant neglect of another's limitations. The more and the less of life are constants. But for most of us the eye goes to the one who has more. Possessions define us. We compete with others about who has more and who has less. A consortium continues only where there is a willingness on the part of the members to live there, to be there, to share in common.

Our second word is *participatio.* It denotes especially sharing in a common table. Participation implies that everyone has a place, each one accepts the place of the other, and together there is a harmony. Sharing a common table in the Rule is not limited to diet. A shared table is a sacred event to which all accede as one (*RB* 43.13). Benedict envisions gathering into one as a quintessential hallmark of monastic assemblies or the school of the Lord. There is to be shared table, shared listening, shared communion. These gatherings are symphonies of the disparate, and such a symphony is maintained only when each member is attentive to the well-being of the others. The dominant rules of table become the rules for the school of maturity. 'Brethren are to serve one another in love' and are to 'silently anticipate the needs of the other' (*RB* 35.6; 38.4).

Our last word is *colloquio*. Shared words are important in this school of formation. Silence is more fitting, but the heavy emphasis on listening guards against wrong conversation. In the guarded heart of the monk there is always a conversation. It is between God and the self. To speak with another is not so much an interruption of this inner conversation but a revelation of the heart in which there are humble words, joyful words, loving words. With the help and guidance of many in the school of the Lord's service, the monastics support one another and await the day when they will become companions of Christ in his kingdom (Prologue 50).

16. Shaping Holy Lives

ROWAN WILLIAMS

'God's workshop'

Benedict is, as usual, uncompromisingly prosaic in describing the monastic community as a workshop; it is a place in which we use specific tools – listed with blunt simplicity in Chapter 4 of the Rule – which are lent to us by Christ, to be returned on the Last Day, when we receive our wages. It is an imagery that conjures up a landscape in monochrome, a grey sky, a stone wall: the tools worn smooth with long use and skilfully patched up over time, taken from the shelf each morning until finally hung up when weariness and age arrive. The holy life is one in which we learn to handle things, in businesslike and unselfconscious ways, to 'handle' the control of the tongue, the habit of not passing on blame, getting up in the morning and not gossiping. A monastic lifetime is one in which these habits are fitted to our hands. Simone Weil wrote somewhere about how the tool is for the seasoned worker the extension of the hand, not something alien. Benedict's metaphors prompt us to think of a holiness that is like that, an 'extension' of our bodies and our words that we have come not to notice.

In an essay on Benedictine holiness, Professor Henry Mayr-Harting describes it as 'completely undemonstrative, deeply conventual, and lacking any system of expertise'.[1] Perhaps the most important thing to emphasize is the 'deeply conventual': the holiness envisaged by the Rule is entirely inseparable from the common life. The tools of the work are bound up with the proximity of other people – and the same other people. As Benedict says at the end of Chapter 4, the workshop is itself the stability of the community.

Or, to pick up our earlier language, it is the unavoidable nearness of these others that becomes an extension of ourselves. One of the things we have to grow into unselfconsciousness about is the steady environment of others.

To put it a bit differently, the promise to live in stability is the most drastic way imaginable of recognizing the otherness of others – just as in marriage. If the other person is there, ultimately, on sufferance or on condition, if there is a time-expiry dimension to our relations with particular others, we put a limit on the amount of otherness we can manage. Beyond a certain point, we reserve the right to say that our terms must prevail after all. Stability or marital fidelity or any seriously covenanted relation to person or community resigns that long-stop possibility; which is why it feels so dangerous.

At the very start, then, of thinking about Benedictine holiness, there stands a principle well worth applying to other settings, other relationships – not least the church itself. How often do we think about the holiness of the church as bound up with a habitual acceptance of the otherness of others who have made the same commitment? And what does it feel like to imagine holiness as an unselfconscious getting used to others? The presence of the other as a tool worn smooth and grey in the hand? The prosaic settled-ness of some marriages, the ease of an old priest celebrating the Eucharist, the musician's relation to a familiar instrument playing a familiar piece – these belong to the same family of experience as the kind of sanctity that Benedict evokes here; undemonstrative, as Mayr-Harting says, because there is nothing to prove.

The 'tools of good works' listed include the Golden Rule, several of the Ten Commandments and the corporal works of mercy (clothing the naked, visiting the sick, burying the dead, and so on); but the bulk of them have to do with virtues that can be seen as necessary for the maintenance of stability as a context for growth in holiness. It is as though Benedict were asking, 'What does it take to develop people who can live stably together?' He does not begin by commending stability, but by mapping out an environment where the long-term sameness of my company will not breed bitterness, cynicism and fear of openness with one another. If you have to spend a lifetime with the same people, it is easy to create a carapace of habitual response which belongs at the surface level, a set of standard reactions which do not leave you vulnerable. It is the exact opposite of the habitual acceptance of otherness though it can sometimes dangerously resemble it. With a slightly artificial tidiness, we might see the practices Benedict commends for nurturing the stability of the workshop under three heads: transparency, peacemaking and accountability. Let's look at these in turn.

Transparency

Those who belong to a community such as Benedict describes are required 'not to entertain deceit in their heart' (*RB* 4.24) in the list of 'tools of good works', and, intriguingly, not to give false peace (*RB* 4.25); to acknowledge their own culpability in any situation of wrong (*RB* 4.43), a principle regularly stressed by the Desert Fathers; to be daily mindful of death (*RB* 4.47); to deal without delay with evil thoughts, breaking them against the rock of Christ, and to make them known to the spiritual father (*RB* 4.50-51), another precept familiar in the desert. These and other precepts suggest that one of the basic requirements of the life is honesty, principally honesty about yourself. It is necessary to know how to spot the chains of fantasy (which is exactly what 'thoughts', *logismoi*, meant for the Desert Fathers), to understand how deeply they are rooted in a weak and flawed will, and to make your soul inhospitable to untruth about yourself. Exposure of your fantasies to an experienced elder is an indispensable part of learning the skills of diagnosis here. In the background are the analyses of Evagrius and Cassian, pinpointing what simple boredom can do in a life where ordinary variety of scene and company is missing. The mind becomes obsessional, self-enclosed, incapable of telling sense from nonsense; the reality of the other in its unyielding difference is avoided by retreat into the private world where your own preference rules unrestricted. Hence the stress on making thoughts known: it is a simple way of propping open the door of the psyche, a way of making incarnate the consciousness that God sees us with complete clarity in every situation (*RB* 4.49).

To become in this way open to your own scrutiny, through the listening ministry of the trusted brother or sister, is to take the first step towards an awareness of the brother or sister that is not illusory or comforting. The recommendation against 'false peace', I suspect, belongs in this context: one of the ways in which we can retreat into privacy is the refusal to admit genuine conflict, to seek for a resolution that leaves me feeling secure without ever engaging the roots of difference. If we are to become transparent, we must first confront the uncomfortable fact that we are not naturally and instantly at peace with all.

This could of course read like a commendation of the attitude which declines reconciliation until justice (to me) has been fully done; but I do not think this is what Benedict is thinking of. The recommendation follows two precepts about anger and resentment (*RB* 4.22, 23), which, taken together with the warning against false peace, suggests that being wary of facile reconciliation is not about a suspicion of whether the other has adequately made reparation but about whether I have fully acknowledged and dealt with my own resentment. It is a hesitation over my honesty about peace, not the other's acceptability.

Peacemaking

Monks and oblates should be peacemakers. The precepts are clear enough: there should be no retaliation (*RB* 4.29–32), no malicious gossip (*RB* 4.40), no hatred or envy or party spirit (*RB* 4.65–66). And the climactic items in the list of tools make the priority of peacemaking very plain indeed:

72 To pray for one's enemies in the love of Christ.
73 To make peace with one's enemy before the sun sets.
74 And never to despair of the mercy of God.

Stability requires this daily discipline of mending; it is the opposite of an atmosphere in which one's place always has to be fought for, where influence and hierarchy are a matter of unceasing struggle.

Peacemaking, then, is more than a commitment to reconciling those at odds. On its own, a passion for reconciliation can be a displacement for unresolved angers and resentments. What it may put into circulation is anxiety or censoriousness, certainly a situation of tense untruth when there is pressure to 'make peace' at all costs. The peace which the Rule envisages is more like this 'currency', a habit of stable determination to put into the life of the body something other than grudges. And for that to happen, the individual must be growing in the transparency we began with, aware of the temptations of drama, the staging of emotional turbulence in which the unexamined ego is allowed to rampage unchecked.

It is all quite difficult for us in the twenty-first century. We have been told – rightly – that it is bad to deny and repress emotion; equally rightly, that it is poisonous for us to be passive under injustice. The problem, which half an hour on the street outside will confirm, and five minutes watching 'reality' programmes on television will reinforce as strongly as you could want, is that we so readily take this reasonable corrective to an atmosphere of unreality and oppression as an excuse for promoting the dramas of the will. The denial of emotion is a terrible thing; what takes time is learning that the positive path is the education of emotion, not its uncritical indulgence, which actually locks us far more firmly in our mutual isolation. Likewise, the denial of rights is a terrible thing; and what takes time to learn is that the opposite of oppression is not a wilderness of litigation and reparation but the nurture of concrete, shared respect. The Rule suggests that if concern with right and reparation fills our horizon, the one thing that we shall not attain is an unselfconscious respect as another of those worn-smooth tools that are simply an extension of the body.

None of this is learned without the stability of the workshop. The community that freely promises to live together before God is one in which both truthfulness and respect are enshrined. I promise that I will not hide from you – and that I will also at times help you not to hide from me or from yourself. I promise that your growth towards the good God wants for you will be a wholly natural and obvious priority for me; and I trust that you have made the same promise. We have a lifetime for this. Without the promise, the temptation is always for the ego's agenda to surface again, out of fear that I shall be abandoned if the truth is known, fear that I have no time or resource to change as it seems I must. No one is going to run away; and the resources of the community are there on my behalf.

This describes the Body of Christ, not just a Benedictine community. But how often do we understand the promises of baptism as bringing us into this sort of group? How often do we think of the church as a natural place for honesty, where we need not be afraid? Hence the need for these localized, even specialized workshops, which take their place between two dangerous and illusory models of human life together. On the one hand is what some think the church is (including, historically, quite a lot of those who actually run it): an institution where control is a major priority, where experts do things that others cannot, where orderly common life depends on a faintly magical command structure. On the other hand is the modern and postmodern vision of human sociality: a jostle of plural commitments and hopes, with somewhat arbitrary tribunals limiting the damage of conflict and securing the rights of all to be themselves up to the point where they trespass on the territory of others – so that the other is virtually bound to be seen as the source of frustration. The community of the Rule assumes that the point of authority is not to mediate between fixed clusters of individual interest but to attend to the needs and strengths of each in such a way as to lead them forward harmoniously, and it also assumes that each member of the community regards relation with the others as the material of their own sanctification, so that it is impossible to see the other as necessarily a menace. Neither simply hierarchical nor individualistic, the Rule reminds the church of how counter-cultural its style of common life might be.

Accountability

At the simplest level, this is almost identical with the transparency already discussed; but it is made very clear that the exercise of the abbot's rule has to be characterized by accountability. Although what the abbot says must be done, without complaint (Chapter 5), the abbot is adjured at some length to recall his answerability before God, his call to be the image of Christ in the monastery and to 'leaven' the minds of those under his care, and his duty to ignore apparent claims of status. Authority exists so as to create adult persons in Christ's likeness, and all discipline is directed to this end – with the added emphasis in the Rule of attention to the requirements of different temperaments (*RB* 27 is the most humanly subtle of the various accounts of this in the text).

The abbot makes distinctions not on the basis of visible difference (rich or poor, slave or free) but on the basis of his discernment of persons. You could say that his accountability is both to God and to the spiritual realities of the people he deals with. And this perhaps fills out the significance of the idea of accountability in the Rule as a whole: we are answerable to the other. Everyone in the community envisaged by the Rule is responsible both to and for everyone else – in different modes, depending on the different specific responsibilities they hold, but nonetheless sharing a single basic calling in this respect. The workshop is manifestly a collaborative venture with the aim of 'mending vices and preserving love' (Prologue).

So the Rule envisages holiness as a set of habits – like goodness in general, of course, but not reducible to goodness only. The holy person is not simply the one who keeps the commandments with which the catalogue of tools for good works begins, but one who struggles to live without deceit, their inner life manifest to guides and spiritual parents, who makes peace by addressing the roots of conflict in him- or herself, and, under the direction of a skilled superior, attempts to contribute their distinctive gifts in such a way as to sustain a healthy 'circulation' in the community. The product of the workshop is people who are really there; perhaps it is as simple as that. What Benedict is interested in producing is people who have the skills to diagnose all inside them that prompts them to escape from themselves in the here and now. Benedict regards monastic life as a discipline for being where you are, rather than taking refuge in the infinite smallness of your own fantasies. Hence he can speak, in one of those images that continue to resonate across the centuries, of the expansion of the heart that obedience to the Rule will bring. The life is about realizing great matters in small space: *Cael neuadd fawr/ Rhwng cyfyng furiau* – 'inhabiting a great hall / between narrow walls'. That is the definition of life itself offered by the Welsh poet Waldo Williams in one of his best-known poems, *Pa Beth Yw Dyn* (*What is Man*), and it is not a bad gloss on the Rule.

I have already hinted at some of what makes the Rule hard reading these days, and I want to reflect just a little more on this, so as to suggest where the Rule is salutary reading for us, individually and corporately. The idea fundamental to the Rule (and to practically all serious religious writing), that there are some good things that are utterly inaccessible without the taking of time, is probably the greatest brick wall. And it is not just a matter of personal neurosis; given the 24-hour pattern of news provision, we are discouraged very strongly from any suspicion that the significance of events might need time to understand. But the truth is that serious and deep meanings only emerge as we look and listen, as we accompany a long story in its unfolding – whether we are thinking about the meaning of a life (mine or anyone's) or the meaning of a period in international affairs. Stability is still the key, a 'staying with' that gives us the opportunity ourselves to change as we accompany, and so to understand more fully.

And what we have been thinking about in relation to peacemaking has an uncomfortable pertinence today. Are we capable, as western societies, of peace that is not 'false' in Benedict's terms? That is, are we sufficiently alert to the agenda we are bringing to international conflict – resentments, the sense of half-buried impotence that sits alongside the urge to demonstrate the power we do have, the desire to put off examining the unfinished business in our own societies? And, for that matter, there is the falsity that can also afflict would-be peacemakers, who are more concerned with condemning what's wrong than with planning for what might change things, and who derive some comfort from knowing where evil lies (i.e. in someone else, some warmongering monster). What do we do to help our culture discover or recover habits of honesty? Is there a healing of the 'circulation'? 'Peace work', writes Donald Nicholl, 'demands a far higher degree of self-discipline, spiritual preparation and self-knowledge than we are generally prepared to face.'[2]

As for accountability – we tend these days to pride ourselves on taking this seriously; we have introduced the notion of audit into most of what we do, and are encouraged to challenge anything that looks like non-accountable exercising of authority. But I suspect that all this is rather a long way from what the Rule has in mind. First of all, the accountability of the Rule depends on a clear common understanding of what everyone is answerable to: the judgement of Christ. In the Rule all the lines lead to Christ, the central instance of authority rightly used and attention rightly directed to God and the immediate other. There is no interest at all in the Rule in challenging authority on abstract principle. There is a clear commitment to listening, as a central and necessary aspect of making decisions, listening even to the most junior (*RB* 3); the possibility of explaining difficulties and asking for consideration of special circumstances (*RB* 68); and the repeated insistence that the abbot is measured by and must measure himself by the standard of Christ's pastoral service, with its focal principle of self-gift for the sake of the life of the other.

The Rule is in no way a primitive democratic document, and its appeals to obedience are undoubtedly countercultural these days. But what the discomfort arising from this misses is the sense of standing together before Christ, becoming used to Christ's scrutiny together. In this way, we both see ourselves under Christ's judgement and see others under Christ's mercy; and we are urged not to despair of that mercy even for ourselves. Not to despair of mercy is the last of the tools of good works; we could say that the final point of accountability before Christ was that we should have as the extension of our natural bodily being the habit of hope, trust in the possibilities of compassion.

So the Rule's sketch of holiness and sanity puts a few questions to us, as church and culture. It suggests that one of our main problems is that we don't know where to find the stable relations that would allow us room to grow without fear. The church which ought to embody not only covenant with God but covenant with each other does not always give the feeling of a community where people have unlimited time to grow with each other, nourishing and challenging. We have little incentive to be open with each other if we live in an ecclesial environment where political conflict and various kinds of grievance are the dominant currency. And, believers and unbelievers, we'd like to be peacemakers without the inner work which alone makes peace something more than a pause in battle. We are bad at finding that elusive balance between corrupt and collusive passivity that keeps oppression alive and the litigious obsessiveness that continually asks whether I am being attended to as I deserve. And no, I do not have a formula for resolving that; I only ask that we find ways of reminding ourselves that there is a problem.

So we'd better have some communities around that embody the stability that is at the heart of all this. 'Each [religious] house is meant to be a model – an "epiphany" rather – of the condition of mankind reconciled in Christ', wrote Fergus Kerr in an essay around 1970.[3] And he goes on to say that this is impossible unless we face the real condition of unreconciledness in and between us; which is why religious houses are not always exactly easy places.

But in the terms of these reflections we should have to say that without the stability the work is not done; the tools do not become extensions of the hand in such a way that the other's reality really and truly ceases to be an intrusion and a threat. How right Benedict was to say that it is only when community life has done its work that someone should be allowed to take up the solitary life: only when the other is not a problem can solitude be Christ-like – otherwise it is an escape, another drama.

A monochrome picture? Perhaps, but the self-indulgent techni-colour of what are sometimes our preferred styles needs some chastening. The workshop is at the end of the day a solid and tough metaphor for that spirituality which is a lifetime's labour, yet also an expansion of the heart; just as all good physical work is an expansion of the body into its environment, changing even as it brings about change. Holiness is a much patched cloth, a smooth-worn tool at least as much as it is a blaze of new light; because it must be finally a state we can live with and in, the hand fitted to the wood forgetful of the join.

Based on an address given at 'Shaping Holy Lives', a Conference on Benedictine Spirituality, Trinity Wall Street, New York, April 2003, the full text of which is available on the Archbishop's website, www.archbishop ofcanterbury.org

Notes

1 Stephen Barton (ed.), *Holiness, Past and Present*, T&T Clark, London and New York, 2003, p. 261.
2 Donald Nicholl, *The Testing of Hearts: A Pilgrim's Journal*, Darton, Longman & Todd, London, 1989, p. 224.
3 John Coventry, Rembert Weakland and others, in *Religious Life Today*, Tenbury Wells, n.d.

17. Stability

NICHOLAS BUXTON

A tree cannot bear fruit if it is often transplanted.[1]

In his description of the four kinds of monks, Benedict gives a clear indication of what he believes to be the positive attributes of, and negative hindrances to, the religious life. The two types of monk of which he approves, *cenobites* and *anchorites*, are both characterized by the qualities of perseverance and rootedness. The former by virtue of the fact that they commit to a community and its rule, the latter because they have 'come through the test of living in a monastery for a long time' (*RB* 1.3). By contrast, fickle restlessness characterizes the 'disgraceful way of life' of the two kinds of monks he finds so detestable. The *sarabaites*, who 'do whatever strikes their fancy', embody the pick-and-choose mentality so prevalent today, while the *gyrovagues*, the 'spirituality shoppers' of late antiquity, drift around from monastery to monastery, 'slaves to their own wills and gross appetites' (*RB* 1.11).

We tend to think that travel broadens the mind, but according to Amma Syncletica, an early female desert ascetic, wandering from place to place is more likely to have a detrimental effect, just as 'If a hen stops sitting on the eggs she will hatch no chickens.'[2] This sentiment is reflected in Benedict's reluctance to allow his monks to travel, a restriction that might sound a bit harsh to those of us accustomed to frequent overseas holidays. In the Rule he writes that no one may leave the enclosure without permission, nor speak about what they've seen outside when they return, because it would be disruptive for the rest of the community (*RB*

67). For Benedict, therefore, staying put – to be understood, as we shall see, at various different levels – was arguably *the* central concern of monastic life. So important is the promise of stability required of novices entering the monastery that Benedict sees fit to mention it twice (*RB* 58.9, 17). But the principle of stability isn't only of relevance to the monastic life. Benedict also maintains that 'stability in the community' is one of the necessary conditions for spiritual growth (*RB* 4.78), and this, I suggest, applies to us all. In what follows, I will explore the meaning of stability in both the obvious and outward terms of perseverance and commitment, as well as the inward or spiritual sense of 'being present'. Before that, however, and in order to appreciate the importance and value of stability, we must first consider its opposite.

Restlessness

Born a few generations after the sack of Rome, the young Benedict grew up in a volatile world plagued by constant warfare and widespread social and political insecurity. Although many of the institutional structures of empire remained more or less functional, the days of the *Pax Romana* were long past and the future was looking increasingly uncertain. Little has changed. Today there are wars on every continent, and even in peacetime many people live under the threat of terrorist attacks. An attitude of 'spend now, pay later' takes the waiting out of wanting, but also leads to the creation of a crippling debt culture that makes us all vulnerable to housing-market crashes and stock-market meltdown. Perhaps even more alarming is the fact that the natural world, thanks to our carelessness, is also becoming increasingly unstable with unpredictable climate change threatening to cause global environmental catastrophe. At the same time, rapid technological progress, which may be exciting for some, leaves many disoriented and confused, and requires us to continually upgrade in order to keep in step with the pace of change. Indeed, consumerism has become an end in itself: its purpose is not the satisfaction of our needs but their constant stimulation. Far from being a recipe for happiness, greater choice only fuels increasing discontentment, while keeping one's options open brings not freedom but insecurity. It doesn't take much to realize, therefore, that we live in a world of great instability.

Modern life has, for many of us, become deeply fragmented, to the extent that we even talk about our work life, our home life, our family life, our social life, and our spiritual life, as if we have several separately compartmentalized existences. Social roles and expectations have become so blurred and ill-defined that many young people are deeply troubled by a real anxiety about life and their place in the world, taking up residence in virtual worlds of 'celebrity culture' and escapist entertainment, or indulging in hedonistic excess, to ward off their thinly veiled despair. Identities are in flux, if not crisis: we are no longer souls but consumers, defined by where we shop and what we watch on TV. Buying into brand labels, we acquire not only an image, but also a set of values to live by. Indeed brand loyalty may amount to the only semblance of community that some people in today's world are likely to experience, and even that is pretty shaky, as anyone in advertising knows. Meanwhile, many of our familiar and time-honoured social structures are disintegrating around us. Ever-increasing divorce rates make the traditional family unit seem like a nostalgic fairy tale, while job security is, for most of us, a thing of the past.

Perhaps there are some people who have relatively stable lives, and do not see their personal experience reflected in this bleak apocalyptic scenario. I suspect, however, that many more will be aware of at least some of the factors of instability that I have mentioned. In any case, we can also think about instability in more universal and psychological terms. Most people are familiar with the experience of thinking that the grass is greener on the other side of the fence and, presumably too, the subsequent realization that it very rarely turns out to be so. Recognizing that we can be fickle creatures, and wary of commitment, Benedict says: 'Do not be daunted immediately by fear and run away from the road that leads to salvation' (*RB* Prologue 48). In other words, unless we persevere in a task, we cannot expect a fruitful outcome. Yet in spite of this obvious truth, we constantly allow ourselves to be put off by the slightest inconvenience, or sidetracked by what appear to be more attractive options. Too ready to give up, always seek-

ing the quick fix, we have a tendency to blame external circumstances for our frustration and unhappiness when, more often
than not, the problem is as likely to be our lack of willingness to
take responsibility. There is much talk of a dependency culture,
but we are not just passive victims of forces beyond our control:
we cause much of this instability ourselves, which suggests that it
is born of a fundamental inner restlessness. We crave constant
stimulation and distraction, and are unwilling or afraid to be alone
and silent. This is a symptom of a problem very familiar to the
monastic tradition, which even has a special term – *acedia* – to
describe the restless boredom which gnaws insidiously at the
monk, inducing him to 'forsake his cell and drop out of the fight'.[3]
It should be clear by now, I hope, that all of us, not just monks and
nuns, could probably use a bit of stability in our lives.

Perseverance

Often, when I talk about the value of stability, perseverance and
rootedness, I am met with a certain amount of resistance, as if I am
talking about something rigid and oppressive that can only lead to
stagnation. Like the prisoners in Plato's cave, we have grown so
accustomed to our chains of slavery to the idols of individualism
and consumerism that any attempt to remove them is seen as a
threat to our freedom. But of course, stability isn't about stagnation at all; it is not about stunting growth, or stifling creativity. As
the Cistercian monk Michael Casey says, 'Stability is not a matter
of immobility or resistance to change but of maintaining one's
momentum'.[4] In other words, stability is not about sticking our
head in the sand, but rather, it is precisely that which enables us to
rise to the challenges of life's inevitable changes – the necessary
precondition, and the other side of the coin, to the conversion that
the religious life calls for. Re-forming the self in the image of
Christ comes about as a result of 'the blunders and blemishes of
social interaction', as Casey puts it: 'Stability prevents us from
running away from necessary development'.[5]

Having stability implies engaging fully with the situation at
hand, persevering in the face of obstacles and in spite of what

might initially appear to be more appealing prospects. Stability is about being centred, remaining focused and undistracted. It is, in other words, to realize and accept that wherever we are, we are in the right place at the right time. But this is not the same as being fatalistic – the situation we are in may require us to contend against it – nevertheless, in order to engage more effectively with any situation, we have to understand that wherever we are, we are there to do a job that needs to be done. Failing to take responsibility by blaming others or constantly flitting from one thing to another will be more likely to increase our frustration. Growth, by contrast, comes from persevering through difficulty. An anonymous desert monk said that if you give up and flee in the face of temptation, 'you would find that the temptation you were fleeing would go with you to the next place'.[6] Admittedly, there are some things in life that simply *cannot* be avoided – death and taxes, for example, not to mention illness, or simply not getting our own way all the time – but the point is that if we can maintain an attitude of stability with respect to the little things we can control, it may shape our approach to more serious matters.

So in spite of the times when everything in life seems dark, irritating or futile, it is stability that gets us through – not quitting when we don't want, or can't be bothered, to carry on. Unfortunately, however, we are all too often unwilling to make any more effort than the minimum required to achieve immediate results. In his chapter on humility Benedict says, 'Under difficult, unfavourable or even unjust conditions, his heart quietly embraces suffering and endures it without weakening or seeking escape' (*RB* 7.35–37). The rationale is simple: 'We shall through patience share in the suffering of Christ that we may deserve also to share in his kingdom' (*RB* Prologue 50; cf. 7.39). The belief that present sacrifice is justified by future reward shows that the value of stability cannot be isolated from the context of faith: it takes a degree of trust to make a commitment for the sake of an outcome that cannot be known in advance. But this too is a fact of everyday experience. We know there are some things that can't and don't just happen instantly, but require sustained commitment, and time – perhaps a whole lifetime – to grow and mature. Getting to know somebody, for example, does not happen straight away, but is the outcome of a long-term process. Moreover, the relationship may only really deepen after weathering periods of trial and difficulty, after working things out and coming to a greater level of trust and acceptance as a result. The fruit of perseverance is vividly illustrated by the story of John the Short, a desert monk whose teacher took a dead stick, planted it in the ground, and instructed him to water it every day. After three years, the stick turned green and blossomed.[7]

Being present

I once spent a month in solitude and silence with the Carthusians at Parkminster. 'The first 48 hours are the worst,' I was cheerily informed by a Benedictine of my acquaintance, 'If you can get through that you'll be fine!' Well, the first couple of days were pretty tough; it certainly wasn't much fun. The Carthusian reputation for austerity is well earned, and at times I found it hard to see being there as anything more than an endurance test. But I persevered, and although I can't say I ever got comfortable, I nevertheless settled in a bit and, after a while, even started to appreciate something of life in the artificial desert of the Charterhouse. I noticed how the discipline of silence and, paradoxically, the enforced stability of the enclosure – apparently so restrictive – actually allowed for the opening up of an interior space that I am seldom aware of in my normal everyday life.

But the really difficult thing was just being present, and fully attentive to what is. Abba Moses, one of the most celebrated of the Desert Fathers, famously said: 'Go and sit in your cell, and your cell will teach you everything'.[8] This was something that Dom Cyril, the novice master, would repeatedly emphasize when he dropped by every few days to check up on me. 'Just be here,' he would say. And for the first week or so he would keep asking me whether or not I was there yet. It took me a little while to fully understand what he meant. How often, for example, do we really give our whole attention to whatever is in front of us? In the Rule, Benedict says that the cellarer is to 'regard all utensils and goods of the monastery as sacred vessels of the altar' (*RB* 31.10). This is to say that the whole of life should be treated as sacred, including – or even, especially – the mundane reality of just *being*. With little to occupy my mind, and completely removed from all my usual daily activities, I became very aware of how much of my time was being spent elsewhere – anywhere and indeed everywhere but here and now – thinking about all the things I could or should be doing, the people I might be seeing, what I would do when I got out, and so on. Indeed, much of this idle daydreaming was taken up with making plans for the future, surely the most pointless of enterprises, and a clear sign of a distracted, restless and unfocused mind.

When a desert monk complained that he could not control his wayward thoughts, his teacher answered, 'Go on sitting in your cell, and your thoughts will come back from their wanderings'.[9] If we sit quietly and observe our minds, we may find that most of our mental activity consists of either reliving the past or fantasizing about the future. In doing this we construct a world of projections, which we superimpose over the simple reality of what is. Stillness is not, however, about *forcing* the mind to be quiet, but simply a state we reach when, like a fire deprived of fuel, distractions and restlessness naturally fade away. To be silent is to let go of all this needless preoccupation with the past and the future so that we may become aware of the still centre behind the surface activity of consciousness, thus allowing the possibility of an encounter with what is. This is to make ourselves present to the presence of God. According to the Benedictine nun Joan Chittister, 'it is the clamour of the self that needs to be brought to quiet so that the quiet of God can be brought to consciousness'.[10] In the gospel, Jesus says 'where I am, there will my servant be also' (John 12.26), and therefore, vice versa, God is to be met in the present moment, in the stillness and silence of the human heart. To be present to the presence of God is not to be floating in fantasy or memory, not to be thinking that the grass is greener elsewhere, but to be right here, right now. During my stay with the Carthusians, I noticed how most of the time we are simply not present; not even to ourselves and each other, never mind God.

Being present to God, however, comes at a price. It entails being open to scrutiny and the attendant risk of having to give up our cherished notions of who and what we think we are, and accepting who and what we really are. Benedict says, 'While he guards himself at every moment from sins and vices of thought or tongue, of hand or foot, of self-will or bodily desire, let him recall that he is always seen by God in heaven, that his actions everywhere are in God's sight and are reported by angels at every hour' (*RB* 7.12–13). To live as if we truly believed that God sees everything would be totally transformative. The fact is, I would not do or say half the things I do if I really believed it was all seen and recorded, and that I would be held accountable on the day of judgement. This is why stability is the necessary foundation for spiritual growth: it implies taking responsibility for our actions, and acknowledging a measure of truth beyond one that we simply decide for ourselves. As Anselm Grün puts it, 'Living in the presence of God, we encounter ourselves at every turn. God, in turn, confronts us with our own reality so that we can recognise it and allow it to be purified by God'.[11] By cultivating stability, we encounter God, the deepest reality of what we are, in the silent emptiness that is the heart of being, the place where, emptied of ourselves, we participate in that in which 'we live and move and have our being' (Acts 17.28).

Notes

1 Benedicta Ward, *The Desert Fathers*, Penguin Books, 2003, p. 72.
2 Ward, *The Desert Fathers*, p. 63.
3 William Harmless, *Desert Christians*, Oxford University Press, 2004, p. 325.
4 Michael Casey, 'The Value of Stability', *Cistercian Studies Quarterly*, 1996, p. 288.
5 Casey, 'The Value of Stability', p. 293.
6 Ward, *The Desert Fathers*, p. 71.
7 Ward, *The Desert Fathers*, p. 141.
8 Ward, *The Desert Fathers*, p. 10.
9 Ward, *The Desert Fathers*, p. 70.

10 Joan Chittister, *Wisdom Distilled from the Daily*, HarperCollins, 1990, p. 169.

11 Anselm Grün, *Benedict of Nursia*, Liturgical Press, 2006, p. 23.

18. Obedience

MARIA BOULDING

'Obedience *to* Christ, obedience *with* Christ': this is how the Rule's teaching has been summarized. It is a good summary, but we need to unpack it.

Obedience to Christ, to God

God calls his creatures into being from nothing, creates them for their good and for his glory, and calls them back to himself as their ultimate fulfilment. Among them he has chosen to have free creatures, persons capable of responding to him with a 'Yes' of love. He has sovereign rights over us, and our most truthful attitude before him is humility. Benedict is conscious all the time of God's holiness, God's presence, God's knowledge of us. He calls this awareness 'fear of God'; it is not a craven fear but joyful, a continuous mindfulness of where the truth lies, a trustful, awed, obedient attitude: 'A monk should constantly remember everything God has commanded . . . and recall that he walks always in God's sight.'[1]

The God who creates also speaks, revealing himself and his love. Throughout the Old Testament a people created for the purpose of listening to God's word listened only fitfully, yet the call to faith and obedience was never silent. 'Today, if you hear his voice, do not harden your hearts.'[2] This invitation is repeated in the Prologue to the Rule, which begins with the command, 'Listen'. The listening ear, the listening heart, are the foundation of obedience. The Word of God was made flesh and speaks in human words. His first preaching reiterated this call to repentance, faith and obedience: 'Repent, and believe the good news.'[3] Obedience to God now becomes indistinguishable from obedience to Christ. In many passages of the Rule, Christ is called simply 'God'; so, for instance, the abbot is called 'Abba', 'father', because he holds the place of Christ.[4] Obedience to God is an act of love on the part of 'those who love Christ above everything else'.[5]

Christ said to the apostles, 'He who listens to you, listens to me',[6] and the authority of the apostles is passed down in the church. One tradition in early monasticism, represented especially by *The Rule of the Master* and taken up in some parts of the Rule of Benedict, saw the apostles' authority as inherited particularly by the elders or teachers. In the desert tradition it was normal for an experienced monk to gather a few disciples, who listened to his teaching and found in it their way to give up their own wills and seek the will of God. Something of this passed into the cenobitic tradition; Benedict's picture of the abbot is partly that of a teacher, and the monks' obedience is the obedience of disciples who listen and learn. The abbot 'holds the place of Christ', and in obeying him the monks take the hard, laborious road of obedience back to God.[7]

Obedience with Christ

The road was trodden first by Christ himself. All we know of his public life hinges on his steady resolve to seek the Father's will. It is like a lodestone. He spends nights in prayer, attuning himself, opening himself to it. He is always ready to abandon his own plans when circumstances suggest that the Father wants something different. He is inwardly free and adaptable, because he wants only one thing. With regard to his miracles, we may wonder whether the workings of nature and the resources of the human mind and body look different where God is perfectly obeyed.

But Jesus also accepts limitations as part of the Father's will – the comparative narrowness of his situation, the lack of travel, the slowness of the disciples. He can work within the limitations. All this is part of the Father's will, and he says 'Yes' to it all. He is practising for what is to come.

The Letter to the Hebrews makes an astonishing statement about Jesus: 'Although he was a Son, he learned obedience through what he suffered, and being made perfect he became the source of salvation to all who obey him.'[8] He learned obedience! He was human, he could learn as humans do, and grow towards the perfect maturity of his obedience to the Father. The life of God, the ecstatic life of the Trinity, is total self-giving: the Father's delight is to give his all to the Son, the Son's delight is to surrender his whole self to the Father, and the mutual gift of each to the other is the love of the Spirit. This is what 'obedience' is at the level of God's own inner life. When the Son is made man in Jesus, his ecstatic 'Yes' to the Father is expressed as human obedience – to Mary and Joseph in his childhood, to the Father's will in all things as his mission works out. But it is now not in the perfect joy and bliss of God that it happens, but in the conditions of a sinful world among sinful men and women, amid all the messy, ambiguous, imperfect situations we know so well. And this finally means obedience unto death, even the death of the cross. He accepts the Father's inscrutable, baffling will that his mission shall end in what seems total failure, ignominy, suffering, abandonment, death. He has nothing left but reliance on the Father's trustworthiness: 'You are all I have left in the land of the living.'[9] He has become obedient with all his human mind and heart and will, and it has brought him to death, even death on a cross.

This is why John's Gospel insists on the unity of cross and resurrection, for both are the revelation of the glory, the exaltation of Christ. His resurrection is not a reversal of all that went before, but rather the revelation of its secret reality. In his pre-Calvary life Jesus had obeyed in the conditions of a sinful world, amid the malice of sinful human beings, but the obedience itself was something glorious. The resurrection reveals it in all its glory and beauty and joy. It is glorious because Christ's human obedience was the translation into a human life of the relationship of the Son to the Father within the Trinity, in the unimaginable joy of God. His human 'Yes' to the Father's will was the human expression of the infinite rush of love, the ecstasy, that carries the Son to the Father and the Father to the Son in God's inner life, and their love is the Holy Spirit. In his Easter glory Christ pours out his Spirit on us, the Spirit of Easter life and joy and love, the Spirit of sonship who reveals obedience as a participation in the glory.

This paschal perspective is as clear in the Rule as the teacher–disciple model mentioned earlier, particularly in the second, third and fourth rungs of the ladder of humility described in Chapter 7:

> The second rung is not to be in love with one's own will . . . but to imitate the Lord who said, *I came to do not my own will, but the will of the One who sent me.* The third rung is to submit to a superior out of love for God, in imitation of the Lord, of whom the apostle says, *He was made obedient unto death.* The fourth rung is climbed when, if obedience brings hard things, someone clings to patience with a silent mind, not giving up or evading the issue . . . for scripture says in the name of those who suffer, *For your sake we are being slain all day long, no better than sheep for slaughter . . . yet in everything we are more than conquerors, because of him who loves us.*

Obedience to one another

Obedience in and with Christ, paschal obedience, makes special demands in community life. In Chapters 71–72 of the Rule, St Benedict, less influenced here by the *Rule of the Master*, gives us insights into his own experience of the love that makes community possible. Obedience is a good thing, a sure way to God, and it becomes indistinguishable from love when the Rule speaks of relationships between persons, and the humble acceptance of one another as we live together:

> Obedience is of such value that it is not enough to show it to the superior: all members of the community should obey one another, knowing that this way of obedience is the sure road that will take them to God. . . . Let them strive to be first to show respect to one another. Let them bear with the utmost patience each other's weaknesses, whether of body or of character. . . .

No one should pursue what is to his or her own advantage, but rather what is for the good of others.[10]

This give and take, mutual forgiveness, loving awareness of the rights of the other and readiness to give up one's own will and put someone else's interests first, are familiar to everyone in marriage and in family life, as in monastic communities. Within these ordinary, everyday experiences, in the daily exercise of patience, the paschal mystery happens.

It will be obvious that these chapters are full of echoes of the New Testament, and especially of the letters of St Paul. 'Christ too did not please himself . . . Let your love show itself in mutual affection; reckon others more highly than yourself . . . Bear with one another and forgive . . . Forgive one another, as God in Christ has forgiven you.'[11] The church is holy, the body and the bride of Christ; but in this world she is also the church of sinners. She carries sinners like a load on her back until the end. But we are all the church, and we are all sinners; therefore we are all carried on the church's back, and we are all called to do our share of carrying. We all bear with one another, and we are all borne with. Benedict was vividly aware of it.[12]

Practical applications of the Rule's teaching in secular life

The Rule deals with obedience within a monastic community, but teaching of such breadth and depth has a bearing on every Christian life. Faith, hope and charity all require an acceptance of the unknown, a leap beyond ourselves. So does prayer, for we can pray only from an attitude of open-hearted listening and obedience to God. We listen in prayer and silence to his word; we listen to the word in the scriptures, in our own lives, and in our encounters with every other person who, as the Rule often reiterates, is Christ to us. Within each one who is alive in Christ the Spirit dwells, the Spirit who inspired the scriptures and enables the church to hear the living word of God.

Obedience may often entail a long, hard process; the Rule speaks of 'the labour of obedience', and of disobedience as a form of laziness.[13] Christ's obedience was brave, adventurous and intelligent. He could see through to the heart of every situation. Our obedience may sometimes demand an intelligent, patient search for the right way forward, consultation with others, listening, trying to read the signs, and in the end making what seems to be the right decision, without any comforting certainty that we have got it right. There are times when we know we are immersed in a sinful world, and to some extent complicit with it, yet we have to make an effort to see where God's will lies in mixed situations, in political decisions when no party is wholly right, or when we feel we have to choose between two unwanted results. There are many such situations in all our lives.

When a legitimate authority commands something that conflicts with our conscience, how can our obedience to God be expressed? The Rule does not deal directly with this dilemma; probably Benedict did not think it likely to arise. However, no abbot or abbess is either infallible or sinless, and in *RB* 4.61 it is recognized that the abbot's own conduct may be at variance with his teaching. Benedict is content to warn the abbot repeatedly that he is accountable to God for everything he decides or commands. It is not so simple, however, in today's world and today's church. This is a difficult area of tension, and there is certainly a place for conscientious protest.

A different question may arise when one is part of a group to which one owes loyalty, and a collective decision is to be made. There should certainly be a place for discussion and disagreement before the matter is settled, but what if one believes the final decision to be unwise, though not morally objectionable? Must I still obey?

Every case needs to be considered on its own merits, but there are a few principles that should be kept in mind. First, conscience is always sovereign, and must be followed; no authority, even the highest, can override anyone's conscience. But, second, conscience needs to be informed and educated, and everyone needs to remember that he or she has no monopoly of wisdom. Third, some issues may take a long time and much patience to resolve. The passage of time may show up a problem in a different light. There can be a learning process.

Christ's obedience moved from the active, intelligent obedience
of his public life towards the acceptance and helplessness of the
cross. Ours too may sometimes require simple acceptance of
things, persons and situations that are less than ideal. Amid the
concrete realities of the church, in skirmishes on the parish front or
frustration with the local liturgy, there is scope for patient, faith-
inspired obedience. Your most fundamental obedience to God
may be acceptance of yourself – yourself as you are, with all your
particular strengths and weaknesses, your gifts and limitations, all
the baggage you carry from your remote and immediate past, all
that your life has made you. This person is what God wants, and
you must want it too; but such obedience is not a static programme, because it means consenting to become through God's
grace the person he wants you to become. At Christmas we listen
to Christ's genealogy as recorded in the first chapter of Matthew's
Gospel. It is a grubby record for the most part, but he took it all
on, took on history, Israel's story, humanity's story, all the load of
sin and struggle, all the network of relationships and decisions in
which we are enmeshed. He made it his own, and redeemed it. And
so you take on your own history, your part in the story. To accept
yourself and other people, to accept joyfully the conditions of life
in a flawed, inconsistent, sinful but redeemed humanity, is an obedience to the creator. The Rule is realistic about this. The abbot is
to accept the diversified, weak, quirky human material in his
community in a peaceful and compassionate spirit. It has been
remarked that he envisages every kind of misdemeanour, from
oversleeping to murder.

Benedict also accepts, and respects, material realities like the
seasons, weather, daylight and darkness, and tools for work.
Responsible stewardship of the material and animal world is
another aspect of obedience to the creator. According to Chapter
2 of Genesis God entrusted to Adam a sovereignty over the rest of
creation: not a freedom to do what he liked with it, but a duty of
Godlike care. Adam's obedience was meant to include this, but
when he disobeyed God, his relationship to the earth, and by
implication to its non-human inhabitants, went awry. The enor-
mous problems of justice and responsibility for one another and

the world amid today's complexities may daunt the bravest, and we can feel helpless to change anything. Yet to look only at material contributions that seem absurdly inadequate may be to miss part of the truth. No one can measure the effects of faithful living, personal integrity, prayer and willed solidarity, on however small a scale.

Obedience may be a very stretching experience. It sometimes means acceptance of roles or responsibilities to which one does not feel equal, if the call is insistently there. It may involve failure and making a fool of oneself, but it may also call out energies, gifts and capacities one never knew one had. The Rule hints at something like this in Chapter 68. When a monk is assigned a job for which he feels he is not equipped, he is given the opportunity to explain to his superior why he thinks it impossible. But if after discussion the superior sticks to the original order, the monk or nun, 'confident in the help of God, must lovingly obey'. There is a hint of heroism here, but many, many good things have probably been done under those conditions.

Conclusion: Christian life

The life of an oblate, as of any Christian, may sometimes feel like a lonely struggle to obey the will of God, and within the conditions of our own sinfulness and a sinful world it can be painful and dark, like Good Friday. But it is neither solitary nor simply a matter of individual resolve. Because we have the Holy Spirit in us we can obey with and in the Easter Christ, and one day the glory will be revealed. Our identification with Christ, obedient unto death and resurrection, is not a mere external imitation of him. Christ's obedience is diffused throughout his body and we all participate as beloved sons and daughters of God, empowered to cry 'Abba!'

Christ is the human, tangible presence of God, the sacrament of God to us. The church is the great sacrament of Christ, risen, glorious and present through his Spirit. Benedict's Rule is deeply sacramental; it hears Christ in the scriptural word, the abbot, the sick, the guests and the brethren. Within this sacramental faith obedience makes sense, because it reaches through the human signs to touch God. We have a small part within a mystery that began with God's *fiat* at creation and the *fiat* of Christ that inaugurated the new creation. We are kin to the saints of old whose obedience to God anticipated Christ, like Abraham, and to those who were immediately involved in his saving work during his lifetime, like Mary, who welcomed God's word in her spirit before conceiving the Word made flesh. The same consent to God continues still in all the saints down the ages until the last, when Christ's body will reach its full stature. We are all taken up into his self-offering, as we are in the Eucharist. Our personal, humdrum, seemingly inglorious obedience to God is like the bread and wine we bring: human, limited, imperfect, but taken up by Christ into the glory of his priestly offering.

Notes

1 *RB* 7.11, 13.
2 Ps 95.7–8; Heb. 3.7–8.
3 Mark 1.15.
4 See *RB* 2.2–3.
5 *RB* 5.2.
6 Luke 10.16; *RB* 5.6.
7 Prologue 2.
8 Heb. 5.8.
9 Ps. 142.5.
10 *RB* 71.1–2; 72.4–5, 7–8.
11 Rom. 15.3; 12.10; Col. 3.13; Eph. 4.32.
12 Different currents of influence meet in Benedict's Rule when it deals with obedience. The individual, ascetical, hierarchical notion examined earlier and derived from *The Rule of the Master* sees Christ as the tip of a pyramid, and the superior as in some sense the heir to the apostles. The will of God is mediated downwards. The community aspect, that of obedience to one another, shows rather the influence of St Basil and St Augustine, for whom community comes first, and the superior is necessary to promote and organize the community. To point out the differences like this is too strong, however, for all the early fathers looked to the scriptures and to the growth of charity.
13 Prologue 2.

19. Moderation: The Key to Permanence

MICHAEL CASEY

The Rule of St Benedict and the various social institutions based on it have been in existence for nearly fifteen hundred years. This tradition has survived an astonishing range of social upheavals: barbarian incursions and their aftermath, schism, the Aristotelian invasion of the West, the Black Death, the Protestant Reformation, the Council of Trent, the French Revolution, the *Kulturkampf* and its cousins, not forgetting the unspeakable brutalization characteristic of the twentieth century – fifteen centuries of change by which the continuing vitality of the Benedictine tradition has been subjected to challenge and recurrent diminishment. And yet there are still men and women in all six continents who continue to hold Benedict's 'little rule' in high esteem and allow its beliefs and values to shape the way they live.

The fact of the tradition's longevity is remarkable enough. What is more spectacular is its manifest capacity continually to reform itself after periods of degeneration. Even when monasteries have been confiscated or destroyed and their communities dispersed it often happened that, when the tyrants departed, the monks returned and began to rebuild. The different forms of Benedictine monasticism existing today are not, as some of its buildings may be, merely monuments to past achievement. They are testimony to a living and growing organism that survives by adapting itself to the ever-changing environment, and usually outliving the forces that threatened it and necessitated change.

It is, therefore, futile to look for a 'pure' form of Benedictinism. The charism survives through a process of hybridization.[1] By blending the received tradition with elements of the local culture, the *Zeitgeist*, the needs of the church and the particular giftedness of persons, new expressions of the Benedictine are constantly being created. There is no such thing as normative Benedictinism, nor are Benedictines cast in a single mould. Think of Bede, Bernard of Clairvaux and Columba Marmion: different centuries, different situations, different personalities. Each of them, however, recognizably belongs to the same broad Benedictine tradition.

Furthermore, we should not be too ready to believe that change occurs only at the level of practice: bells are computerized, the sick are sent to the hospital, and flogging ceases. No doubt such obvious adaptation is necessary and in accordance with common sense. There is, however, another more radical form of change evident in the rethinking and development of the whole philosophical basis of monastic life and the organic incorporation into the monastic belief-system of values that come from elsewhere. Everyone knows how much things changed after the Second Vatican Council, not only in the visible life of monastic communities but in the inmost rationale that animated observance. Other absorbed values are the gift of the surrounding society: the abolition of slavery and serfdom, respect for persons and human rights, fiscal responsibility, care for the environment, concern for world peace. These are not alien to monasticism, but they were long undiscovered. If we search diligently, perhaps we can find what Augustine would have termed the 'seeds' of such concerns in classical monastic sources, but in general they are positive outcomes that would have been mostly unfamiliar to St Benedict, at least in the way that we understand them.

It is only since the 1970s that the term 'inculturation' has been used in the church to denote the double movement that needs to take place in the process of evangelization. It refers to the dialogue whereby a local culture is enriched by welcoming the proclamation of the gospel and the simultaneous enrichment of the gospel by the very fact of its being received and expressed in a new language and cultural ambience. Monasticism likewise is enriched as it spreads and adapts to new situations. Benedictinism has survived because of its capacity to change: that is to say, because of what might be termed its 'dynamic adaptability'.

The underlying source of this capacity for adaptation can be found in the moderation inherent in the Benedictine tradition – a certain reserve about total identification with passing trends, an instinctive recoil from extremes, and an acute sensitivity to the complexity of human life typical of those with deep spiritual experience.

Polarity of values

There is a wise maxim reminding us that it is possible to have too much of a good thing. We all know persons who are entirely praiseworthy in the pursuit of particular goals but are so single-minded that their total practice begins to exceed the boundaries of common sense and decency. We usually call such people 'fanatics'. According to the insight of ancient Greek philosophy, a virtue becomes a vice when it is not governed by the cardinal virtue of temperance. *In medio virtus stat;* a tendency can be regarded as virtuous only to the extent that it pilots a course between two extremes. Virtue is equally opposed to both extremes, not only to one. Overwork and idleness are opposite possibilities; the virtue of avoiding idleness must be protected equally from overwork. It is not virtuous to eat either too much or too little. Moderation is obviously the opposite of the vice of superfluity and extravagance (*RB* 36.4; 55.11; 61.2; 61.6), but it is also the opposite of penury and niggardliness. Sometimes monastic administrators and cellarers seem to forget this. Note, however, that between generosity and meanness there could be seen to exist a whole spectrum of virtues, each located closer to or farther from the mean: magnanimity, liberality, reasonableness, abstemiousness, austerity.

The *abbas* and *ammas* of the Egyptian desert had strong tendencies to extremism in their practice of virtue, though this was often subjectively balanced by personal kindness, gentleness and discretion. They were solitaries and, supposing they were also wise, they were able to reach their own individual equilibrium in the expression of gospel values. The case of a cenobitic lifestyle is different. For the good of community it is necessary that individuals either curb their fervour somewhat or try a little harder in order that all the group may stay together. The basis of communal observance must be the highest common factor, the best that is possible for all the members of the community, neither too demanding nor too lax, 'so that the strong have something to desire and the weak do not run away' (*RB* 64.19).

Benedict was the heir of a sober and even phlegmatic tradition, formed by centuries of efficient administration. Roman thinkers gave priority to the values of possibility, practicality and adaptability. Through John Cassian, Benedict may also have imbibed something of Stoicism. We find, for example, that 'moderation' was a word much used by Cicero, and with it a whole family of near-synonyms. He believed that everything is to be governed according to its appropriate mode and measure. Extremes are to be excluded: sufficiency, suitability and appropriateness are desirable norms. Any who wish to live by the law of moderation must practice temperance, and this usually involves continence – restraining themselves somewhat, holding back, keeping something in reserve. In the midst of the chronic disorder of the early sixth century Benedict desired to create an environment in which order ruled – foreseeing and forestalling any possibility that the monastic life could be shaped by random subjectivism.[2] Furthermore, the fact that Benedict's Rule belongs to a quasi-legal genre means that there is an a priori supposition that what is prescribed will generally be middle-of-the-road practice rather than the expression of eccentric fanaticism.

In the Rule of Benedict such practical discretion comes into play concerning the measure of food and drink, the hours of work and sleep, the clothing given to the monks. Great care is taken by Benedict to ensure that the demands made on his monks are not excessive and thereby counterproductive. *Ne qui nimis*, according to the often-quoted saying of the Roman poet Terence (*RB* 64.12). Food is provided according to strict measurement in order to avoid giving any occasion to the spirit of gluttony (*RB* 39.7–8). Sufficiency is to be the norm. In defiance of ancient monastic tradition, wine is permitted, but only a half-bottle; monks are to drink sparingly, not to the point of satiety, much less as far as drunkenness (*RB* 40.5–6). Even the liturgy is subject to the law of moderation; there is no place for liturgical extravagance in a Benedictine monastery. So there is provision that Sunday Vigils should not be too long (*RB* 11.2). On the other hand, while the content of the *Opus Dei* may be modified, the quantity of psalmody must not fall below the minimum of a weekly psalter (*RB* 18.22–23). Benedict legislates so that there is a measure or proportion between the fault and its punishment (*RB* 24.1), noting that there ought to be different measures of punishment for monks of different ages and different levels of intelligence (*RB* 30.1). We can understand such provisions in regular discipline as expressions of what may be termed 'quantitative moderation'.

More important, as far as the survival of the charism is concerned, is 'qualitative moderation'. This is based on the recognition that contrary values exist and that sometimes the choice is not between good and evil, but between two good things. In such cases it is important to affirm both poles of the dialectic to avoid a distorted outcome. We find good examples of such even-handedness in the Rule of Benedict.

- Solitariness is balanced by commonality.
- Communal prayer is balanced by personal prayer and *lectio divina*.
- Physical work is balanced by prayer and reading.
- Austerity is balanced by *humanitas*.
- Occupation is balanced by leisure.
- Ideal self-sufficiency is balanced by practical economy.
- Separation from the world is balanced by hospitality.
- Authority is balanced by consultation (and supervision).
- External order is balanced by interior freedom.

The capacity of a community to interact creatively with the real world is a function of its being able to determine the correct proportion between these contrary values. The correctness of the determination, however, is not reached mathematically, as though there were some mid-point that could be computed once and for all. A creative solution is found by continually moving forward, reading the data accurately and responding to it in the light of traditional wisdom. This is what the early Cistercians were promoting when they advanced the ideal of alternation: moving from one activity to its complement under the guidance of a single goal. It is clear that monastic seniority and experience play a significant role in understanding the potential monasticity of particular options. This is to say that maturity and experience are the best assessors of monastic moderation. This kind of practical wisdom seems to have been a quality Benedict himself had in abundance.[3]

First of all it is to be noted that inevitably, in a particular situation, one of the polar options will present as being the more urgent. If communitarian values are being neglected in the monastery the solution can never be to expel solitude and replace it with community. Rather, some common ground needs to be found between the opposite values (for example, the importance of peace and harmony) on which the opposites can be simultaneously affirmed. Both community and solitariness are essential components of Benedictine life; we cannot hope to build one by destroying the other. Silence and communication need to cooperate to assist the members of the community to realize their goal of perfect love of God and neighbour. The magic is to be found in the interaction of opposite poles, not in the elimination of one of them.[4]

Second, everyday life is always more complicated than theory. In a transitional phase the incoming value will be emphasized at the expense of the outgoing one. For example, when a reform calls for more poverty, initially it is normal that there will be a period of excessive severity until things settle down. Moderation will be suspended in the short term, but will gradually reassert itself. The Golden Mean cannot be achieved instantly.

Third, there is more than one value or virtue in monastic life, and the different areas of moral significance impact mutually. For example, the ideal balance between work and leisure may be modified by the economic indigence of the community (*RB* 48.7), by the subjective incapacity of members of the community to use leisure profitably (*RB* 48.23), by the monks being employed in other more useful occupations (*RB* 35.5). This is why there is no place for fundamentalism in applying the Rule: the tradition is received by all, re-expressed, applied and administered by the abbot, and reshaped by the manner in which the community allows itself to be led. Although Benedict gives full authority to the abbot, he is fully aware that monks of our times cannot always be persuaded to follow the more perfect path (*RB* 40.6), and sometimes it is necessary to adopt Plan B.

Both qualitative and quantitative forms of moderation are important for the long-term survival of a monastic institution. Opposite virtues need to enter into dynamic tension without either polarity moving into a zone of excess, and the end result of this balance is harmony, good order and peace.

The Benedictine bane

Historic Benedictinism has exhibited an enduring tendency to degenerate. This is the reason why the Benedictine tradition has undergone many necessary reforms in the course of the centuries. The pursuit of moderation carries with it a hidden danger. Too often the related virtue of *epieikeia* (fairness or equity) is invoked only to support a claim for mitigation of the Rule. Yet obviously it also has a role to play when it prompts increased severity as a means of redressing an existing imbalance. Opting for a 'more balanced life' cannot always mean choosing to be less austere. [5]

Moderation can be positive or negative. Positive moderation is achieved when opposite virtues flourish: when, for example, both the values of community and the values of solitude are equally strong. Negative moderation results when the tension between opposites is dissipated and neither value is pursued with any degree of fervour. A community in such a dire state may be at peace simply because all typically monastic goals have been abandoned and the only consensus is to pursue a non-challenging, easygoing existence. The monastery becomes a Country Club. After all, another word for moderation is tepidity, the state of being neither hot nor cold. Although in Latin the term *mediocritas* is more descriptive than evaluative, in current English 'mediocre' is almost always used in a pejorative sense. A community that is wishy-washy may believe itself to be moderate in all things but is, in fact, a mockery to the term – being neither contemplative nor active, neither cenobitic nor eremetical, given neither to manual labour nor to intellectual tasks.

This is a communal form of the well-chronicled monastic vice of *acedia*, a chronic inability to make and sustain commitments, the time-filling pursuit of variety and entertainment, and the listlessness and dissatisfaction that come from having no meaning in life. The community unconsciously develops a culture of entitlement in which the rights claimed are not complemented by obligations accepted. The absence of a sense of an ultimate goal and immediate objectives, such as John Cassian described in his first *Conference*, is a sure recipe for a dissipated and bootless existence.

Monastic life as envisaged by St Benedict depends on a great passion for the unseen world of spirit. This good zeal powers a move away from the world of sense and external involvement. The *apatheia* praised by the Desert Fathers was not apathy or listlessness in the ordinary meaning of those words, but a progressive desensitization to carnal and secular excitement – the lusts of the flesh, obviously, but also the allure of a comfortable life and worldly status. In the analysis often proposed by Gregory the Great, first comes the attachment to the hidden treasure and only then do detachment and worldly dispossession follow. The completeness of a monastic's disengagement from alternative sources of gratification is proportionate to the intensity of his or her spiritual experience. Having had a slight encounter with God makes the monk desire a more complete experience. Such desire is the prime mover in the monastic impulse. The monk is meant to be passionate in the search for God. Bernard of Clairvaux regards lack of affective drive (to be *sine affectione*, as in Rom. 1.31) to be the source of decline in monastic life. A dry heart, lacking the sap of maturity and wisdom, becomes harsh and judgemental.[6] Inevitably the monk so afflicted begins to seek for more immediate gratifications than those offered by a fervent monastic life.

An urbane and comfortable existence easily escapes any charge of extremism, but is it going anywhere? Does it have any purpose except continuance of existing forms and insulation against any challenge to renewal? This moderation is no virtue. It makes no contribution to the attainment of the monastic goal except that it may eventually provide a point of departure for a radical conversion that God's grace may provoke at some time in the future.[7]

Stability and moderation

Perseverance is the quality Benedict demands first of the prospective monk, who is to demonstrate that he has such constancy even before he joins the community by patiently enduring whatever obstacles are placed in his way (*RB* 58.3). On entering the novitiate, long before he is invited to make his vows, he is expected to promise stability or perseverance (*RB* 58.9). When eventually he makes profession, it is its irreversibility that Benedict emphasizes (*RB* 58.15–16).

Moderation is the key to perseverance, not only in the sense of avoiding excess but also as keeping to whatever is appropriate to the monastic way of life: *pro modo conversationis* (*RB* 22.2). The heart of the word is *modus*. Moderation respects the specific modality of the monastic lifestyle. Gluttony or buffoonery are utterly rejected because they have no place in a monastery (*RB* 39.8; 6.8). In St Benedict's mind a monk can never be merely moderately gluttonous. Of its nature gluttony has no place in the monastic mode of living. What is appropriate in a monastic ambience does not necessarily correspond with what is acceptable in a secular workplace, a diocesan curia, or a university common room. Monastic life is different and it is shaped by different modalities. A whole-hearted acceptance of the necessary limitations and boundaries inherent in the monastic calling is the fundamental element in eventual perseverance. Struggling against these restrictions or constantly trying to subvert them is demoralizing and lessens the person's chances of final perseverance.

One who intends to remain a lifetime in a monastery needs to develop a sort of marathon-mindedness; going forward at a deliberately reduced pace so as to ensure that sufficient energy remains at the end. Benedict is quite fond of running metaphors, but he gives the impression that the speed of running increases with time. The astonishing thing about monastic life is that it begins slowly because the novice arrives burdened with many obstacles. As these are shed with the passage of years, fervour and single-mindedness increase and the monk begins to do joyfully and naturally what used to be accomplished only with much inward groaning (*RB* 7.68). At the end of a long journey of growth the good monk will become extremely holy, but it is an extremism that is built on years of moderation.

Notes

1 See Michael Casey, 'The Dynamic Unfolding of the Benedictine Charism', *American Benedictine Review* 51 (2000), pp. 149–67. Reprinted in Michael Casey, *An Unexciting Life: Reflections on Benedictine Spirituality*, St Bede's Publications, Petersham MA, 2005, pp. 133–54.

2 See Michael Casey, 'Saint Benedict and Order', *Tjurunga* 73 (2007).

3 See Michael Casey, '*Quod Experimento Didicimus:* The Heuristic Wisdom of Saint Benedict', *Tjurunga* 48 (1995), pp. 3–22. Reprinted in Casey, *An Unexciting Life*, pp. 69–100.

4 For a discussion of how this difficulty was resolved among the twelfth-century Cistercians, see Michael Casey, 'The Dialectic of Solitude and Communion in Cistercian Communities', *Cistercian Studies* 23 (1988), pp. 273–309.

5 See Michael Casey, '"Balance" in Monastic Life', *Tjurunga* 9 (1975), pp. 5–11.

6 Bernard of Clairvaux, *SC* 50.4, *SBOp* 2, 80, 10; *SC* 44.5; *SBOp* 2, 47, 21–24. He attributes to St Paul the opinion that this condition is to be numbered among the greatest crimes, typical of non-believers (*AssptO* 15; *SBOp* 5, 274, 3; *OS* 5.6, *SBOp* 5, 365, 14).

7 Bernard of Clairvaux speaks eloquently against the ultimate unkindness of allowing a monk's focus on the goal to become dissipated through the institutionalization of self-indulgence. See *Apologia* 16–30; *SBOp* 3, 95–107.

20. Benedictine Hospitality

ROBERT ATWELL

There are three tables in a monastery. There is the Lord's table around which the community gathers to celebrate the Eucharist; the chapter table around which it transacts its business; and the refectory table at which meals are eaten and shared. As members of the community participate in the dynamic that links these three tables so the life of the monastery deepens and acquires the spiritual coherence that Benedict desires. If liturgy and prayer are not balanced by taking responsibility for the day-to-day management of the monastery then its worship will never be earthed, and both need to be complemented by its ministry of hospitality to stranger and pilgrim, for, says Benedict, 'Christ is received in their very persons.' For Benedict, until and unless I see Christ in the stranger sitting next to me in refectory I will not know him in the breaking of the bread at the Eucharist.

Hospitality has always been one of the characteristics of Christian monasticism. 'Life and death are with my neighbour,' said Antony the Great. The Desert Fathers and Mothers withdrew from ordinary society and sought solitude in the desert. They lived radically simple lives given to prayer and fasting, but their aim was not solitude or asceticism but God, and the way to God was charity. Monastic life was shaped by the two great commandments: to love God, and to love your neighbour as yourself. They received guests as Christ would receive them. They lived austerely themselves, but when visitors came they would hide their austerity and welcome them.

The early monastics loved to ponder the text from the Epistle to the Hebrews: 'Remember to show hospitality. There are some who by so doing have entertained angels unawares' (Heb. 13.2). Pachomius (*c.* 290–346), the founder of cenobitic monasticism, had a special guesthouse built near the entrance to his monastery in Egypt, and in Caesarea Basil constructed an entire village to care for the destitute. 'Whose feet do you wash?' was Basil's great question.

From the desert emerge fascinating stories of monastic hospitality. One of the most famous is of a young monk who was puzzled by the way one monk would receive visitors whereas another monk would not. Which was the authentic monastic way? He visits Abba Arsenius, an austere hermit who received him graciously but sat down to pray with him in silence. Eventually the young man feels so uncomfortable that he leaves and goes to consult Abba Moses, an Egyptian and a converted robber. He greets him with open arms, they share a lentil stew and talk all day. That night the young monk has a dream in which he sees two boats travelling down the river in parallel. In one sits Abba Arsenius in silent contemplation, eyes fixed firmly ahead, with the Holy Spirit in the rear of the boat holding the tiller. In the second boat he sees Abba Moses having a party with the angels and eating honey cakes. The point of the story is that both boats are travelling in the same direction: both ways lead to God.

Benedict was the receiver of this rich tradition and it informs his own understanding of monastic hospitality, as a result of which Chapter 53, entitled 'On the Reception of Guests', stands as one of the great chapters of the Rule. His teaching, however, is in marked contrast to that of *The Rule of the Master*, whose anonymous author is generally suspicious of guests because they may steal the community's property and consequently requires them to leave the monastery after only two days' stay. Benedict is both more generous and more courageous.

Benedict was writing in the sixth century, an age of political instability which witnessed the gradual disintegration of the Roman Empire. Feelings of insecurity were widespread. People no longer felt safe to travel, with marauding bands of armed mercenaries on the lookout for unsuspecting travellers. For good reason

Benedict stipulates that a monastery, if at all possible, should be constructed so that within its walls 'all necessities, such as water, mill, and garden are contained, and various crafts can be practised' (*RB 66*). Benedict removed the need for monks to travel outside the monastic enclosure because he deemed it not to be 'good for their souls'; the fact was, it was also dangerous. In the midst of the chaos into which Italy was falling, Benedict's households of God were stable and economically self-sufficient units. They were not only places of prayer and learning, they were safe havens for weary travellers, the weak and the vulnerable. Monasteries were valued places of hospitality and refuge.

Benedict fosters a culture of trust and friendship by taking people's suspicion and hostility, and converting it into hospitality. He is wise and practical in the advice he gives. Guests, including complete strangers, are to be welcomed 'with all courtesy of love'. In our own age of anonymous cities, when people die alone in flats and are never missed, and when in some sections of society there is a collapse of trust, it is difficult to hear his words and act upon them. We not only do not talk to strangers, we actively view them with suspicion in case they are terrorists. Benedict would understand our fears better than we think, but would still bid us take risks, confident in the knowledge that 'perfect love casts out fear' and because hospitality is an act of God.

A monastery, Benedict notes, 'is never lacking in guests' and he is alert to the danger of a community becoming overwhelmed by their demands. He therefore insists that things be so organized that the monastery's life is not unduly disturbed. He recommends that a porter be on hand to welcome visitors and field inquiries, and suggests that in large monasteries a separate kitchen be provided for guests who, he notes, often turn up at unseasonable hours. He provides for a guesthouse and deputes a brother to administer it efficiently and 'prudently' – always a favoured virtue in Benedict's mind. Food and wine, and the creature comforts of a bed with decent bedding, are all considered necessary. He calls the guest-quarters 'the house of God', a title which reveals the high esteem in which he holds the ministry of hospitality.

As elsewhere in the Rule, Benedict makes no artificial division between the spiritual and the material, as if one is good and the other evil, and exhibits a wonderful attention to detail which is the mark of all good hospitality. Care for another is indeed shown in small things: carrying a suitcase, arranging for a taxi to take someone to the station, putting flowers on the table, or simply listening. Hospitality is expressed by what we do for others, but even more by the way we do it.

Benedict is prepared to go to extraordinary lengths to ensure that a genuinely warm welcome is extended to guests. The Rule is for everyone, including the abbot, and yet everyone is a potential exception to it. Thus Benedict permits the greater silence at night to be broken in order that late arrivals can be accommodated, and allows the abbot to relax his fast to share supper with a guest. Not even asceticism is counted as holy as care for another. At the same time, however, Benedict is determined to protect the regular life of the community. He wants the legitimate needs of guests to be met but defends other members of the community from needless or endless distraction. He knows that if silence and prayer are disregarded the monastery will have nothing distinctive to offer its guests. There are limits to the welcome a community can extend.

Every monastery, for example, has a private area (an enclosure) to which guests and even oblates are not normally invited, and there may be times of the year when guests regrettably cannot be received. A culture of generous hospitality cannot flourish if boundaries are not observed. No one can be available all the time and no monastic community can meet a guest's every need. Indeed some guests may leave disappointed that the closeness of friendship they sought during their visit has not been met.

There is a delicacy about Benedict's language throughout this chapter. Good manners and courtesy are to be shown to guests at all times. Guest and monk are to pray together in order that they may be united in the kiss of peace. *Pax* is another Benedictine watchword. Conversation is to be gracious and never superficial or insipid. The scriptures are to be read and every kindness shown. In this way the monk is to share not only his meals, but his faith and hope with these strangers. It is through such encounters that strangers become pilgrims, and pilgrims become disciples and friends of God. This quality of gentle engagement is very different from the more intense and frantic spirituality of our own day which seeks to accumulate 'experiences' and expects instant gratification. Benedict invites guests to move into a different rhythm and to share in the holistic way of life of the monastery.

Guests are always to be received humbly, and the abbot is to provide water for their hands. Humility is not a popular virtue today, but the humility of which Benedict speaks is not a contrived depreciation of the self, but a humbling experience of being loved by God which opens a person to the gift of the other. The community is to wash the guests' feet and this recalls Christ's own action at the Last Supper when, laying aside his clothes, he assumed the job of a house-slave, kneeling before each of his disciples to wash their feet. The monks are to recite a verse from the psalms as they perform this ritual: 'O God, we have received your mercy in the midst of your temple.' In welcoming the stranger I am welcoming the mercy of God into my life. It is not enough to offer food or accommodation: I must recognize the One who comes to me incognito, disguised as a stranger or pilgrim.

The reason Benedict is so determined that guests should be properly cared for is a religious one: like the sick, they represent Christ. In the Rule he refers specifically to the gospel text, 'I was a stranger and you took me in' (Matt. 25.35). This quotation from the parable of the sheep and the goats reminds me that Christ will repeat those same words to me on the Day of Judgement. My attitude to others will form a criterion by which I will be judged by God.

Benedict's theology is strongly incarnational. No less than three times he states that guests are to be received, welcomed and adored. 'By a bow of the head or by a complete prostration of the body, Christ is to be adored because he is indeed welcomed in them.' Benedict uses the same Latin verb meaning to sustain, receive or welcome guests, as he does in the *suscipe*, the formula of monastic profession: 'Receive me, O God, according to your promise and I shall live; and let me not be disappointed in my hope.' Receive and welcome one another, Benedict says to his monks, as Christ has welcomed you in your monastic profession.

This quality of hospitality will be a hallmark of the life of a Benedictine oblate as much as of the monastic community to which he or she is affiliated, though inevitably it will be exercised in different ways according to domestic circumstances. The question for the oblate, as for every Christian, is one of stewardship: what does God want me to do with the good things he has given me? Gifts are for sharing: how can I welcome others to my home and to my table to share the good things of life that I enjoy? The answers to these questions will vary, but they will be informed by the principles and values that Benedict upholds. The challenge is always to love people as they are, not as we would wish them to be.

Like monastics, oblates need to know their limitations and how to conserve their time and energy. Attentive listening does not necessarily mean lengthy conversations. Hospitality is about creating internal space so that there is room to receive the gift of the other. I need to value my privacy so I can be genuinely open to others, and will need to withdraw from time to time to safeguard my inner life; otherwise I will become exhausted and 'extroverted out'. This pattern of withdrawal and engagement is as important for the well-being of an oblate as for the cloistered monastic.

The manner and customs with which we greet and welcome people today, whether in the street, in our homes or in a monastery, have changed enormously over the centuries and it would be ludicrously artificial to reproduce Benedict's instructions today. The issue now as then is how to honour a person without embarrassing them. We need also to examine our motivations and general attitude to people, as Benedict's monks had to in their day. 'In the reception of poor people and pilgrims,' Benedict says, 'special attention is to be shown because in them more particularly is Christ received; our awe of the rich already guarantees them respect.' Personally I find it easy to give the important, the intelligent and the attractive my attention. Benedict challenges me to give the same quality of attention – in fact more – to the dull, the lonely and the boring. These are today's poor, and to them, says Jesus, belongs the kingdom.

In most monasteries on the wall above the abbot's table hangs a crucifix, cementing in the mind of monk and visitor alike the link between the oratory and the refectory. In some Benedictine houses the refectory may also have a copy of Andrei Rublev's icon of the Trinity. Based on the Old Testament story of the angelic visitation to Abraham and Sarah recorded in the book of Genesis, it depicts the three angelic visitors gathered around a table on which sits a cup, representing Christ's self-offering. It is an icon of divine hospitality: God invites all people everywhere to sit and eat at his table in his kingdom. Celebration belongs to God's kingdom: he has prepared a rich banquet for us.

Icons such as this remind us that the source of hospitality is the generous heart of God who shares his bread with sinners. In Benedict's vision the monastery is to be a sacrament of the hospitality of God, making visible God's invitation to share his life and love for eternity. It is this vision which inspires an oblate's ministry of hospitality in the knowledge that we can all find ourselves 'entertaining angels unawares'.

Part Two Living the Oblate Life

V THE OBLATE IN THE WORLD

21. Was Blind but Now I See

JANICE DAURIO

My husband Paul and I are oblates of St Andrew's Abbey, Valyermo, California. Valyermo is a small monastery pressed against the San Bernardino Mountains in the blazing sun of the high desert about 90 miles from Los Angeles. As oblates we presume that we share a certain vision of reality with other oblates, but what is that vision? It is the sacramentality of the universe, and especially of ordinary days and ordinary objects.

Not long ago I called one of our oblate friends, Colin. We had not spoken for a while, but, as often happens with good friends, we talked as if we had been in touch all along. He recounted a recent troubling but not uncommon incident.

Some non-religious (indeed, anti-religious) people he met at a dinner party found out he was Catholic. Up to that point the conversation had been typical of dinner parties: casual, superficial, and friendly. Now it became focused, adversarial, and asymmetrical. How can you believe all that stuff? What about child abuse by priests? How can you be religious in an age of science?

The conversation was asymmetrical because they could grill Colin but he couldn't grill them. He had religious beliefs and they did not. This was not like a conversation you might have with, say, evangelical Christians, or Muslims, who also have religious beliefs – comparatively rich and complex ones. Or is it?

I have been in situations like this, and probably you have, too.

When I was in college, one friend, particularly well informed about Catholics, delighted in trying to stump me. When I asked him what he believed (I confess that I was uncharitably motivated by the desire to make him uncomfortable in turn), he said, 'Nothing.' Even at the time that struck me as odd.

Ex-Catholics are often the most troublesome – and helpful. At the college where I teach philosophy one such ex-Catholic, John, an anthropologist with whom I meet to plan conjoined courses, is articulate and knowledgeable about defects – real or only apparent – in the Catholic view of things. I have learned a lot from this experience.

For one thing, I've learned how to engage in dialogue. My goal is listening, not speaking; learning, not teaching. The Rule of St Benedict opens with the admonition to listen. Just as Mother Teresa found Christ 'in a very strange disguise' in the poor, so we can find Christ in the words of our anti-Catholic colleagues and friends. Listen for that still, small voice.

For another thing, I have learned that authenticity requires that I take criticism of my being religious seriously: why *do* I believe these things? It is hard (but helpful!) to be around people who explicitly reject what we explicitly accept and what means so much to us. If you want to know what you really believe, surround yourself with those with whom you disagree. Doubts are good: they are normally the way from childish to adult faith.

Finally, from the anthropology class I have learned about religion: every culture has one. People who call themselves secular humanists have one. Although twenty-first-century Americans talk of 'religion' as one topic among many, most cultures don't even have a word for 'religion': it is just the way things are.

As I thought about Colin's and my own experiences, I wondered about religious beliefs. First, why do some people lack them? Second, why did formerly religious people give them up? Third, why are there so many religions? Last, are non-religious people more rational than religious people?

First, then: Why do so many people have no religion? Answer: They do have religion, but they don't realize it.

All yearn to respond to the attraction of the transcendent. All desire to understand themselves against a horizon that goes beyond the ordinary or, more accurately, sees the value of the ordinary. Christian theology has a word for that: sacramentality. Benedictine life embodies it: the holy in the ebb and flow of the ordered day, with its meals and work and sleep and play.

Religion is incorporation into a community with a *creed*, *code*, and *cult*.

The *creed* is the community's set of beliefs, whether those beliefs are well worked out or operate implicitly. Every culture has a creed of some sort. The American creed might be the Declaration of Independence or the Preamble to the Constitution. The secular humanist's creed is about human value and human progress. A *code* is the community's expectations of the behavior of its members. In Saudi Arabia, self-appointed enforcers of appropriate dress wander the streets checking to see that no hair is peeping out from under a woman's headscarf, and that men are wearing loose clothing. Acceptable American behavior is, unfortunately, revealed by television, where 'undress' is the dress code. The *cult* of a community is its formalized rituals. Americans have rituals for courtrooms, presidential funerals, and baseball games. Secular humanists have 'christening' ceremonies. In so far as everyone belongs to a community, and in so far as every community has its own creed, code and cult, everyone has a religion.

Religion also refers to your comprehensive view of the way things are – of *reality*, *value* and *meaning*.

Your dinner hosts or co-workers who say they are not religious nonetheless have their own view of *reality*: even the most scientific among them accept the existence on faith of all kinds of things they can't see, such as quarks, black holes and minds. I am surprised when I find people who demand high standards for acceptance of Christian beliefs but readily accept karma, astrology, reincarnation, or fate.

Your supposedly non-religious friends also have strongly held *values*: for example, they might fight for human rights or the preservation of mountains and rivers. True, they don't call marriage sacramental, but they value fidelity over adultery. They find *meaning* in human relationships, absorbing work, and art. A self-described agnostic is moved to tears by Gothic cathedrals and

Bach's *St Matthew's Passion*. They are on to something, even if they don't realize it.

We all want the void into which we peer to peer back. We want the darkness to have a face. We desire that there be answers to 'why' questions, even if we don't know the answers. Even those who think the 'why' questions have no answers *want* there to be answers. All desire that life *matters*.

All want the Benedictine vision, even if they don't realize it. All who see value at all in the ordinary have that view of *reality* Christians call sacramental. The careful attention to a daily *ordo* points to the holiness not just of prayer times but all times. The careful attention to the linens and chalices in the sacristy of the monastery chapel invites attention beyond itself to the holiness of all 'the work of human hands'. The homage Christians pay to the divinity of Christ includes, in the eucharistic liturgy, the desire that by this mystery we may come to share in that divinity. The high is brought low; the low is brought high. Separate categories of supernatural and natural blur in one grand vision of the new heaven and the new earth, seen in the birth of a child or in the embrace in friendship of former enemies.

In its loving description of the most ordinary events like sleeping and the most ordinary objects like knives, the Rule of St Benedict invites a rich way of seeing. Your hours of sleep continue the rhythm of the Rule, made holy by the act of consecration of your life to God. Your trip to the supermarket is a pilgrimage. Your folding and putting away the clothes is a participation in God's ongoing act of creation, making order out of chaos. Benedictine formation is learning to see this way.

The hobbits of the Shire in Tolkien's *The Lord of the Rings* are Benedictines! They know the holiness of the little things: good meals shared with family, friends, and anyone who shows up, and cultivating gardens in peace. They undertake great dangers only for the sake of preserving and returning to the quotidian. It is Benedictine, as well as hobbit-like, to see the extraordinary value of ordinary things. Non-religious people who love *The Lord of the Rings* have adopted this sacramental view of reality without knowing it. They are on to something, even if they don't realize it.

Days spent in a hospital bed (few of us will escape) give glory to God; all has *value*, especially suffering. For the Benedictine, ordinary days – bringing the cares of home and job to prayer, and bringing the rewards of prayer to home and work – afford endless opportunities for finding the sacred in the secular; or better, for obliterating the distinction between the sacred and the secular. ✓ The sacred is pressed down and overflowing in the so-called secular. The source and summit of Benedictine life is the eucharistic liturgy, where with self-forgetfulness we can see Christ in word, in bread and wine, in the community, especially the 'unimportant' and easily overlooked members of the community. Emphasis on humility in the Rule gives witness to this search for the holiness of the other in self-forgetfulness.

After a lifetime of such training in proper seeing, the Benedictine oblate at the point of death is ready for what T. S. Eliot calls the familiar unknown. Our eyes close in death and open to see that Face we have searched for our whole lives, often without knowing it.

If we define religion broadly, everyone has one. The religion of some people is like a dry, weary desert without water. For Benedictines it is a lush, wild rainforest, saturated with meaning and value, with purpose and eternity.

Second: why do some people give up religion? The short answer is, they don't.

What appears to be giving up religion is really changing religions, exchanging one view of reality, value, and meaning for another. People change their understanding of who they are by identifying with a new community with its own creed, code and cult.

The next time someone says to you that she is no longer religious but is now 'spiritual', ask her what the difference is. It's very hard to say, but for Americans spirituality seems to refer to positive, solitary, subjective experiences that make people feel good about themselves. Religion – especially so-called organized religion – is associated with what is not emotionally rewarding: responsibility and external, communal, ritualized prayer. *(to some)*

So understood, spirituality complements religion. Spirituality without religion risks self-absorption; religion without spirituality courts superficiality. Spirituality and religion are the two eyes of the Benedictine Rule. We see spirituality and religion in the *lectio divina* and spiritual reading. However personally rewarding it may be, one can't spend all day praying or all day working. Spirituality and religion are honored in *ora et labora*. Our community calls us to the responsibility of our work, undertaken for the transformation of the world.

Third: Why are there so many different religions? Because there are so many plausible, consistent accounts of reality, value, and meaning and because so many are partly true, and none is complete. There are so many different religions because there are so many coherent answers to questions about the meaning of life and because reality will always elude our best attempts at systematization. Religion is even more ambitious than science in striving to achieve a comprehensive account of reality. Religion aims to know everything; the more you try to describe, the more room there is for error.

Furthermore, although we know how to use words, when we speak of God we don't know what we mean. Mystics caution against overconfidence in even the best theological formulations. If some religious traditions have more truth than others, all fall short of the whole truth.

The Benedictine Rule balances the claims and limits of truth. Chapter 6 of the Rule praises silence, witness to the incompleteness of even the Bible. Prayers ought to be short (Chapter 20) because mystery is large. In the last chapter Benedict praises the Bible and the church fathers, but he also notes that even full observers of the Rule are just beginners. The Rule spends much space on the ordinary, and very little on theology.

Finally: Are non-religious people more rational than religious people? No, if there is more to reality than what meets the eye, and if it is rational to see more, rather than less, of what is really there.

There are two kinds of people: the Nothing-Buts and the Yes-Buts.

For the Nothing-Buts, what we perceive is nothing but its most basic components. You might *think* of your best friend as a person, but she's *really* nothing but a bunch of cells. Praying is just synapse firings of the neurons in the cerebral cortex – meat doing some interesting things with chemicals. You might be overwhelmed with the beauty of the sun as it dips slowly toward the horizon, but the sun is nothing more than a gigantic ball of atoms and ions. In short, for the Nothing-Buts, the value of anything is less than what it seems.

Just as the blind and the deaf are deprived of one of their senses, Nothing-Buts are missing one of their senses – what theologians call the *sensus divinitatis*. The Yes-Buts see more; Benedictines see better. The Yes-Buts see more than what is, in a simplistic sense, visible to the eye.

Your friend is made up of cells, but she is a person, and a person is more than the sum of her cells. She is a future citizen of heaven; if you could see her as she really is you would be tempted to worship her, as C. S. Lewis put it. Synapse firings accompany prayers, but prayers are the doors to the sacred.

Yes-Buts see the sun and think of the countless suns in an incomprehensibly large and rapidly expanding universe, the gift of a frolicsome, playful, utterly vivacious Creator of everything out of nothing. The beauty of the sunset points to Beauty himself. The beauty of our friend's face is the reflected beauty shining on the face of Christ. Even the best human experiences are teasers, promising more than they deliver.

Isn't it odd that the Rule of St Benedict says so little about supernatural things as such? But it does have a lot to say about what to serve at meals (Chapter 39, two kinds of cooked food), how much to drink (Chapter 40, one hemina of wine), what to sleep on (Chapter 55, straw mattress) and how to care for tools (Chapter 32). Could the message be that the supernatural is another way of seeing the natural? I think so. The Benedictine, sacramental view is a 'seeing as': seeing the temporary as eternal, the ordinary as extraordinary. Religious people don't wear rose-colored glasses; anti-religious people wear cloudy glasses.

In a dialogue from Willa Cather's *Death Comes for the Arch-*

bishop, a miracle is defined as the pulling back of a curtain to reveal what has been there all along. In a burst of Benedictine insight, the grandmother in Flannery O'Connor's short story *A Good Man is Hard to Find* goes from seeing the Misfit as a criminal to seeing him as her son.

The Benedictine way of life is a 'Seeing Eye Dog'. The ordered life of the Rule offers guidance for the development of the *sensus divinitatis*, a natural human faculty. Religious people don't see more than what is there; they see the more that *is* there – even at the most surprising times and in the most surprising places, God in a very strange disguise.

22. Creation

ESTHER DE WAAL

At the very end of his life comes that amazing moment in which St Benedict saw the entire world gathered up 'as it were in one ray of light'. As he records this in the *Dialogues*, St Gregory is giving us a glimpse into what is so apparent throughout the Rule: the prayer-filled love and reverence with which St Benedict approached all created things. It is reflected in every aspect of a Benedictine's life: in the handling of matter and the earth itself no less than the tools of daily life, and not least our own physical beings. St Benedict's concern is always to form the underlying attitude and motivation, 'the disposition of the heart', which determines the way in which we see and handle our lives. He helps us to approach the world around us with love and yet with detachment, enjoying it as gift but also accepting it as responsibility.

'And God saw all that he had made and indeed it was very good . . .' (Gen. 1.31). St Benedict wants us to see this world as a continual outpouring of God's love, to be cared for and rejoiced in as God's generosity and blessing, to which the daily response can only be one of praise and gratitude. Sacredness is vested in matter; the spiritual and the material, if handled aright, are both paths to God. Time and space, the two primordial dimensions of reality, are among the greatest of these gifts. If we are to live by the insights of the Rule we are bound to ask ourselves whether we do violence to time, whether we are sensitive to space? For St Benedict knows that a balanced and holistic life requires a framework which will bring a sense of order and structure. The gentle rhythm that he establishes for each day allows for both the meal times and the times of prayer to be determined by the coming of light and darkness and the changes of the seasons. The importance that he gives to space is shown by the way in which places are allotted according to their specific activities. He makes a telling point in what he says about the oratory: 'the oratory must be simply a place of prayer, as the name implies, and it must not be used for any other activities at all nor as a place of storage of any kind'.[1] For a well-ordered community brings conditions in which both the individual and the institution can grow and thrive. Muddle and confusion mitigate against a focused energy. The monastic practice of *statio* is an example which establishes something from which we can all learn. By entering the chapel a few minutes before the start of the saying of the office, monks and nuns ensure that they are totally present to themselves, to the moment, to the presence of God – body and spirit are brought together, alert and attentive to the Word.

Those chapters which when I first read them seemed so utterly mundane – the instructions about the serving of food, about clothes, about sleeping arrangements – I now realize were giving me extremely profound theological insights in a most practical and immediate way. Everything matters. We are to own up when something gets broken not out of guilt but simply because every single thing, even a simple cooking pot, matters. St Benedict's concern to ' handle with care' applies to people as well as to material objects and, of course, above all to the earth itself. Care encourages enjoyment, delight. We have only to read those passage in which he speaks of food to know that he honours it, and wants there to be a choice of dishes, properly served, with appropriate wine, to know that St Benedict is no puritan.

We are, however, to consider nothing as our own – the verb *habere* used in Chapter 33, which asks whether monks ought to have anything of their own, may be translated 'to consider' rather than 'to have'.[2] Characteristically St Benedict explores this idea of everything being ours only on loan in a chapter apparently dealing with the mundane matter of the abbot issuing tools to the brothers. For us, outside the monastery, the figure of the abbot, *abbe*, father, is of course Christ who, as he entrusts the work tools to each of us, makes a list. Why? Because each matters, is to be cared for, not treated carelessly, for it will be collected after use – with the implication of something being brought to fruition, achieving fullness through the responsible action of a faithful steward.

Fr Joe of Quarr Abbey was clear just how important the idea of non-attachment is in today's competitive and consumerist society. 'Possessions are extensions of the self, you see. They become the walls of that prison of the self. The more possessions the less likely will be your release from the prison . . . '[3] Talking with a young man living in New York who knows only too well that the more of the latest fine product anyone possesses the more formidable they appear, Fr Joe insisted that owning things was not wrong in itself, any more than the pleasure that they brought was wrong. But the question is one of attitude: how you *see* them – can you hold them with detachment?

All this applies most powerfully to the earth itself. Here we have an aspect of the Rule that speaks most immediately and urgently to all of us today as we watch greed, exploitation and destruction wantonly ruining God's gifts. For far too long this aspect of St Benedict's prophetic voice has been overlaid because Christian concern for creation has been associated with Celtic Christianity or with St Francis. Yet, as Dom Aidan Bellinger of Downside has pointed out, for anyone living under the vow of stability the environment is bound to be of the greatest importance. Stability brings not only the commitment to staying in a relationship with the people around one but equally with the surrounding land.[4] Being tied to the soil carries immense practical implications, in the context of St Benedict's understanding of care with detachment and corporate concern not only for the present but for the future as well. It was a challenge that the American Benedictine sisters recognized 25 years ago, and their challenging statement then needs to be recalled:

We must choose here and now. What can Benedictines of this century offer in a world which lacks a community conscience, a vision of the sacredness of creation, a commitment to the dignity of life?

Our answer is monastic stewardship; that we use what we are and what we have for the transformation of culture because creation is the Lord's and we are its keepers; we hold it on trust. We must remember that the earth is not so much inherited from our parents as borrowed from our children. We owe a debt to the next generation.[5]

St Benedict's strong sense of respect for the locality means accepting restraints, responding to what is found, discerning rather than imposing; clothing, for example, is to use whatever materials come to hand in the neighbourhood. Recognizing the particular character of a place brings the timeless, basic wisdom of learning how to live in accord with local specificity.

Life is determined by concern for the common good, for the shared life. There is no competition or exploitation. One of St Benedict's favourite words is 'sufficit'. He cautions against wastefulness (13.1), against eating too much (39.7), or drinking too much (40.6). He tells the monks not to be greedy for profit but to sell their goods at comparatively low prices (57.8), and if anyone has more than they need they are to distribute to the poor. Everything is in moderation, with enough to satisfy basic needs. If this simple lifestyle involves a little self-restraint then, as a recent commentary puts it, 'here we have a primary asceticism and one which is important for the health of the planet'.[6]

Simplicity and stability, however, do not prevent development and the enhancement of the environment. St Benedict recognized the place of the intellect so that Benedictines have always brought a trained mind to bear on manual labour. Already the Rule, in mentioning a mill, which was something quite new in the sixth century, shows us that right from the start their way of life accepted technological advance. In the Dark Ages they were known for their handling of both plough and book, and subsequently they showed skill in every field of enterprise from land reclamation and drainage to hydraulic engineering.[7] Yet always the goal remained corporate, the common good. 'May he bring us all together . . .'

Notes

1 Chapter 52. The translation is that of Patrick Barry OSB.

2 See an article by Terrence Kardong in *Cistercian Studies*, 985, no. 20, p. 188.

3 Tony Hendre, *Father Joe: The Man who Saved my Soul*, Random House, New York, 2004, p. 120.

4 See Bellinger's review of *Monasteries and Landscape in North East England* by Bryan Waites in *The Downside Review*, vol. 116, no. 403, April 1998, p. 149.

5 *Of All Good Gifts: A Statement on the Nature of Stewardship in the Lives of American Benedictine Sisters*, Benet Press, Erie, 1980.

6 Terrence Kardong, *Benedict's Rule: A Translation and Commentary*, Liturgical Press, Collegeville MN, 1996, p. 341.

7 A twelfth-century prior of Canterbury who was a pioneer in hydraulic engineering installed a system that brought piped water to the community and its extended household throughout the Middle Ages.

23. The Oblate Life: Spirituality at Work

DERMOT TREDGET

One of the factors that frequently motivates an individual to become a Benedictine oblate is the way in which the Rule of Benedict brings under the broad heading of work a number of indispensable aspects of Christian life, namely prayer, work, rest and study, which together provide a foundation for a Christian spirituality of work. Although a full-time commitment to the Benedictine life was seen primarily for 'professional religious', many who have made a commitment to live the Christian life in the world, and in the lay state, now have come to realize that the Benedictine Rule, with its spirituality of work, has a great deal to offer the individual grappling with real issues about work–life balance, integrating prayer and work, coping with difficult relationships at work or discerning what is the right thing to do in difficult situations. Additionally, the Rule provides a framework for a routine, stability and rhythm which all too often is difficult to sustain in our rapidly changing work environment. Benedict recognized that work, in its different forms, had a transformative power. For the monastic, work is seen as a principal means to seeking God. One of the great strengths of the Benedictine oblate movement is that it too opens people's eyes to the fact that every working activity, paid or unpaid, can be the means to salvation. Finally, the Rule of Benedict can be of value in assisting any conscientious oblate to discover the true meaning and purpose of work.

When Benedict set out to compose his Rule his primary aim was to provide a distinctive form of Christian life and commitment based on earlier forms of monasticism. The first monastic communities were nurtured in a civilization which on the whole disdained work and manual labour. The essential daily chores of life, domestic work, farming, construction and such like were done by slaves or bonded servants. One of the first challenges that Christianity and the earliest monks faced was how to make work not only respectable but an integral part of Christian living and a duty to God and one's neighbour. Benedictine monastics have always had to work to earn their living. Down the centuries, the Christian church, deriving its inspiration from holy scripture and tradition, has had to find ways of adapting its teaching to accommodate new ways and types of work. It has also had to come to terms with phenomena such as globalization, the Internet and the powers of secularization. In spite of their choice to deliberately place themselves on the margins of society and to be 'other-worldly', monastics have not been exempt from these changes. It is their ability to adapt, while preserving the fundamental core values and aims of the Rule of Benedict, that makes a Benedictine spirituality of work so attractive.

Benedict does not speak of a spirituality of work as such, although the relationship between prayer, the life of the spirit and work is immediately apparent. Because of this connection some people have even suggested that *orare et laborare* (to pray and to work) could be a Benedictine motto. In sixth-century Europe there was not the preoccupation with defining, compartmentalizing and systematizing human behaviour that there is today. With ease, and without thinking, the monastic moved from one work activity to another. The day was seamless, balanced and rhythmical. There is no doubt that Benedict's disciples were immersed in the life of the Spirit. In the Prologue to the Rule he encourages the monk to listen to the Spirit. Quoting from the book of Revelation 2.7 Benedict writes, 'You that have ears listen to what the Spirit says to the Churches.' Soon after, Benedict concludes what is probably one of the most important chapters in his Rule, that on the 12 steps of humility (*RB* 7), with the words:

Now, therefore, after ascending all these steps of humility, the monk will arrive quickly at that perfect love of God which casts out fear (I John 4:18). Through this love, all that he once performed with dread, he will now begin to observe without effort, as though naturally, from habit, no longer out of fear of hell, but out of love of Christ, good habit and delight in virtue. All this the Lord will by the Holy Spirit graciously manifest in his workman now cleansed of vices and sins. (*RB* 7.67–70)

Contemporary definitions of spirituality emphasize that spirituality underpins our relationship with God. Through prayer, through listening, we come to know God better and he hears our prayers. A spirituality of work brings another dimension into this relationship. If our connectedness to God is characterized by a vertical axis then our connectedness to our work is symbolized by a horizontal axis. Part of this horizontal relationship is with our neighbour and God's created world. Thus the spiritual and the ethical are inextricably linked. We cannot speak about a spirituality of work without talking about an ethics of work. Our spirituality of work determines how we relate to others in the workplace, whether we encounter them as co-worker, boss, customer or supplier. Not surprisingly Benedict places great emphasis on community and loving the brethren. For this reason a spirituality of work can only grow and flourish in the midst of community where we put ourselves at the disposal of one another.

A close examination of the Rule will reveal several words or phrases such as the work of God (or *Opus Dei*), manual labour, toil, craftsmanship, artisanship and good deeds. The work of God or corporate worship was the most important work that a monastic engaged in. 'Let nothing be preferred to the work of God,' says Benedict (*RB* 43.3). This duty formed the backbone and framework for monastic life. All other tasks and activity revolved around this corporate worship, the praise of God. In between the work of God was inserted other kinds of work, such as manual labour, which could take the form of doing the necessary domestic chores, labouring in the fields, milling the corn, tending the animals, curing the skins for leather, tailoring the clothes, making the sandals and so on. As monasticism became established the ingenuity and creativity of monastics transformed and enlarged the variety of work to the extent that it had a civilizing effect on those around them. For instance, the copying and reproduction of books, some of them elaborately illuminated, helped preserve much of the literature of ancient antiquity including sacred scripture, commentaries and sermons. For today's monastics much of the work they do is intellectual rather than manual, such as scholarly research, studying, pastoral work, teaching and so on.

But, it is important to recognize that Benedict only envisioned monastics doing manual labour four to five hours a day. In the same chapter on manual work (*RB* 48), additional provision is made for a further two to three hours to be spent in sacred reading or *lectio divina*. Although this reading was primarily a preparation for meditation and prayer, it is also a form of intellectual work in so far as it required discipline, application and could be toilsome. In other words it engaged a different skill set, that is intellectual rather than manual, and provided on a physical and psychological level a respite from the demands of manual labour.

In the monastery there were often individuals who possessed some skill or art. Benedict refers to them as the artisans. Here we are presented with an important lesson about the nature and purpose of work. Benedict warns the artisan against becoming puffed up with pride because of the status or economic advantage that the artisan is bestowing on the rest of the community (*RB* 57). It is not difficult to see this caution as a rebuke to much of the utilitarian thinking that characterizes the modern work ethic. How easy it is for us to fall into the same trap! We value others, or inflate our own importance, according to what we do rather than for who we are. We lose sight of the fact that our work is primarily about service to others. Consequently, we fail to remember that an individual's most important qualities or contribution cannot always be measured or quantified. This is certainly the case with the spiritual life.

What is also important about this chapter on manual work is not only what it tells us about the kinds of work activity monastics were engaged in but also the relationship between them. Although the Benedictine oblate now lives in a world of work where there is greater opportunity for leisure, does this non-work time spiritually nourish? Is it genuinely re-creational in so far as it enlivens and sustains the human spirit and allows the Holy Spirit to enter in? This is probably one of the greatest challenges facing the world of work. On the surface Benedict makes no provision for leisure, at least not as it is generally understood in our modern world, but he does make provision for *lectio divina*. In fact Benedict studiously avoids the term leisure as commonly understood in antiquity, probably wanting to avoid its elitist connection to an ideal which eschewed manual labour or work. 'Idleness (or boredom) is the enemy of the soul,' he reminds us (*RB* 48.1). Instead, what Benedict's Rule does in recommending *lectio divina* is to encourage a form of activity that could lead the reader to contemplation. Paradoxically, for philosophers of ancient antiquity such as Aristotle, this was one of the nobler aims of leisure. Therefore the Benedictine oblate ought to consider *lectio divina* as a way of redeeming leisure from the perilous state it is now in, where the majority of activities that pass for leisure are new or novel forms of offering from the marketplace that never fully satisfy the consumer's spiritual thirst. What the practice of *lectio divina* can do for the oblate is to help restore the contemplative dimension to leisure which, hopefully only temporarily, has been lost. With this important aid in their spiritual toolbox the oblate has the ability to see work in a new light.

Finally, we come to the last type of work and that is inner work, or as Benedict calls it the work of conversion. One of the three vows that a Benedictine monastic takes is 'conversion of life'. It is so easy to forget that this is the case, but all other kinds of work, namely the *Opus Dei*, manual and intellectual work, practising crafts, sacred reading, study or any other form of work, are directed to this inner work of conversion. Certainly the same can be said of the life of the oblate or anyone else following in the footsteps of Christ. However, as Benedict constantly reminds us, we do not achieve this conversion by ourselves. We achieve it only by the gift of grace, freely given through the Holy Spirit.

These people fear the Lord, and do not become elated over their good deeds; they judge it is the Lord's power, not their own, that brings about the good in them. They praise the Lord working in them, and say with the Prophet: 'Not to us O lord, not to us give the glory, but to your name alone.' (*RB* Prologue 29–20)

24. Cyberspace, Community and the Oblate

CAROL LEWIS

I often ask myself why it is that people like to dwell on the negative: others' shortcomings, material deprivation, the bad news – is it really more dramatic than the wealth of riches that may be found in the same situations: the sacrifice of rescuers, kindness and gentleness, the generosity of gifts to the needy; or does it just give us a chance to comment and appear wise . . . ?

Well, the Internet is, it seems, no exception. Negative reactions vary from fear of the technology to outright condemnation of the information to which it gives access. I have even heard the view that people shouldn't have access to the Internet or even to computers in case of temptation to evil ways. Yet I have never heard anyone condemn on such grounds that other great information resource, the library.

Why such wariness? Perhaps it is the juxtaposition of familiarity and the immense and hitherto undreamed of opportunities to reach the unknown. This, of course, is a fundamental human need – to know the unknown and to strive to know the unknowable. This dichotomy presents a danger in itself – that in turning to the Internet in pursuit of the latter aim we lose sight of the truly Unknowable. Do we, who seek in so far as we may to follow the Rule of St Benedict, blast ourselves into cyberspace believing the sum of all human knowledge to be an end rather than a means? In our lonely wanderings in that mysterious land, do we lose sight of the *community* of endeavour and growth through *lectio divina*, so especially important within the Rule? We may be isolated from our monastic community by the natural constraints of our worldly obligations but the idea of community should, nevertheless, remain present. While accepting that the only true communion is within the Mass, we may nevertheless profitably consider the implications for community of this great resource.

In his excellent paper 'The Postmodern Desert: Solitude and Community in Cyberspace',[1] Elisha Emery obl.osb calls upon us to look beyond our traditional interpretation of the concept of community, made possible by current technology. He illustrates one aspect of community by reference to mother and baby. There are many other aspects but such a short paper can only take one for further thought. Emery points out that mother and baby cannot represent beings or concepts in isolation from each other, since each is necessary in the interpretation of the other. The term 'mother' is capable of being viewed from two aspects. First, that of 'object' providing the physical necessities of life to the baby during its physical formation. Second, that of a 'holding environment' representing the point of reference for the baby during its personal, spiritual and mental formation. Both aspects are vital to the development of a healthy, whole human being; you are unlikely to find such a being formed in isolation from all or part of one of these functions.

Thus, because there is a sense in which mother and baby are separate entities, their coming together within the holding environment represents a community within which solitude is possible. The solitude within this environment enables the baby to form as a whole person with its separate identity, yet inextricably linked with its mother through the environment they have shared.

This has obvious parallels with the Benedictine environment. Emery draws the comparison with an abbot who creates and sustains an environment within which each monk, while sustained in every respect in the material sense, can find 'the solitude of the desert as the medium through which develops an authentic openness and purity of heart'. Similarly, each oblate must seek to enter the environment that makes this possible in order to achieve his or her own 'proper encounter with the living God'.

Such a physical place on earth has been the desert wilderness –
for the church fathers and many mystics since. The utter openness
of the desert, the lack of spatial or ideological markers and absence
of obstruction has produced a fertile place for that 'authentic
openness and purity of heart' that unconditionally admits the love
of God.

Emery says:

> As a holding environment, the desert is a cauldron where the
> soul is refined. . . .
> Each day begins clean and promising in the sweet cool clear
> green light of dawn. And then the sun appears, its hydrogen
> cauldrons brimming – so to speak – with plasmic fires and the
> tyranny of its day begins. (Abbey, 1968).

Can we apply this evocative analogy to the great wilderness of the
Internet where our intellect may wander at will? This description
mirrors the best and the worst of the Internet where knowledge
can be acquired and love and support expressed in social communications, but where also the human mind can slide into the
cauldron where right judgement and discipline are not exercised.
To join the countless community of contributors and explorers in
cyberspace necessitates the exercise of care and wisdom.

Here we should consider what attracts the growing oblate commitment – community for sure, but, perhaps more specifically, the
liberation of the desert within which to grow towards grasping the
Unknowable while assured of the safety of the collective wisdom
and guidance of the community?

Oblates live within one community, be it family, educational
establishment or whatever, but also spiritually within *and physically apart from* their monastic community – isolated yet within
that community. Physical attendance can be sporadic, even non-
existent, yet each seeks their proper encounter with the living God
by the prayers of, and intercourse with, their community within
the Rule of our holy father Benedict so far as is appropriate to their
station. Most of us need the support of community in the desert
but, clearly, that does not mean physically within the community.

As oblates we are held neither by residence within the community nor by the traditional monastic vow of stability, but by the gravitational field of shared spiritual commitment. The abbey is the 'holding environment' within which we grow, mature and make our response, just like mother and child. Since the notion of community holds fast despite physical separation, so it can as well apply in the wilderness of cyberspace. The Internet is a marvellous tool which facilitates communication with ease and immediacy and should be used to foster that community of endeavour which we have entered. It represents a valuable facet of community in the Benedictine sense, contributing to the mortar that binds us, being a channel outward to a seemingly limitless resource in pursuit of our common aim.

We are urged to use the Internet in the same way as all other media to benefit others individually and collectively in every way possible.[2] To use the Internet positively we must be familiar with it and its potential. We must, in effect, know how to allow it to transport us to every corner of that cyberspace which has become such a pivotal tool in the human endeavour to acquire and to disseminate knowledge. There we meet each other through social communication and the sharing of knowledge; there there is no distance between myself and other oblates, whether or not we have ever met; there we can go directly to the information source which may otherwise have been misrepresented by those who would distort our understanding; there our community has transcended its boundaries and, while recognizing that prayer is the single most important resource open to us, the community of shared endeavour, learning and faith can be nourished.

In considering how to use the Internet properly we must always hold in front of us that 'the fundamental ethical principle is this: the human person and the human community are the end and measure of the use of the media of social communication; communication should be by persons to persons for the integral development of persons'.[3]

We must, therefore, be discriminating in our use of the Internet. In my own view it is arguable that not all knowledge is neutral, specifically by reference to its intended use. Where is the neutrality, taking intention into account, in a formula to make ricin or a homemade explosive? What about trivial or useless information or pornographic images? They waste time and effort which could be better used. It takes discipline in a greater or lesser degree to discriminate, and that ethical principle of the common good forms a vital measure.

And so, where is all this leading? The golden thread running throughout the garment of our lives should, when we have the balance right, be the seeking in all things the path that leads to God. For most people this is more fruitful within a community, but a community that allows access to the desert. The desert must be sought all around us and includes the nowhere place of cyberspace. To explore fully this desert we need the sustenance of our holding environment, our community from which we derive the strength to seek out its mysteries. This strength derives from love, an essential element of every healthy community. This enveloping love renders physical presence in the community unnecessary and is, therefore, the secret of community in cyberspace. The desert stretches out seemingly featureless – where to seek God in such a place? We need to remind ourselves that he is sometimes not visible because he is standing right behind us.

Notes

1 Elisha Emery, 'The Postmodern Desert: Solitude and Community in Cyberspace' in 'Book II, Reading the Signs of the Times: The Good News of Monastic Life', Pre-convention Reflection Papers in Preparation for the American Benedictine Academy Convention 2000, St Meinrad IN, pp. 5–10.

2 Pontifical Council for Social Communications, 'The Church and Internet, Part III Recommendations and Conclusions'.

3 Pontifical Council for Social Communications, 'Ethics in Communications', n. 5.

25. Serving the Local Community

WIL DERKSE

The communities in which oblates have the opportunity to cultivate the virtue of humility – see my etymological description of 'humility' as the 'courage to serve'[1] – will of course vary, depending on their spheres of life, age, abilities, responsibilities and influence.

Most oblates live in small households (my own at present consists only of my wife and me); but they will have ties with a wider network of family relations; they may work professionally in schools, university departments, business enterprises, or not-for-profit organizations; and they might have civic responsibilities at local, municipal, state or even national level.

Yet it is quite possible to point to some basic attitudes that are connected with St Benedict's Rule, which for such a long time has been a flexible, adaptable, and nevertheless solid, guide for religious communities and their associates in different circumstances and eras.

The opening sentence of the Prologue to the Rule of St Benedict gives the basic clues to these attitudes:

> Listen carefully, my child, to the teaching of the master, and bend close the ear of your heart. Readily accept the advice of your loving father and faithfully put it into practice.
> *(translation by Catherine Wybourne OSB)*

Probably the best service we can offer any community is to put this opening sentence into practice: to have an attentive ear, to put in our hearts, to respond and act. 'Listening and responding' is perhaps the briefest summary of Benedictine spirituality. Fruitful responsibility – and responsibility is the art of responding – is impossible without careful listening, without an attitude of affection (listening with the ear of the heart), and without action. These three dimensions are necessary prerequisites for responsible behaviour. If one of them is lacking, we are being irresponsible.

A small and seemingly innocent example may illustrate this. During a break in a student seminar on the interaction of science and religion (this particular seminar being the little community I was serving at that moment), an international exchange student from Turkey asked a question on the paper that she was required to write for the course. While she was talking to me, I was looking into the notes I needed for the second half of my class. This already was irresponsible behaviour. My heart was in my notes, and I was not really listening to her. Now, happily, I noticed my un-Benedictine behaviour and put down my notes to give her my full attention. Full attention? True, I listened to her seemingly practical question and gave my likewise practical answer. But I nearly overlooked little signals of a deeper anxiety, which may have been due to her being the only non-Christian student in the group (which likely had influenced her attitude concerning the course subject) and also to her being rather confused by our local examination rules. If I had responded only to the first signal – and merely made an appointment to talk a bit more in detail about the topic of her paper – but not to her concern about exam rules, I would not have responded fully. Only when I also offered to walk with her to the student administration office after class to discuss the second matter, had I really taken my responsibility in the sense Benedict suggests, and acted in the student's service.

An example like this also shows that service involves conversion and humility. Conversion, first, from my lecture notes towards the student. Humility, as I have to '*bend* close the ear of my heart', so I have to bend, bow and incline, and not only because of a sense of duty (laudable as that may be) but because of affectivity: my *heart* must bend toward this 'guest', and as Benedict says in the chapter on receiving guests, any guest can be the Lord.

Conversion also involves the more fundamental sense, that in listening and responding the cause and centre of my attention is external to my ego; it is the matter or the person at hand that deserves my attention and dedication. Service implies, as I suggested in my essay 'Serving the Local Church', an ex-centric orientation.[2]

An excellent opportunity to put this attitude of careful listening and active responding into practice is to let it direct our behaviour in meetings where we discuss and deliberate, which also present ample opportunities to cultivate the Benedictine virtues of stability, conversion and obedience, the latter being equivalent to 'listening and responding'. Meetings where decisions are made are treated in Chapter 3 of the Rule. The more important a matter is for the community, the more the community has to be consulted by the abbot. The abbot has to clearly put forward the *matter* at hand (and thus *not* his intended decision) and to listen carefully to the advice of his brethren and bring it close to his heart (*tractet apud se*, in Latin), implying the art of discernment. And then he has to decide what is best and fruitful – not for his own ego, of course, but that the community might flourish. All should be consulted, including the young: 'The Lord often reveals what is better to a younger person' (*RB* 3.3).

This can be applied in non-monastic contexts. Our eldest daughter some years ago met a woman in the local bookshop. The woman was the owner and director of a middle-sized business that produced technical equipment. The firm was doing quite well, but she was a bit anxious about the fact that young engineers did not stay very long and were rather rapidly head-hunted by other firms. While on a train journey she had read a book of mine in which Chapter 3 of Benedict's Rule is treated and 'translated' to non-monastic contexts.[3] This proved to be a little eye-opener. Until then she had made all the really important decisions on her own, discussed less important matters with her management team, and, in the rather infrequent meetings of all employees, put only minor matters on the table. After her train journey she decided to turn this decision pyramid upside-down, as Benedict suggests: small matters were her exclusive responsibility, more important deci-

sions were discussed with her management team, and for fundamental matters the whole 'community' was consulted. She told my
daughter that this really had changed the commitment of her
employees and that in particular the younger engineers stayed
longer with her firm.

Oblates serving their local community may also find inspiration
in the chapters St Benedict devotes to fruitful leadership. When we
have leadership responsibilities within small groups, it will prove
fruitful to cultivate the qualities of a good abbot. Chapters 2 and
64 give an extensive treatment of these qualities, but in quite a
number of other chapters there are additional suggestions for good
leadership. One such chapter that will inspire us in serving our
community is the one on the qualities of the cellarer (*RB* 31).
Columba Cary-Elwes OSB comments:

> Here is a character sketch of a person we should like to be or at
> least to have as a good friend. He has all the qualities of a com-
> munity man; in fact as St Benedict says, he is 'like a father to the
> whole community'.[4]

In serving our communities we must beware of presumption. We
must appropriate the Benedictine virtues ourselves, rather than
point them out explicitly to others.

But sometimes a more explicit stance may be appropriate, for
instance, when asked to do so, or when someone knows about
your oblate background, as a concluding example illustrates.

I once chaired a seminar on the topic of leadership and Benedictine spirituality; both young as well as experienced executives
attended. All of them had participated in a previous course on this
theme and had read a number of relevant sources. Anselm Grün
OSB, the cellarer of the Abbey of Münsterschwarzach in Germany
and a fruitful and influential author, was our guest. The participants had been asked to bring pressing questions with them. One
question that many had written down was: how do you act when
you have to live under the governance of a bad 'abbot'? 'Bad'
meaning not possessing the qualities St Benedict hopes for in
Chapters 2 and 64 of his Rule. Father Anselm formulated advice,

which I briefly summarize: Don't start a power struggle (the abbot will win); take some inner emotional distance from your disappointment; try to find some kindred minds in the department in which you bear responsibility, and start working not *against* the abbot but on a *positive* project within your responsibility (one that you would like the abbot to adopt for the whole company); tell the abbot at a good moment and with a careful choice of words about the fruitful results of your department project. Then he might adopt your proposal.

Two years later I met one of the participants as a guest in a Trappist monastery. Over a beer Gerard told me that he had applied Anselm Grün's lesson. He had had a conflict with his CEO and took the very steps Grün had suggested. The conflict was fruitfully resolved, and the CEO, who apparently had noticed the inner change in the approach of his deputy, explicitly asked how this had come about. Gerard promised him an essay to explain things. The CEO read the essay, 'From Gerard to Benedict', and is now himself reading books by Grün, and the climate in the corporation has fundamentally changed for the better.

This was a good reason for us to ask the monk serving at the bar for a refill. Serving the community is not a sour duty; it is often accompanied with fruits and little joys that deserve some celebration.

Notes

1 See my chapter, 'Serving the Local Church', p. 226.

2 See p. 226 below.

3 Wil Derkse, *The Rule of Benedict for Beginners: Spirituality for Daily Life*, Liturgical Press, Collegeville MN, 2003.

4 *Work and Prayer: The Rule of St Benedict for Lay People*, Commentary by Columba Cary-Elwes OSB, with a new translation by Catherine Wybourne OSB, Burns & Oates, Tunbridge Wells, 1992, p. 90.

VI THE OBLATE IN THE CHURCH

26. Serving the Local Church

WIL DERKSE

In the guidelines for the contributors to *The Oblate Life*, the authors were kindly invited to bear in mind that this book will be read in English-speaking countries all over the world, and for that reason to avoid local or parochial references and terminology. In this little essay on serving the local church as an oblate, however, it will be inevitable that local and parochial experiences and references must be my starting points. In my own language the word for 'parish' is actually *parochie*, having Greek roots, of course. Yet I do hope that my experiences and reflections may have a wider applicability than the specific local context that happens to be my own.

Serving is a basic Christian attitude: Christ, speaking to us through the gospels, gave marvellous examples. St Benedict gives the virtue of service a prominent place in his Rule. The longest chapter therein, Chapter 7 on humility, can be read specifically as encouraging the reader to serve. The Dutch and German equivalents of humility, *deemoed* and *Demut* respectively, have an etymological root which means 'the *courage to serve*'. You need real courage to develop a realistic insight into your limitations *and* your possibilities to grow in a serving attitude. Service always implies that your care, attention and affection are directed towards someone or something you esteem higher than yourself. You are serving an external cause, so service has, as it were, an ex-centric character. This in no way implies a lack of self-esteem (of course the notion of humility has sometimes been misused to put people down), but it does imply a certain asymmetry. Paradoxically, quite often your own self flourishes when it serves a highly esteemed cause, such as your loved ones, doing a good job, offering an attentive ear to someone needing your attention. Likewise, serving the local church can sometimes offer small pleasures and enjoyments.

Serving the local church – your parish, your congregation, your diocese – as a Benedictine oblate will offer ample opportunities to cultivate the basic Benedictine virtues of attentive listening with the ear of the heart, stability in sustaining the local church, keeping an alert eye for quality improvement (*conversatio morum*) and obedience (which is basically the art of responding). Of course, there is no necessity at all to proclaim publicly that your serving the local church is part of your oblate life. Just being there and available, and taking your responsibility in accordance with your limitations, talents and practical possibilities will be enough. It is somewhat comparable to the presence of a monastic community in a local region. It normally is not a proselytizing but rather a welcoming community; its presence has a value of its own, a value with probably many dimensions, of which, in my view, the most important is *being there*.

Yet occasions may arise where it is quite appropriate to give the Benedictine charism a more explicit place in your serving of the local church, for instance in providing information about monastic life, giving reading and retreat suggestions, giving a presentation on Benedictine spirituality, or writing on relevant aspects of monastic life in your parish newsletter. Again, much depends on your personal talents and possibilities, and on what is appropriate in the local context.

It is at this point that I must deliberately write from a 'parochial' perspective. For quite a long period our family was involved with parish life connected with the medieval St John's Cathedral in 's-Hertogenbosch, The Netherlands. Our two daughters received their first Communion in this marvellous church, I led our eldest to the altar when she married in the cathedral, and I was active as a deputy organist (playing an impressive seventeenth-century instrument) and, later on, also as a member of the church council, with a special responsibility for church music, organs and spirituality.

In this period my attachment to St Willibrord's Abbey developed as well. My first visit there was in 1982; I became an oblate in 1993. In the beginning there was no reason at all to proclaim this bond with a Benedictine community, but of course in private contacts and conversations this matter turned up, and some fellow parishioners felt stimulated to make contacts with monastic life themselves. As a churchwarden, I had the opportunity to develop, in collaboration with the cathedral priest, a spirituality programme in which a number of Christian spiritualities were presented and investigated, including Benedictine spirituality. Quite a number of parishioners participated and were surprised to learn how this form of spiritual life, with such a long history, is apparently flexible and adaptable enough to serve as a guide for monastics, oblates and associates worldwide: a real treasure-house for the present world and the local church.

Another situation that offered some appropriate occasions for bringing in my oblate background was while I was a professor of philosophy at the diocesan seminary. Not only when reading, for instance, St Anselm or St Aelred, who over the years have become my personal friends, and whose thought is deeply connected with their monastic contexts and with St Benedict's Rule, but also in a more informal and colloquial way. During coffee breaks and recreation time I sometimes had the opportunity to discuss matters connected with spirituality with my students. I pointed out to them that there is no such thing as a 'diocesan spirituality' but that, on the other hand, our diocese hosts quite a lot of spiritualities. What I suggested was that they should take their bicycles during their holidays and visit and 'investigate' the main religious houses of our diocese, the Augustinians, Franciscans, Capuchins, Poor Clares, Norbertines, Trappists and Trappistines. I suggested they do so just to find out which of these spiritual climates agreed with their own characters and inclinations, not with the intention of joining these communities but with the perspective of having an attachment with a spiritual home when they would be secular priests. Most of them would be living on their own, would be very occupied, and would really need a spiritual anchorage where they could be regular guests to be refreshed and inspired. Some seminarians followed my informal advice, and I have the impression that this did not do them any harm.

Since 2002 my wife and I have lived in the city of Nijmegen. There we became involved in the Ecumenical City Chaplaincy, which is, of course, quite different from a Roman Catholic hot-house like St John's Cathedral. Nevertheless, it gave us the opportunity to celebrate in the city-centre church of St Stephen, which was consecrated by St Albert the Great in the thirteenth century.

In what is now 'our local church', we enjoy the best elements of the Roman Catholic and the Reformed traditions. Catholic priests and Reformed pastors preside in turn, always keeping in mind what the teaching of their particular churches holds as being litur-gically appropriate. There is a strong interest in spirituality in this community. This is also expressed in the backgrounds of those who celebrate and teach in our services: we have two Dominican priests (one of them had been a Protestant minister) and a pro-fessed lay Dominican (Albert would like that!), a Benedictine priest (connected with St Willibrord's Abbey), as well as a Protestant minister who is also an oblate of our monastery. The members of the community know about my Benedictine affilia-tion, so they sometimes ask advice about monastic retreats or just being a guest. When invited to do so by the editor, I have written essays for our monthly newsletter. I was also given the opportunity to participate and contribute in some evening group meetings concerned with Benedictine spirituality, connected with the study of some appropriate texts. Gradually the wish has become vocal in our Ecumenical City Chaplaincy to participate for a weekend in monastic life. Of course the two oblates and the monk involved in this chaplaincy will be quite willing to assist and moderate.

One of the experiences I would like to share, finally, is that in serving the local community as an oblate one must be aware of three potential pitfalls. The first is idealizing monastic life; it is important to be realistic. The second is Benedictine 'overkill', bringing in your oblate background and reading time and again. The third pitfall is connected to the others. It is the presumption that Benedictine spirituality has a definite answer to anything and that you possess the tools to provide these answers. But there is an excellent antidote to these inclinations: reread Chapter 7 of the Rule again and again . . .

For information on the monasteries in the Low Countries, see www.monasteria.org

27. Building Christian Unity

MAXWELL E. JOHNSON

Oblates of St Benedict increasingly find themselves to be members of an ecumenical 'school for the Lord's service' (*RB*, Prologue 45) that cuts across denominational boundaries and ecclesial affiliations. While Roman Catholics remain, undoubtedly, in the majority, membership in the oblate movement today has become decidedly and even intentionally ecumenical in nature, with members coming from almost every imaginable Christian tradition in existence, including those that are often called 'non-liturgical' or 'Free Church' traditions. In some monasteries today, in fact, the sheer number of oblates other than Roman Catholics is so great that without them the very survival of their individual oblate programs might be jeopardized. In some monasteries, guidelines for the admission of oblate candidates have been revised to reflect this trend. At St Vincent's Archabbey in Latrobe, Pennsylvania, for example, the answer to the question of membership requirements is phrased as follows:

Membership in the Oblates of Saint Benedict of Saint Vincent Archabbey is open to all those who have committed themselves to follow Jesus Christ through Baptism and have completed the fourteenth year of age and who wish to deepen their commitment to the Christian life by studying and following the Rule of Saint Benedict. A Roman Catholic seeking membership should be in full communion with the Catholic Church (confirmed and receiving the Eucharist regularly). A non-Catholic Christian should be in good standing with his or her particular denomination. A person, whether lay or clerical, should not have official affiliation with another religious community.[1]

In a 1973 'Guidelines for Directors and Oblates', Benedictine oblates were called explicitly to an ecumenical orientation:

> They foster the ecumenical spirit as called for by Vatican II. They will meet with those not of the Catholic faith, strive to understand the religious beliefs and customs of others, look for teachings on which others agree with them, enter into friendly discussion of teachings on which there is disagreement, put aside all prejudice, and foster the spirit of universal brotherhood in God our Father.[2]

But if in 1973 this was directed obviously to Roman Catholic oblates, Mary Collins OSB, reflected in 2004 on the fruits of this orientation, writing:

> Recent popes have given Benedictines and other monastic orders a special mission in the church. At the turn of the twentieth century, certain monasteries in Europe were asked to be places of ecumenical hospitality. It was believed that Catholics, Protestants and Orthodox Christians who welcomed one another as brothers and sisters in Christ might overcome the centuries-old estrangements within the churches East and West. It was hoped that committed believers who came to know one another and to pray together might grow together in unity. They would also experience both the possibility and the difficulties of true reconciliation. These early initiatives helped prepare the way for today's greater mutual understanding among all Christians who are baptized into the one Body of Christ. Now we see that Benedict had long ago prepared the way for such twentieth-century monastic dialogue. He taught that all guests were to be received as Christ, and that strangers who visited the monastery might well be messengers of God.[3]

It is precisely from and within these sorts of monastic encounters in Benedictine houses all over the world that ecumenism continues to grow and develop among those who are oblates. Not surprisingly, one of the most popular commentaries on the Rule of St Benedict was written by an Anglican,[4] and one of the most popular books on the Benedictine experience today was written by a Presbyterian.[5]

What is it about Benedictine monasticism, however, that engenders this type of ecumenical spirit in the first place? Collins rightly pointed to the Benedictine focus on hospitality, the reception of guests 'as Christ'. Other monastics explain it this way:

> Monasticism is a way of life in which the desire and search for God is all-important. Its spirituality is a process of transformation into Christ through self-emptying in order to be totally available to God. As such it is not necessarily tied to any single belief system. Since it predates the separation of the Christian churches, monasticism forms an ideal basis for ecumenism in today's world. The main forces transcending all our differences are the deep love of God, of Sacred Scripture, prayer, and our genuine love and concern for one another.[6]

Similarly, in addition to these, the so-called values discerned from St Benedict's Rule, including community, stability, hospitality, attentive listening, obedience, *lectio divina*, balance, and work, are themselves surely ecumenical values. What is more, the very center of Benedict's Rule is Christ. It is the relationship with Christ that grounds community, provides stability and balance, and forms hospitality. And in the Rule this Christocentrism is focused especially in prayer, in the liturgy of the hours, the divine office. For, says Benedict, 'We believe that the divine presence is everywhere . . . But beyond the least doubt we should believe this to be especially true when we celebrate the divine office' (*RB* 19.1–2). Indeed, if Christ is the absolute center of Benedict's Rule, so is the *Opus Dei*, the liturgy of the hours, central for those who would live according to that Rule. As Abbot Patrick Regan has written: 'Benedict urges us to prefer nothing to the love of Christ . . . But since Christ is especially present at the office, he can likewise declare that we should prefer nothing to the work of God (Rule 43:3).'[7]

It is this spirituality of prayer as it is expressed primarily in the *Opus Dei* that explains why the Benedictine oblate movement is and remains ecumenical and counts among its members laity and clergy of so many different Christian traditions. Quite simply, Benedictine monastics have taught oblates how to pray, and the content of that prayer encountered in the Benedictine office is precisely the systematic arrangement of psalmody and the organized reading of scripture. And what could be more ecumenical or ecumenically appealing and inviting than the singing and proclamation of the scriptures on a regular daily basis? It is here, in common liturgical prayer and association with monastic communities, that Christians of varying traditions other than Roman Catholic have encountered Roman Catholicism itself, not in some stereotypical fashion but as a living reality, one centered in the classic early Christian tradition long before the crises and controversies of the Reformation took place. In such fashion misunderstandings, biases, and prejudices have given way to friendships, community, collaboration, and new forms of unity.

Drinking deeply from this Benedictine spirituality, centered in Christ and the *Opus Dei*, Benedictine oblates cannot but be catalysts in the world in seeking and building greater Christian unity, because they have experienced within Benedictinism a unity in Christ that transcends denominational and ecclesial boundaries and they refuse, therefore, to settle for the status quo of a divided Christianity. They function this way as catalysts simply by living out this Benedictine spirituality in their home, work, and parish communities. If in no other way, they work at building Christian unity by daily prayer for that unity, as they are united spiritually across all boundaries in the daily prayer of the divine office.

Several years ago Jesuit theologian Karl Rahner urged theologians to take more seriously what he termed 'actual faith' rather than 'official faith' in the pursuit of Christian unity. At the level of the 'actual faith' of Christians within differing traditions, Rahner said:

Their sense of faith . . . is identical with that of Christians belonging to another denomination. They believe in God; they entrust their lives to this living God of grace and forgiveness; they pray; they are baptized and celebrate the Lord's Supper; they recognize Jesus Christ, the crucified and risen Lord, as the definitive guarantor of God's saving bestowal of himself on them; they live the gospel; they know, too, that to be a Christian in this sense obliges them to participate in a corresponding community of faith, the Church. The traditional points of controversy between the Churches . . . are unknown to them, or are unimportant, or are at most noted and accepted as part of [a] provisional and relative character . . . and which is accepted nowadays as belonging naturally to the historical contingency of the human situation.[8]

Elsewhere Rahner referred to this unity at the level of the 'actual faith' of Christians as constituting a kind of 'Third Church', that is, not a new denomination separate from the churches, but as constituting a common Christian ground within the churches seeking and moving toward greater realization in a greater Christian unity.[9] Such unity is often the experience of Benedictine oblates and such is the gift that the oblate movement can bring to the churches themselves.

Once, in a Roman Catholic Benedictine monastic context, during the communion rite at a daily eucharistic liturgy, I looked up to see a Russian Orthodox, a Presbyterian, a United Church of Christ member, and a United Methodist, all Benedictine oblates, in the communion line approaching the altar from the choir stalls for the reception of holy communion. Soon, I, a Lutheran, would be in that same line. While some would have been and would still be scandalized by such an event, I remember uttering a short prayer of thanksgiving that at that surprising moment I had been privileged to see, if only for an instant, the very church of the future, the 'Third Church', the 'one' church that already exists among us. May Benedictines and their oblates continue to serve that church and bring this kind of unity to a fuller reality.

Maxwell E. Johnson

Notes

1 St Vincent Archabbey, *Oblate Formation Booklet*, Latrobe PA, St Vincent Archabbey, 1996, C.1. http://www.osb.org/sva/obl/oblaform.html#Who%20Is

2 http://www.osb.org/obl/guidelns.html

3 Mary Collins OSB, 'From the Prioress', *Threshold*, Mount Saint Scholastica (Winter 2004), 1.

4 Esther de Waal, *A Life-Giving Way: A Commentary on the Rule of St Benedict*, Liturgical Press, Collegeville MN, 1995.

5 Kathleen Norris, *The Cloister Walk*, Riverhead Books, New York, 1996.

6 http://www.benedictinesisters.org/oblates/oblatesgeneral.html

7 Patrick Regan OSB, 'Encountering Christ in Common Prayer', *Worship* 59/1 (January 1985), 52.

8 Karl Rahner, 'Is Church Union Dogmatically Possible?' in Karl Rahner, *Theological Investigations*, vol. XVII: *Jesus, Man, and the Church*, Crossroad, New York, 1981, p. 209.

9 Karl Rahner, 'Third Church?' in Rahner, *Jesus, Man, and the Church*, pp. 215–27.

28. Benedictine Oblates and Interreligious Dialogue

LUCY BRYDON

My own spiritual journey as a Benedictine has led me for many years down the enriching pathway of dialogue, mainly with Buddhists.

Some oblates of our monastery also have long been deeply involved in interreligious dialogue as a normal part of their own professional life-style (mainly in education). I know of three who see this as essential to their Benedictine vocation, and others who have the same attitude to ecumenical dialogue with other Christians throughout the universal Church. Such oblates say that they chose to become oblates of Turvey Abbey because this would be part of their lay Benedictine life.

The world has changed radically since the days when it was forbidden to Roman Catholics to pray even with other Christians, for fear of endangering their faith. The huge difference in attitude towards ecumenism, including recently the wider 'ecumenism' of interreligious dialogue, came about through the pioneering lives, study and work of such people as Thomas Merton, Henri le Saux (known in later life as Abhishiktananda), Jules Monchanin, Bede Griffiths, Raimundo Pannikkar, William Johnston, Murray Rogers and other 'smaller' heroes and heroines who in foreign countries and at home, often through their daily work and life, formed bridges of friendship, respect and mutual learning between themselves and people of other religions.

Beginnings of interreligious dialogue

On the official level the biggest change came in 1965 with the document *Nostra Aetate* of Vatican II,[1] which acknowledged the presence and working of the Holy Spirit in other religions and gave the go-ahead to Catholics for a serious engagement with people of other religions from that time, as dialogue, not as proselytism.

In the forefront of the work of active dialogue were Benedictine men and women, in many cases after years of quiet prayer, study and correspondence with people of other faiths. John Paul II specifically asked that Benedictines should take the lead in the work of interreligious dialogue.[2] In response, an association of monks and nuns of the Benedictine tradition was set up in the 1970s to promote the work of interreligious dialogue in each country. MID (Monastic Interreligious Dialogue) commissions were formed in many European countries and in the USA to promote this kind of engagement between monks and nuns.[3] Interreligious dialogue became an outstanding feature of Pope John Paul II's teaching and example. The whole world was moved by the first Assisi Encounter in which the Pope and leaders of other religions prayed together for peace. Exchanges began to take place with monks and nuns of other religions, particularly Buddhists and Hindus. I was privileged to take part in the most recent exchange, the tenth of its kind, spending a month in Zen Buddhist monasteries in Japan in 2005.[4]

Following on his predecessor's work, and in his own very different style, Pope Benedict XVI has also indicated that the work of interreligious dialogue is an integral part of our Catholic faith journey, 'not an optional extra'.[5] He places the same emphasis as Pope John Paul II on the double aspect for Catholics of proclaiming Christ and at the same time being in friendly and equal dialogue with non-Christians.

Oblates and interreligious dialogue

So much for monks engaging in the dialogue of spiritual exchange with monasteries of other religions. But what about oblates? For many years as the practice of inter-religious dialogue grew, it *was* strictly *inter-monastic*, at the official level, only engaging monks and nuns. Then in 1991 came a full exploration of the relationship between the two aspects of interreligious dialogue as the Catholic Church sees it: proclamation and dialogue. The Vatican issued an authoritative document in 1991 called *Dialogue and Proclamation*.[6] It outlines four interdependent approaches to dialogue with people of other religions, laying great stress on the primacy of *theological* dialogue.[7] With this document, oblates can not only come into their own and take part in it equally with monks and nuns, but in some areas they can enter more deeply into it. There are areas and approaches which seem appropriate for monks and nuns and others which are particularly suited to oblates.

Furthermore, we must remember that the word 'monastic' has far deeper connotations than merely signifying men or women living in a monastery. The word comes from 'monos', 'monachos' and the related feminine forms, and it means 'single' – not in the sense of single meaning 'not married', but in the sense in which Jesus uses the word 'pure of heart' in the Beatitudes. It means people who are single-minded in their pursuit of the 'one thing necessary', people who 'truly seek God' as the Rule of St Benedict puts it.[8] Raimundo Pannikkar, in his book *'Blessed Simplicity'*,[9] spoke of the 'archetype of the monk' present in all of us. Just as there is deep within each person the archetype of Father, Mother, Child, Warrior, Wise Person, Witch/Wizard and so on, so he would maintain, we have within us the archetype of Monk. I have found over the years that this idea rings loud bells and has a 'Eureka!' sense for oblates who take their oblation as a serious commitment to seeking God in their own life. Now would seem to be the right time to re-affirm the Benedictine dimensions of dialogues for oblates already engaged in this work; and to encourage **all** oblates to realize that they are also called to the work of interreligious dialogue – *monastic* interreligious dialogue. This is particularly true now in the aftermath of 9/11 and 7/7 (the terrorist attacks on New York and the Pentagon in 2001 and London in 2005) when everyone realizes the need for Christians, Jews and Muslims – the 'People of the Book' as the Qur'an calls them – to be

Lucy Brydon

engaged in dialogue with each other as well as with the ancient religions of Hinduism and Buddhism. In the Muslim and Jewish faiths there is no monastic order as such. It would probably be true to say that Muslims and Jews have ambivalent feelings about the idea of men and women serving God as monks and nuns. Marriage and children are so very important as part of God's will, in both these faith traditions. But they would readily recognize the commitment and devotion of laymen and -women serving God with their whole heart.

Dialogue and Proclamation – Programme for Action

It is worth outlining the four areas of dialogue indicated in *Dialogue and Proclamation*, Paragraph 42. It is immediately obvious that oblates can engage in all of them, whereas monks and nuns are sometimes limited by their commitment to enclosure and to community life and duties:

1 *The Dialogue of Life*, where people strive to live in an open and neighbourly spirit, sharing their joys and sorrows, their human problems and preoccupations.
2 *The Dialogue of Action* in which Christians and others collaborate for the integral development and liberation of people.
3 *The Dialogue of Theological Exchange*, where specialists seek to deepen their understanding of their respective religious heritages, and to appreciate each other's spiritual values.
4 *The Dialogue of Spiritual Experience*, where persons, rooted in their own religious traditions, share their spiritual riches, for instance with regard to prayer and contemplation, faith and ways of searching for God or the Absolute.[10]

I would like briefly to consider each of these in turn and how vital it is for oblates to fulfil their Benedictine vocation by taking part in this kind of dialogue in so far as it falls within the parameters of their lives.

The dialogue of life

It is almost certain that oblates living in large towns will be within reach of communities of people of different religions living around their local place of worship – mosque, temple, synagogue etc. Second generation immigrants live widely dispersed and lay oblates may well relate to them as students, colleagues or line managers in the workplace. Basic to all our religious faiths is the notion of God as Love. A very important and basic form of dialogue is to show genuine respect and loving kindness to neighbours and colleagues of different religions from our own. This is particularly important in the present climate of suspicion of people of other faiths, especially Muslims since the terrorist attacks of 9/11 and 7/7, and Jews in the current crisis in the Middle East. At a conference at Heythrop College, University of London, in 2005, one of the delegates spoke of this kind of dialogue in the area where she lived, how much she had learned and how rewarding it was for everyone concerned.[11] She compared the need to go slowly and to tread sensitively in this kind of dialogue, to making friends with the fox in *The Little Prince* by Antoine de Saint Exupéry.[12] It is equally important to engage with locally-born Muslims, Jews, Hindus et al on terms of respect and obedience, in the Benedictine sense, within the professions and the workplace, and in such voluntary works as multi-faith chaplaincies.

The dialogue of action

One of the areas where the union of the great religious faiths can have a major impact on our society is that of moral and social ethics. Most world religions are agreed on the larger issues of social concern for justice, and the rights of the poor, young children, the helpless, the aged. Further, we share with people of other religions the experience that a faith stance may often be counter-cultural in a society that behaves in a materialistic, uncaring manner. To join with people of other religions in a peace march, or vigil or any of the other social activities can be a tremendous experience of unity and can lead to more personal, individual forms of dialogue. One delegate at the same Heythrop conference spoke of the importance for her of the realization that she was one with people of many different faiths, when there was a peaceful protest walk in which all took part and prayed, walked and talked *together* after a race riot in which a policeman was killed in the council estate where she lived in the Midlands and similarly an anti-Iraq war march was a very enriching experience for another Turvey oblate. Enclosed monks and nuns are not easily able to participate in this kind of dialogue.

The dialogue of theological exchange

This form of dialogue requires 'specialists',[13] but these are not only to be found now among the clergy or in the monasteries. Moreover there is a valuable kind of informal theological dialogue that takes place when neighbours or colleagues speak to each other of their Faith practice and beliefs. Some oblates may be attracted by the various theological courses on different religious faiths which are offered, for example, by The Centre for Christianity and Inter-religious Dialogue (Heythrop College) of the University of London.[14] It seems to me that nowadays it is *particularly* important for laymen and -women oblates to become involved in this. After many years of dialogue with Buddhism and Hinduism, it is clear from the current political and social scene that the new frontier or cutting edge of interreligious dialogue is with the Abrahamic faiths. The 'People of the Book' must come together to grow in understanding of each other. Judaism and Islam do not have a monastic dimension (as such) in their religions. Here is a special area for oblates. As with other forms of dialogue, it will be immensely enriching for their own personal faith journey as well as contributing to the wider church.

The dialogue of spiritual experience

In some ways this is the most challenging of all the ways of dialogue. It touches the mind, heart and soul, and can lead to a very profound experience and sense of unity with the people whose faith experience we share. It seems to me that it is easier with Buddhism than with any other religion, because of the tradition within Christianity (and especially Roman Catholicism) of silent contemplative prayer, a tradition going back to the Desert Fathers, John Cassian and the early monastic traditions of both Eastern Orthodox and Western Roman Catholic practice and faith. Monks and nuns have taken naturally to it.

However, this is above all an area in which oblates in interreligious marriages have a powerful witness to give. Two oblates working in education also speak of the joy of leading Id, Diwali, Channukeh, and Chinese New Year celebrations for staff and students in their schools; and of the immense privilege of being invited to join local interfaith groups in their religious ceremonies, one very moving occasion being the funeral of a young Hindu pupil which the head teacher was invited to attend.

The proviso that it is for 'persons rooted in their own religious traditions' is a very important one to notice.[15] If we are not deeply rooted in our own personal faith in Christ, sadly it is possible to slip into a 'pick'n'mix' attitude or even drift away from the Christian faith altogether. Fortunately this is rare, but it has happened.

Conclusion

The modern 'frontier' situation regarding interreligious dialogue present a new challenge for the dialogue of spiritual exchange, as we try to establish sound contacts with Judaism and Islam while maintaining cherished links with Buddhism, Hinduism and Jainism. It is a challenge which oblates are especially fitted to engage in. It will be a slow process but oblates may be able to gain access especially into all forms of dialogue with Jews and Muslims. Since Judaism and Islam do not have monks or nuns as part of their faith tradition they may welcome dialogue with committed Benedictine oblates on terms of greater equality and understanding of the lay married (or single) lifestyle. This is to practise the Benedictine vocation of hospitality in a very wide and deep sense; not only inviting people and accepting invitations on the everyday level, but being open to receiving, offering and being mutually enriched by each other's understanding of our faith traditions. St Benedict's later chapters on the relationships of community life have many suggestions helpful to the work of dialogue, showing honour, respect and mutual obedience, just to start off![16] In the workplace the challenge will be to work respectfully alongside people of other religions, (or in peaceful subordination to them), listening to each other[17] and learning from each other without condescension.

May the whole Benedictine family – monks, nuns, oblates – continue to hear and follow the call to this important work and may it prosper, 'ut in omnibus glorificetur Deus'.[18]

Notes

1 *Vatican Council II: The Conciliar and post-Conciliar Documents*, gen. ed. Austin Flannery OP, Fowler Wright Books, 1981, no. 58: 'Declaration on the Relation of the Church to Non-Christian Religions' (usually known by its first two words in the original Latin *Nostra Aetate*).

2 See Michael Fitzgerald, *Address to the European DIM/MID Commissions*, in DIM/MID International Bulletin, 2003/2, E 15, pp. 13ff, especially the section 'Why Benedictines?'

3 For a succinct account of this period, see 'Monastic Interreligious Dialogue: A History' by Pierre François de Béthune OSB, and 'Contemporary Witness, Future Configuration: Monastic Interfaith Dialogue' by Peter Bowe OSB, in *Catholics in Interreligious Dialogue: Monasticism, Theology and Spirituality*, ed. Anthony O'Mahony and Peter Bowe OSB, Gracewing, 2006.

4 For a recent personal account see the *Monastic Encounter* Bulletin, July 2005. *Monastic Encounter* is the newsletter of the Monastic Interreligious Dialogue Commission of Britain and Ireland. Visit us at our website: www.mid-gbi.com

5 Pope Benedict XVI has made this comment more than once in recent speeches. See, for example, the report of his meeting with Muslim ambassadors and representatives at Castel Gandolfo following the furore in the media after his Regensburg University speech, on the BBC News website, 14 November 2006, http://news.bbc.co.uk/1/hi/world/europe/5379450.stm

6 I am indebted to John McDade SJ, for his article 'Nostra Aetate and Interfaith Dialogue', in *The Pastoral Review* (November/December 2005),

for his comments on the document *Dialogue and Proclamation* published in 1991 by the Pontifical Council for Interreligious Dialogue and the Congregation for the Evangelisation of Peoples.

7 *Dialogue and Proclamation*, Pontifical Council for Interreligious Dialogue and the Congregation for the Evangelisation of Peoples, 1991, no. 42.

8 *RB* 58.7 *Households of God* – Rule of St Benedict translated by David Parry OSB with explanations for monks and lay-people today. Darton, Longman & Todd, 1980.

9 Raimundo Pannikkar, *Blessed Simplicity: Quest for the Monastic Archetype*, Seabury Press, 1970. Also, by an oblate, Marsha Sinetar, *Ordinary People as Monks and Nuns: Lifestyles for Self-Discovery*, Paulist Press, 1986. The books of Norvene Vest on Benedictine spirituality are well worth studying.

10 The document does not mention interreligious **marriages** but this is one of the most intense and intimate ways of sharing in the dialogue of spiritual experience and learning the riches of another faith. They obviously also have a special role to play in the dialogue of life.

11 See *Monastic Encounter* (July 2005) for a report of the Conference celebrating 40 years of *Nostra Aetate* at Heythrop College, University of London.

12 Antoine de Saint-Exupéry, *Le Petit Prince*, ch. 21, Gallimard Edition Spéciale, Folio Junior 1987 N° d'Imprimeur 77186.

13 *Dialogue and Proclamation*, Pontifical Council.

14 The Centre for Christianity & Interreligious Dialogue, Heythrop College, University of London, runs a course of training in interreligious dialogue called 'Faiths Together'. For detail of the course and its contacts with other faith traditions see their website: www.heythrop.ac.uk or apply directly to the Projects Administrator: j.flannery@heythrop.ac.uk or the Course Director: m.barnes@heythrop.ac.uk

15 For oblates this means not only being rooted in their Christian faith but also secure in their commitment to Benedictine life as they experience it through contact with the particular monastery in which they have made their oblation. Being a lay Benedictine means a vocation to gospel living in the spirit of St Benedict, deep hospitality, and (emphasised in some monasteries) to interreligious and ecumenical dialogue.

16 *RB* 70–72.

17 The first word of the Rule of St Benedict and a distinctive feature of Benedictine life is listening to God in the daily experiences of living.

18 *RB* 57.9, quoting 1 Pet. 4.11.

VII THE OBLATE IN THE HOME

29. Marriage and Family

PAUL KENNEDY

There are tensions at the heart of any family. However, there are also tensions within Benedict's Rule, in the balance of the oblate life, and in the Christian understanding of the Trinity. I would like to explore how the Rule encourages us to see family tensions as essentially creative, in much the same way as holding together the unity and diversity of the Trinity is an exercise in spiritual and intellectual flourishing.

The tension at the heart of the Rule lies in its promises on reception. On the one hand are the promises of stability and obedience, which may be seen as essentially restrictive: on the other hand is the promise of conversion, encouraging progressive change. An oblate, in adapting these to her/his life circumstances, has to do so in a way that encourages any tension to be creative rather than stifling. In the same way, there are similar tensions within family life, including the need to protect children and also to let them go; or the tension between personal growth and development while keeping faithful to the marriage and parental commitments. Once a month I attend the daily Mass at the community where I am an oblate. Often the creative tension feels more like plain anxiety as I rush to get my youngest son to school before I can leave.

Stability and conversion

The promises of stability and conversion can form a fruitful combination when the tradition behind them is better understood. The desert mother Syncletica shows the creative potential of stability using maternal imagery: 'If you happen to live in a community, do not move to another place, for it will harm you greatly. If a bird leaves her eggs they never hatch'.[1] Such imagery is very evocative of the cost of family breakdown.

The promise of conversion is one that may appear to undermine stability. It is a complete openness to change: what Thomas Merton referred to as 'a commitment to total inner transformation of one sort or another – a commitment to become a completely new [person]'.[2] The other promise of obedience is fully considered elsewhere but it does have a particular resonance within marriage as it may still be used as a vow during the service.

Syncletica shows us both the tension and the reward of working at our chosen vocation, in my case marriage:

> Great endeavours and hard struggles await those who are con-verted, but afterwards inexpressible joy. If you want to light a fire you are troubled at first by smoke, and your eyes pour water. But in the end you achieve your aim. Now it is written: 'Our God is a consuming fire.' So we must light the divine fire within us with tears and struggle.[3]

Personal growth

Tertullian, refers to the union of man and woman as the 'seminary of the human race'. Benedict saw the monastery in a similar way as 'a school for the Lord's service' (*RB* Prologue 45). Both the insti-tutions of marriage and the monastery have similar aims. Benedict referred to this as to 'bring you back to him from whom you had drifted' (*RB* Prologue 2). If the God from whom we have drifted is seen as the fullness of life, then living life to the full would be the goal of parents as they raise their children and the wish of spouses for one another.

To understand what is the fullness of life, it is necessary to enter into a process of discernment, where tensions are balanced. This process can be enriched by an appreciation of the Rule which Gregory the Great termed 'notable for its discernment'. The need for balance in life is particularly emphasized by Benedict in the tradition known as *ora et labora*. Guidance covering prayer, work, eating and reading shows an awareness of work–life balance centuries before the term was coined. The style of *lectio divina* would also be appropriate in avoiding a stifling unreflective literalism. In ruminating upon the text, openness to new ways of perceiving is vital in discerning how the Bible is speaking to us in our personal situation.

Humility is the other distinctive theme that enriches discernment and personal progress. Twelve steps to humility are mapped out in Chapter 7 of the Rule, but again tension lies here as these steps cannot be taken into the family or marriage context in an unreflective manner. For example, the fourth step refers to 'obedience under difficult, unfavourable or even unjust conditions [so that the] heart quietly embraces suffering and endures it without weakening or seeking escape' (*RB* 7.20). It would be wrong to ask a spouse to stay in an abusive relationship where harshness and injustice were the norm. Indeed, it would be an act of negligence to keep children in a situation where they suffered abuse or neglect. However, there is something fruitful about humility when it is a laying aside of our own ego and accepting our faults and weaknesses. It is the route of self-knowledge, and a trusting family should be the context where we can be truly open and honest. It should be remembered that humility and humus are linked words, and humility can provide the fertile soil of new growth enriching the natural creativity of any family relationship.

Within the long monastic tradition, there is an awareness of the potentially undermining nature of stability and its expression in the daily routine. This is the problem of *accidie*, the weariness of the daily grind and sensory deprivation. Repeatedly feeding a baby in the early hours could well be a cause of *accidie*. One of the ways of tackling this is to approach any task with a spirit of mindfulness, an awareness of God within our everyday activities and a reliance upon his grace in our daily living. This is an openness to the converting potential of all our lives, an 'Easter in Ordinary', as expressed in the Prologue (4): 'every time you begin a good work, you must pray to him most earnestly to bring it to perfection'. The danger of *accidie* is summed up in de Waal's modern interpretation of Augustine's phrase 'Behold, you were within me and I was not at home'.[4] The Benedictine oblate should have the resources to be contentedly at home, both physically and emotionally.

The family community and obedience

Benedict was well aware of what builds up community life and what tears it down. The primary attribute of a healthy community is obedience in the spirit of openness to one another. This is most clearly shown in the need for wide consultation before important decisions because 'the Lord often reveals what is better to the younger' (*RB* 3.3). Taken into the family context, there is no place for a dictatorial parent ignoring the needs of the children when considering future options.

However, it is also up to the younger not to be disruptive, or for spouses not to undermine each other with bickering or criticism. In the Rule there are references to *murmuratio*, a word which may be translated as murmuring or grumbling. It is rooted in the Israelites complaining against Moses during the Exodus, rather than celebrating their emerging freedom. Benedictine obedience is listening to one another in a spirit of love. This breaks down when obedience is given on the surface but the heart is unconvinced and resentment leads to disruptive behaviour; the passive-aggressive partner or the door-slamming teenager. To help prevent *murmuratio* there has to be the habit of listening to one another. The stability of the family must, at the same time, be the opportunity for each member to be a potential instrument of conversion for the others. Discernment of the family's direction and potential is an ongoing conversion process, not despite stability but because of it.

The spirit of obedience in a community, and especially within a family or marriage, is a spirit of mutual discernment. It is only in a community that there can be obedience because it is possible only when we listen to others. Obedience is reaching self-awareness and discernment because we are unable to be sheltered in self-centredness: 'Mutual obedience demands of us a willingness to speak one's truth in trust and then to let go and listen to others'.[5]

Listening and letting go will be at the heart of any loving marriage. In stability, plodding on is not an option.

Conclusion

When I lead marriage preparation Benedict always gets a mention. This is most obvious when talking about the vow to obey within the service. This vow is usually omitted because, in the Church of England, it is only possible for the wife to obey her husband. However, a discussion on the place of mutual intuitive listening ensues. Listening in love enables the balance of stability and conversion to be worked out. So, for example, in the 'forsaking all others' to give stability to this new relationship, what place do the couple's parents have? How will that place change (be converted) over time as circumstances change, perhaps the arrival of children?

Similar questions can be raised over 'all that I am I give to you, and all that I have I share with you'. Resources, material and emotional, are pooled in a demonstration of stability, perhaps symbolized by the opening of a joint bank account, but all such arrangements are provisional and are rightly challenged by the dynamics of family life and ever-changing circumstances.

Notes

1 Hannah Ward and Jennifer Wild (eds), *The Monastic Way – Ancient Wisdom for Contemporary Living: A Book of Daily Readings*, Canterbury Press, Norwich, 2006, p. 56.

2 Esther de Waal, *A Life-Giving Way: A Commentary on the Rule of Saint Benedict*, Geoffrey Chapman, London, 1995, p. 174.

3 de Waal, *Life-Giving Way*, p. 175.

4 de Waal, *Life-Giving Way*, p. 173.

5 Laura Swan, *Engaging Benedict: What the Rule Can Teach Us Today*, Ave Maria Press, Notre Dame IN, 2005, p. 55.

30. The Single Oblate

LORETTA JAVRA

Who is the single oblate? What does the Benedictine oblate way of life have to offer a single person?

There is no one definition of a single person that fits all. People are unmarried for many reasons; they come from a variety of economic, educational and professional backgrounds. Their ages cross generational lines. Some singles choose the single way of life; some were married previously; others hope to marry in the future. Many of them live alone but maintain close ties to their families and married friends. Some single people have satisfying social, religious and professional lives, while others feel a social and emotional disconnect and often experience loneliness.

A Christian way

The apostle Andrew brought his brother Simon Peter to Jesus; Philip invited his friend Bartholomew to 'come and see' Jesus for himself (John 1.41–46). Throughout Christian history, holy men and women called others to Christ and showed them a way to live the gospel message more fully.

Since the sixth century Benedict of Nursia has been doing just that. His message to all who wish to follow Christ endures even today. Countless numbers of people continue to respond to the invitation to live the gospel through the Rule of St Benedict as monastics or oblates. Benedict issues his ageless invitation in the Prologue of his Rule: 'Listen carefully, my child, to the master's instructions, and attend to them with the ear of your heart. This is advice from a father who loves you . . . . The labor of obedience will bring you back to . . . Christ the Lord.'[1]

In the twenty-first century increasing numbers of laypeople are hearing Benedict's message. Single and married people are discovering that the Rule can enrich their lives immensely because it is deeply prayerful, yet practical enough to be incorporated in the busiest of lives.

In what follows I will address four themes from the Rule of St Benedict that can speak practically and powerfully to Benedictine oblates: listening, obedience, prayer, and community.

Listening

What could be more challenging in the era of cell phones, Internet, television, and radio? These marvels of technology give us incessant sounds and images that, for many, crowd out the possibility of a quieter way, leaving many starved for an interior life. When Benedict tells us to listen with the 'ear of the heart' he is saying that surface listening is not enough and we need to listen on a deeper level. That kind of listening calls for both internal and external silence.

There is an ancient story about a man who went to see a holy abbot to get some advice about how to live a better Christian life. The abbot invited the man into his room and, after they sat down, began to pour tea into a cup for his guest. He continued pouring even when the tea reached the rim of the cup and began to run onto the table. 'Stop!' said the man. 'Can't you see that the cup is overflowing?' The abbot looked up and said, 'So it is with you. Your heart and mind are overflowing with so many distractions that there is no room for God to enter in.' And so it is with us. As long as the heart and mind are preoccupied with all manner of noise and busyness, God's voice cannot be heard. Holy people of past and present speak of silence as the place where we can meet God. The prophet Elijah sought God in the howling wind, a fierce earthquake, and a raging fire, but found him in the 'sound of sheer silence' (1 Kings 19.12). Blessed Mother Teresa of Calcutta once said: 'The most important thing in our life is not what we say to

God, but what God says to us. We should be silent in order to listen.'[2]

Benedict insists on the importance of silence and makes it a basic discipline of monastic life. Joan Chittister OSB explains that the goal of monastic silence is respect for others, a sense of place and a spirit of peace. Benedictine spirituality, she says, is founded on listening for the voice of God at all times.[3] Oblates living in the world also learn to make silence part of their lives, for without it there can be no real listening or prayer.

The practice of silence demands, first of all, taking a critical look at the things that encroach on the interior life. For example, when does the cell phone cease to be for me an instrument of communication and become a handy gadget for needless chatter? Do I allow email, Internet, television and other such wonders of technology to become an unnecessary distraction in my life? As oblates, we pledge to be people of prayer. We owe it to ourselves to make silence and prayer everyday priorities in our lives.

Obedience

There is a popular notion that obedience is an outdated service practice that is irrelevant for educated, self-sufficient adults today. But this is not the scriptural meaning of obedience, nor is it what Benedict is proposing. The meaning of 'obey' is rooted in the Latin *audire*, which means 'to hear'. To obey, then, is to hear, and having heard, to respond. Christian obedience is the outcome of prayerful listening for the voice of God in our lives at all time.

The virtue of obedience offers a salutary balance to the lives of single people who live alone and make many of their personal decisions by themselves. Understanding the meaning of Benedict's 'labor of obedience' as a way to Christ, we come to recognize that the scriptures, the tradition of the church, the Rule of Benedict, as well as individual persons, can show us the path to Christ. Obedience takes us out of our small worlds when we learn to pay attention to the things and persons who challenge and advise us. In hearing and responding to truth and wisdom, wherever we find them, we encounter the challenging Christ who calls us to fix our sights on his words and promises while living in a world that has little time for eternal values.

Prayer

Prayer is a way of life for Christians who are striving for holiness. Praying is more than saying one's favorite prayers. It is an attitude and a force that colors all of life. St Paul spoke of that when he wrote: 'Pray without ceasing' (1 Thess 5.17). St Thérèse of Lisieux shares an experience of prayer as a 'surge of the heart and a simple look toward heaven'.[4] St Benedict speaks of the primacy of prayer in the Prologue of his Rule, immediately after calling his disciples to listen and obey: 'First of all, every time you begin a good work, you must pray to him most earnestly to bring it to perfection.'

Benedictine prayer, personal and liturgical, is rooted in the scriptures. The ancient practice of *lectio divina* (sacred reading), pre-eminently a prayer of listening and responding, shapes the daily life of each Benedictine. *Lectio* embodies a variety of prayer forms: scripture reading, listening, meditation, discursive prayer, and contemplation. The entire day of the praying person is shaped by its theme. The practice of *lectio* is essential to the Benedictine way of life, monastic as well as oblate.

Some oblates choose to pray the liturgy of the hours (divine office), sanctifying the hours of each day and doing so in union with all Benedictines and the entire church.

The desire to pray better is one of the reasons people become oblates. It was so for me. My experience of Benedictine prayer during the summers I was a student at St Meinrad School of Theology led me eventually to become a Benedictine oblate.

Community

Single oblates, probably more than others, feel the need to connect with a faith community that will help them in their spiritual lives. As I prepared to write this paper I spoke with a few single oblates and asked them why they chose to become oblates. Every one of them spoke of their need to belong to a spiritual community. Here are a few of the reasons they gave:

- A desire to find a spiritual community that would 'care about me and pray for me'.
- To be part of a community that models prayer and acceptance.
- Need for a spiritual home that would invite me to deeper prayer.

In short, oblates have a need to relate to a community that lives by the motto: 'Let us bring Christ to each other and let us bring each other to Christ.'[5]

Another community dimension that is significant for oblates is connection with Benedictines all over the world. Dorothy Day, one of the best-known single oblates of the twentieth century, saw her oblation as a tie to all Benedictines. She said: 'Now that I am a professed oblate of St Procopius (Abbey) . . . [it] means that I am a part of the Benedictine family all over the world.'[6]

Living Benedictine values

A habit of prayer and receptive listening opens the door for oblates to practice the other values found in the Rule. Hospitality, the trait for which Benedictines are known and admired, exhorts them to 'welcome guests as they would welcome Christ' (*RB* 53). For oblates hospitality is about being available to friends and strangers in their need. In an age when fear and caution can keep strangers at bay one needs to discern how to be hospitable to them. Working through religious and community agencies or contributing financially or by donating blood can be generous and effective. 'Let me be as Christ to you' is a good motto for anyone.[7]

The Benedictine maxim, *ora et labora*, speaks of living a balanced life of prayer and work (and leisure), all done in moderation. For the single oblate who can easily be swept into the maelstrom of overwork and overextension, this is a healthy precept to ponder and live by. Some monastic customs and observances obviously do not apply to oblates living outside of the monastery, yet oblates who reflect on the Rule regularly and avail themselves of spiritual growth opportunities come to understand how to live according to the Rule in ways appropriate to themselves.

Ultimately the Benedictine charism is about conversion of life, the ongoing and lifelong journey of striving for holiness. The scriptures teach that conversion, in its truest sense, is not about what we do but about what we allow God to do in us. All is grace! Our task as oblates, then, is to be faithful to our commitment. So, child of God and single oblate, keep listening to the master's instruction and respond with your whole heart and soul.

Notes

1   *The Rule of Saint Benedict in English*, ed. Timothy Fry OSB, Liturgical Press, Collegeville MN, 1982. All quotations of the Rule in this article are from this edition.

2   Jean Maalouf, *Experiencing Jesus with Mother Teresa*, The Word Among Us Press, Ijamsville MD, 2006, p. 59.

3   Joan Chittister OSB, *The Rule of Benedict: Insights for the Ages*, Crossroad, New York, 1997, p. 60.

4   Quoted in *The Catechism of the Catholic Church*, Catholic Book Publishing, Totowa NJ, 1994, p. 2558.

5   These words are taken from the bookmark printed for the installation of Sister Nancy Bauer OSB, as Prioress of St Benedict's Monastery, St Joseph, Minnesota.

6   Linda Kulzer OSB and Roberta Bondi (eds), *Benedict in the World*, Liturgical Press, Collegeville MN, 2002, p. 62.

7   Richard Gillard, 'The Servant Song'.

31. Friendships and Relationships

MICHAEL WOODWARD

Two are better than one;
because they have a good reward for their labour.
For if they fall, the one will lift up his fellow:
but woe to him that is alone when he falleth;
for he hath not another to help him up. (Eccles. 4.9)

Faithful friends are beyond price:
No amount can balance their worth. (Sirach 6.15)

A mirror reflects a man's face,
but what he is really like is shown by the kind of friends he
    chooses. (Proverbs 27.19)

It is intriguing that the lot for this subject has fallen to me. The
community I currently lead and represent is slightly removed from
the traditional oblate model. However, I hope this is not a dis-
advantage, but rather affords a different perspective on some well-
trodden ground.

It is also a subject of some urgency. A recent survey identifies
most Americans as having no one to confide in, and no one to
whom they could turn in a time of crisis – apart from, in some
cases, their spouses. If this is an American trend, those in the UK
can expect to be but a few years behind.[1]

The Lay Community of St Benedict (LCSB) owes its existence to
the initiative of the first Abbot of Worth Abbey, in West Sussex.
Dom Victor Farwell, a quietly far-sighted monk, responded to the
request of some students who had spent an Easter retreat with the

monks in 1970 and were hungry for a continuing relationship. He offered them the shell of a house to form some more permanent accommodation, and the Worth Abbey Lay Community was born; of water and cement, you might say.

Initially it was for young men with a serious interest in developing a prayer life to live there for a year, sharing the full choir round of the monks while holding down jobs on site or elsewhere, and welcoming a range of groups at weekends for a briefer experience of Benedictine life.

From the monastery's viewpoint it was a hopeful source of new recruits at a barren time; and, indeed, many of the current community took that route, including the fourth Abbot, Christopher Jamison.

However, a little less foreseen was the arrival of the young men's friends. Naturally a number of these were young women. Some, it is true, developed a vocation to religious life elsewhere. However, many more nurtured a vocation to marriage which they were able to share with some of the young men, and before long the community included small children.

To their great credit, the monastic community accepted these changes with a good grace. Truly lifelong and life-changing relationships developed between the young people and the monks. They have wept and rejoiced with us, married us, baptized our children, confirmed us, and buried our dead; as we have mourned theirs. Between these milestones we have shared a lot of life. I would certainly count my friendships with some of the monks among the most significant and enduring of my life. Even with those I know less well there is a special bond, and an ease in relating at considerable depth. In many ways they are an extended family. I feel they know me through and through, and I can feel relaxed under their roof, relieved of the necessity to defend or pretend. I know myself as someone loved, held in positive regard.

No doubt some of the monastic community have tolerated rather than enjoyed the proximity of laypeople, but most have regarded it as an enriching experience.

From the monks' point of view I can guess there is the entertainment of vicarious family life, and a range of committed individuals within a far-flung network that has its uses; there are many examples of cooperation in the vineyard of the Lord at different levels. Several members have contributed over the years to the Abbey's retreat programme; others have brought needy groups to find refreshment at the spiritual water source a Benedictine community naturally creates.

So our own community has modelled itself on this example, while trying to discern its own charisms. One of these is for being the space in which the Holy Spirit creates a dynamic vitality capable of bringing different generations together within Benedict's original vision of the lifelong *schola* of the Lord's service.

Inevitably this looks more like an extended family than is normally prevalent within the oblate model. I see oblates as essentially spokes radiating from a single hub, usually an oblate master or mistress. Sometimes contact, though personal, is limited and occasional. There may be some connection with each other and with other monks, but it is not expected, and the oblate is often ploughing a furrow alone. Many speak of their sense of isolation. Oblates also tend to be mature adults of similar ages.

The LCSB has always striven to be a community in itself. The monastery's invitation to us in 2002 to become independent entailed a good deal of practical work, establishing important but mundane matters like governance and charitable status. It has also challenged us to find more ways of ministering to one another.

We have understood that, while cherishing monastic guidance and inspiration from Worth and from other communities, we also have a responsibility to feed each other. So our focus has shifted more to local and regional groups that often meet in a domestic setting, fostering the deep relationships that form among those who pray together regularly.

The often arduous work of teenage formation has become more important to us, and a clear priority. We are keenly aware that God has given us a huge gift in Benedict's ability to communicate with young people, and give them a compass to sustain them in a disorienting and fragmented society. Often the led become able leaders in their own right, and the teenagers find in their leaders convincing brothers and sisters they want to emulate.

One of our members, Sean Rooney, suggested the idea of prayer partners and most members now have someone to pray for specifically, for a year at a time. This has given us a deeper sense of being an interdependent community, despite our geographical separation.

However, in my experience, the most powerful means of growing in friendship and solidarity is the shared practice of *lectio divina*. The process of slow, meditative reading of the Word of God, the time that we spend absorbing and pondering the Word, the breath of God, and our silent listening for God to speak to us through this Word, is truly faith-forming and nourishing at a personal level.

Depending on the approach chosen, within a group there is often a special emphasis on listening to the response of other people to God's Word, and this can be powerful and inspiring, as well as a means of gelling a group and fostering understanding. The invitation from John's Gospel, 'Make my Word your home', has come to seem a watchword for us as individuals, and as a community.

André Louf has written:

> By listening with his heart to the Word of God for a long time, any believer can learn to listen to his own heart, to perceive an echo of the Word which echoes and is reflected within him. At the same time, his heart is awakened by the Word. It dilates, grows.[2]

And in that growth we find that we share the holy space of the Word with others. Through this 'friendship with the Word' our other relationships are enhanced: 'The Word of God listened to reaches the heart, makes it move and leap, producing the special fruit of a greater sensitivity to the movement of the Holy Spirit.'[3]

Although the Rule does not give direct guidance on friendship, the atmosphere and context it sets has more to offer than the bleak, impoverished ideas that dominate a contemporary cultural barometer like the Wikipedia entry (http://en.wikipedia.org/wiki/Friendship). Perhaps modern freneticism and our tendency to equate busyness with success means that superficial networking attracts more of our energy than the nurturing of deep soul sharing with one or two intimates. This, I suspect, helps to explain the popularity of spiritual accompaniment, where time is taken to explore the inner world with another, something we as a community are beginning to attempt to integrate.

There are many for whom a community relationship is not possible for different reasons and who sorely feel the need for friendships which can sustain and develop a person's exploration of the Benedictine expression of the gospel. A contemporary contribution is the availability of Internet discussion lists on Benedictine themes. Brother Jerome of Petersham has carved out a wonderful ministry by sharing daily wisdom on the Rule in this way, and by acting as a focal point for worldwide prayer intentions from his monastic cell.

One of the oldest and most Benedictine in spirit of these lists is simply called 'Monastic Life'. It features a diverse community willing to tackle any theme, usually with a lot of wisdom and charity. One stalwart member, from New Zealand, has written:

> Monastic life is akin to a cyber cloister where we are separate but supportive of each other's vocation. Online 'recreation' has resulted in some offline more personal & supportive conversations; posting some gifts back and forth; and in my case at least a couple of face to face encounters which have enriched my life immeasurably. It supports in ways that parish life, even colleagues appear not to, in that it focuses so intensely on the spiritual dimension.[4]

Daily life is by no means forgotten, and the list has very tenderly ministered to dying members and their families. It is a long way from Subiaco and Monte Cassino but this form of Benedictine community has a lot to offer the technological world we now inhabit, and in which we are called to incarnate the gospel living that Benedict constantly points us towards.

Michael Woodward

Notes

1 Prof. Lynn Smith-Lovin, from *The American Sociological Review*, 2006.

2 André Louf, *Grace Can Do More*, Cistercian Publications, 2002, p. 16.

3 Louf, *Grace*, p. 15.

4 Bosco Peters, email of 3.7.2006.

262

32. Possessions

ALI WRIGLEY

In his Rule, St Benedict seems harsh about possessions. He suggests that all things should be held in common to all, and as for his monks owning anything of their own: 'if anyone is caught indulging in this most wicked vice, let him be admonished' (RB 33.7). To call private ownership a wicked vice can, at first reading, appear to be somewhat excessive, a hang-over from ancient times like a number of other points in the Rule, but it could be seriously argued that St Benedict has good reason to distrust and dislike this practice, and that it is as entirely relevant to oblates living at the beginning of the twenty-first century as it was to Benedict and his medieval monks.

However, it could also be fairly said that life in the twenty-first century is considerably different from that of fifth-century Nursia, but the sense and balance which Benedict instils into his Rule still has the power to resonate with us some sixteen centuries later. For a piece of writing to have survived for so long and to provide a very solid foundation for many people to live by, there must be a lot more to the Rule than unnecessarily harsh restrictions and admonitions. Common sense would suggest that to be the case, or it would have been tossed aside centuries ago.

To oblates, sometimes it seems that monks and nuns have it easy as far as possession go – they do not really have an option to own things individually, and they also have access to the things which make life good: clothes, books, radio, TV, whatever. All these things are held in common by the monastery, an option which oblates and those of us living outside cannot have. Or can we?

It could be that ownership of possessions is more an attitude of mind, rather than a physical reality. In the Anglican Book of Common Prayer Communion Service, when we offer alms and oblations, the presiding priest says: 'All things come from you and of your own do we give you.' If all things come from God, and we give back to God what was his in the first instance, how did we ever come to own it? I think that the simple answer is that we did not, and to take that one step further, that we do not have the capacity to really 'own' anything. Therefore, our view of possessions, as Benedictine oblates, should differ from that of the world.

Of course, St Benedict grounds his Rule firmly in the Bible, and Chapter 33 is no exception, drawing as it does from Acts 4.32: 'No one claimed private ownership of any possessions, but rather they shared all things in common.' If it was a good enough principle for the early church, then it was good enough for Benedict's monks and should also be good enough for us.

It is easy to get sucked into the hedonistic consumer-driven vortex of ownership which seems to pass for a good lifestyle in this day and age; the idea that we must have the latest version of this game player, or the new and improved edition of that piece of electronic wizardry. My designer clothes will not be really clean unless I wash them in this product, which is designed to get them whiter than white, and then if I have too many buttons on my polo shirt I need to throw it away, no matter how clean it is, as that style is so 'last week'. We read accounts in the papers of children being beaten up because their trainers had the wrong label on them, designers targeting their brand names at children as young as three or four. Get them early and you have customers for life. It seems as though we have become a people who define ourselves by what we have, what we wear and what we look like, and that our children, who learn by example, will simply become just another statistic, just another consumer adding to the endless downward spiral into the self-gratifying and self-indulgent vanity fair of modern life.

That is not to say that we should all walk about in sackcloth looking like a bag of rags, and I do not honestly think that is what St Benedict was getting at either.

It is easy to take the opposite view of ownership. In the Bible we are given the example of the early church whose members held all things in common, but I think it is fair to say that this is not really a practical act for most of us today. We have need of a home, clothes and such, otherwise we would be on the streets, or relying on others to provide for us. However, we can still apply the basic underlying principle of the early church's example, and not consider our possessions to be wholly ours, to be stored and gloated over in private. If God is the creator of all things, which is undeniable, then we, as oblates, should be following his example as given to us in the person of Jesus, or at least trying to. Therefore, if he is generous with his giving, so should we be. If he is prepared to bless us with the good things of this earth, then in turn we should be equally prepared to pass this blessing on. And one way in which we can do this is to be generous with the things which we are fortunate enough to own.

Neither poverty nor affluence is the way of St Benedict, but rather, as with so much in his Rule, it is a balance of the two, a desirable middle ground, which allows us to acquire to our need but yet to stop and not acquire to our greed. It would seem that the ideal Benedictine lifestyle is a modest one, in which we have enough, but do not hoard the surplus.

As babes we are born into this world with nothing. When we die we take nothing with us. This suggests quite strongly that all we manage to gain and acquire in the intervening period of our lives is nothing more than a temporary stewardship. When I die, the house I own will not be taken down brick by brick and buried with me, heaven forfend, but it will stand to be a home to another family as it was before I moved in. I have a loan of it, nothing more.

In *Seeking God: The Way of St Benedict*, Esther de Waal argues this very point: 'essentially [stewardship] should mean trusteeship, the responsible holding in trust of something only temporarily loaned to us for its good usage, and for which we remain accountable to Christ, the one and only master of all goods'. If we treat the rest of our possessions with a transient viewpoint, then we allow ourselves to be distanced from them; with distance comes detachment and detachment allows us to make significant and far-reaching changes into the way we structure our lives and decide what is important to us. As Benedictine oblates we have already laid down a metaphorical challenge to the world, in which we dispute its ideologies and ethics, and suggest that we have an alternative viewpoint which would benefit not only ourselves but also radically improve the lives of others who are less fortunate than we are. Eric Dean discusses this radical effect in *Saint Benedict for the Laity*: 'To live in this fashion would raise significant questions about our relationship to the needy in our society and to institutions that exist to serve the needs of our citizens.' But we can only achieve this radicalization if we are prepared to fly in the face of received wisdom and do what is right, rather than doing what is popular. The two are not always the same. Jesus gives us a fine example of this, never being one to take the easy popular route, he raised controversies which are still raging to this day. If we are to truly be disciples of his, using St Benedict's Rule as a guide, then surely we should be relishing the opportunity to do what is right, and shunning the easy popular ways out of dilemmas. Easy to say, I know, but sometimes seemingly impossible to do.

However, like all tasks, it is best approached in small stages. As the only Christian in my family, let alone oblate, a lifestyle choice which no one much seems to understand, I would be looked on as a complete oddity if I suddenly declared that I was ridding myself of all earthy possessions in order to live a more Benedictine lifestyle. Not only would this be untrue, as discussed above St Benedict calls us to a moderate path, it would also be practically impossible as I do not have the right to inflict my religious beliefs on my husband and father. But I can do small things. I can pass on my books when I have read them, so that others may benefit from them (and this is a very difficult thing for me to do). I can offer people lifts to and fro in my car, even if their destination takes me out of my way. I can recycle clothing which no longer fits by donating it to charity shops instead of just tipping it. I can use the talents which God has blessed me with for the benefit of others rather than just for the benefit of myself.

Small steps, but significant ones. In this consumer-driven world, we can all choose not to fall into the trap of having to have the new and improved version of something if there is nothing wrong with the version we already use. And I think a very important point about possessions is the way in which we use them. It is pointless to own something which we will never use. That is greed and nothing else. It is easy to see this particular trap when it comes to obvious things – do I really need to buy a pair of skis and go on a skiing holiday when the very thought of hurtling down a mountain with two pieces of wood strapped to my feet terrifies the life out of me? The obvious answer to that one is no, and therefore I do not own skis. However, sometimes things are more insidious. Do I really need to buy a new pair of flat black shoes to wear to work when I already have two serviceable pairs? I can only wear one pair at a time, and as I tend to wear them with jeans, do I really need to have some with that particular fancy stitching on them? Again, the answer is no, but it is not always so obvious to me as the first example is, and therefore I do own more pairs of flat black shoes than I really need.

Again it goes back to the principle that we are to have enough to satisfy our need, which will be different for each of us, but not to satisfy our greed.

As Eric Dean states: 'It is not the mere ability to purchase things that gives us the moral right to own them.' It is also easy for me to fall into the idea that I should not really enjoy what I have, that it is somehow a guilty pleasure, and again I think that this goes against the spirit of what St Benedict was saying about possessions. God has created this fabulous planet for us to live on, and he has given people wonderful talents and gifts, and why should we not take pleasure in using all of these things to make our lives more enjoyable? However, if it comes to our possessions possessing us, rather than the other way around, then somehow the balance in our lives has become skewed, and we need to look seriously at our priorities.

I am not for one minute saying that I have got this sorted. I would never be so arrogant, and no doubt if I was, God would soon show me a true image of myself. However, what I would suggest is that St Benedict, rather than being harsh and over the top when it comes to the matter of possessions, instead gives us a practical way to release ourselves from the slavery of earthly things.

Esther de Waal says in *Seeking God*:

> St Benedict's Rule goes against the set of values that assumes that the worth of men and women is to be judged by the size of their pay packet or bank balance, by the area of the town in which they live, or by the kind of holiday they take.

It would be a Godless world indeed if we all viewed each other by that set of standards.

As oblates, St Benedict exhorts us to prefer nothing to the love of Christ. This must encompass possessions as well.

33. Leisure and the Benedictine Oblate

RON O'TOOLE

It would be much appreciated if someone were to produce a 'Cruden's' of the Rule of St Benedict. Looking through many translations I have yet to find the word 'leisure'. Maybe in St Benedict's time life was more gentle than in our frenetic days, and leisure as a subject was just not thought about.

Balance

What does shine through the Rule is 'balance'. Using that Benedictine virtue we will examine leisure for those who seek to follow Benedict as oblates. As a Benedictine, the oblate seeks a well-rounded spirituality, a wholeness in life, a gentle coming together of many elements needed to produce a balanced lifestyle. These elements are there in whatever age or society we live in, and balance is achieved when all are present in a state of equilibrium; all taking their place, none overwhelming the others.

To achieve this can be difficult, we lack the simplicity to see the value of leisure as a necessary part in the jigsaw which when completed, with no bits missing, reveals the life of the Benedictine oblate in the world we live in.

Time

Way back in the 1950s Thomas Merton was highly amused at the expression 'the leisure industry', that a whole new and complex industry should be floated in order to make sure our time free from work produced profits. But do we need others to organize our leisure time?

What should we include in this time at our disposal? First, an acceptance that we need to let go, to step back, and bring into focus all aspects of life, not just some. If we do not have this desire to step back, then we are caught up in the rat race of the day. Yes, even if retired, we can be so involved in many things that the days slip by and we have missed out on the relaxed joys which are the treasure of that time of life.

The oblate will have learned the discipline required to live the oblate life, for the most part on one's own. Time is a gift from God, and should be cherished and used, as all finite resources should.

Do we need leisure?

Yes! Not just as a good idea, a fad. We have needs that can only be satisfied through leisure. We hear these days of 'burn out' when a man or woman arrives at a point where they come to a full stop. In this case they are forced to let go. By then the damage has been done.

Our body requires that we look after it, let it renew its vigour. Remember the old saying about 'All work and no play . . .'? Also scripture thanks God for 'the wonder of my being'. We should rejoice in its complexity, and indulge it in rest and recuperation.

Some leisure activities can fall into the area of exercise – here we are not thinking of pumping iron, or marathon walking, although to each his or her own! As one grows older the body tells us to ease up, ease not stop, change tempo.

The mind and the spirit have their needs, they can become arid and hungry, and have to be fed. Music, literature, art, photography, the theatre, the cinema, yes even television, all of these can feed the soul and the heart; what we have to do is be sure that the food is nourishing, and not harmful.

Benedictine spirituality has always emphasized the need to enjoy and care for the world around us. Scripture tells us it was 'created to be lived in'.

We should be prepared to 'waste' time just marvelling at and *ks ?*
enjoying all that nature has to offer us. There is a strange story
about St Bernard, that one day he rode for miles along the banks
of a lake without noticing it, so deep was his contemplation.
Would it not have been better to contemplate God in his creation?
A well-known British politician during and just after the Second
World War, Hore Belisha, asked the then abbot of Mount St
Bernard Abbey, Malachy Brasil, to explain the difference between
prayer and contemplation – they were on a hill overlooking a
beautiful country scene. 'Look at that tree – examine all its leaves,
notice the colour of the bark – that is prayer.' Then he said, 'Now
just enjoy the whole scene – rest in it, don't analyse it. That is
contemplation.'

Our leisure in the world around us can have that same effect on
us without being forced. We could almost call this unintended
prayer, just enjoying God's work, which after all is what he wants
of us. (Look up Baruch 3.34–3.5) Remember this as we admire the
stars on a clear night. We can also call out, 'Here I am Lord.'

Work, projects, responsibilities

Especially in this achievement-driven age, it can be difficult to step
back and recreate without carrying all the work baggage with us.
My wife and I used to take a couple of detective novels with us on
holiday, now many pack away the laptop and the mobile phone to
be sure they do not miss out on what is happening back in the
office or workplace. It's not a question of feeling indispensable, it
is often worry over retaining one's job in the 'climb over everyone
else and get to the top' society. So letting go can be difficult, but
essential in a Benedictine way of life.

So far all has been about oneself. Now we bring in other needs –
the needs of family, friends, community. We need them to bring
completeness to our lives, and they need us; they need our interest,
our care and our love. Often they will be part of our leisure, visiting, holidays together, meals out – meals in, maybe only a phone
call or email. 'Pie in the sky'? One platitude after the other.
Maybe! However, the oblate has a prophetic vocation today.

The oblate says to the world around him or her, 'There is a better way to live out one's three score and ten (or eighty if one is strong). It is the way of the gospel which promises life NOW, abundant life.' That better way is mapped out for us in the Rule of St Benedict adapted for us who live outside the monastery walls. In it we find an openness, a freshness, a gentleness. All of these are sorely wanted around us. Our leisure should bring us an inward peace, and joy. It is one more of those props which keep the stool balanced; if taken away or left to wither, the whole thing will rock and tumble.

I hope this chapter is read by someone sitting in a comfortable chair and munching a Cox's Pippin apple.

34. Health and Sickness

JANA PREBLE AND CHARLES PREBLE

When Benedict echoes the psalmist asking, 'Is there anyone here who yearns for life and desires to see good days?' (*RB* Prologue),[1] the oblate as well as the monk may cry out, 'I do!' The Rule of Benedict provides the oblate with a framework for a life of health and wholeness, one that supports ultimate healing: salvation in the life of Christ. Believing that Christ desires health and wholeness for persons, Benedict has contributed a manual on the healthy community, a guide that supplies both a way of health and a remedy for illness. He offers wisdom to those who would learn from him, admonishing us actively to pursue health and wholeness of life. This is the desire for life and the longing to see good days.

Including all aspects of life in his Rule, Benedict adopts a holistic perspective that integrates spiritual and physical life. He takes into account work and prayer, the needs of our bodies and the needs of our souls. Wholeness, health, is the context for the monastic life, and Benedict's Rule supports that life.

Benedict realized that our wholeness and health are not found in isolation. He proposes a 'school for the Lord's service', a way for us to 'seek peace and pursue it' together. Oblates may find this companionship with a soul friend, a spouse in Christ, a parish group, an oblate group, and, very specially, a monastic community with whom they make their oblation to Christ. Finding the right community for an act of oblation is not to be taken lightly or without genuine spiritual discernment. Most oblate programs require at least a year of discernment and trial. If we are to follow the way of Benedict, we need others who also are going the way of Benedict. This is part of our health.

In the desire to preserve health of both body and soul the oblate seeks God's primacy in life and supports the desire through prayer, work, the right use of energy, and obedience. The thrust in Benedictine life is toward the preservation and maintenance of health for each person and for the community. What supports this? Benedict gives us guidance: moderation in eating and drink, an appropriate amount of sleep at night, faithfulness to prayer and reading, obedience as appropriate to rightful authorities in our lives, work in moderation, taking care not to undermine our own health or that of others by undue complaining, but rather respecting silence, courtesy, and shared responsibilities.

For the Benedictine oblate as well as the monk spiritual health, peace, and love are the results of a life lived in the search for God in obedience, discipline, and humility. In his prescriptions for those dwelling in the monastery it is relatively clear to whom the monk is answerable in obedience. It may be more complicated for the oblate. One's *abba, amma*, spiritual director, spouse or life partner, or the circumstances of one's life may be the guide to provide the direction toward spiritual wholeness and health, leading to the transformation of life in Christ.

Benedict sees sickness not so much as an aberration from life but as part of life, a part that needs special care, and such ministration is always in the context of greater life. Although he emphasizes the desirability of health, Benedict gives priority to the care of the sick. Furthermore, he recognizes that spiritual health for the followers of Christ is of greater importance than physical health and that illness may afflict the soul and spirit as well as the body.

When times of incapacity, diminishment, and sickness occur, Benedict insists that special attention be given to those who are weak, whether in the spirit or in the body. While the physically ill must be shown every care and consideration, so the soul-sick must also be cared for with mercy and compassion. When we are sick in soul as in body we are part of a community, and we take whatever steps we can toward health. Our own soul-sickness may help us grow in compassion if we accept it with humility, reveal it to a spiritual elder, accept forgiveness and guidance. It may, in ways we never fully understand or experience, help others in their own growth.

Benedict's Chapter 36 on the sick reveals the importance of care for them. Benedict recognizes that in ministering to the sick we minister to Christ himself. As oblates we have a loving obligation to reach out to those who are cast off and alone, especially the sick. Physical sickness is to be borne with tenderness and, in fact, may be the means to greater spiritual health for the community, as the care of the ill demands compassion and a certain self-forgetfulness on the part of the healthy caretakers. In visiting the sick, caring for the sick, praying for the sick, and in advocating for better healthcare for all persons, especially the most vulnerable, we are called to go beyond ourselves, our comfortable daily routine and petty conveniences. Serving the sick, we serve Christ in a very direct way.

In reaching out to those with a loss of spirit we reach out to Christ. In these acts we begin to get a sense of the greater life that Benedict envisages. This vision does not center on the self. God is the true center of our lives and the source of wholeness and healing. Benedict calls us into a greater life that involves not only a genuine obedience to God but a life that sees Christ in others and is obedient to him in serving him in the sick, the guest, the stranger.

We may be especially challenged in trying to live Benedictine values in our own sickness. Just as we are to treat the ill around us with great care, we must treat ourselves with great care if we become ill. Benedict gives us good counsel in this matter. As special service is given to the sick in the community, the time of illness becomes the time to take care of oneself. Perhaps we are overworking to the point where the other aspects of our life and those we care about suffer. Our life may be out of balance, with charity diminishing in us. If we lack love, perhaps we should be ministering to ourselves or permit others to minister to us. We may not have an abbot responsible for us, so we must recognize our own need or allow others to assist us to know our needs. Part of our call is to seek healing and to initiate those things that will support our own wholeness, our own health in the broadest sense.

In physical illness we seek appropriate medical assistance and live obedient to the prescribed plan toward health. We pray for our care-givers and for Christ's healing gifts in them. We are to bear illness patiently and with humility and not be overdemanding of our care-givers or ourselves, knowing that when Christ is cared for in one's illness, Christ provides the care as well.

When we are too ill to pray, in too much pain to even believe that we can cry out in faith, Christ is with us. Christ remains the health-giver, caretaker, companion who descends with us into the hell of suffering and brings us on into his rising.

The oblate may live alone, but the oblate is not in isolation. The oblate's health or sickness remains in the context of community, and oblates recognize their place in Christ's body and their respon-sibilities in both health and sickness to that body. Stewardship of body and soul in health and sickness is called for, so the oblate continues to listen for what that call to stewardship is asking. If we are physically healthy we may use our health to serve others. Perhaps our sickness, even of mind or soul as well as body, may serve too.

In sickness and in health Christ is central. Christ is the healer, and Christ is the companion in illness. Christ in the person of the prioress/abbot/*amma/abba* and in the prayerful concern of the members for one another delivers healing with compassion and mercy. This, according to Benedict's Rule, is how it works in the monastery. For the oblate there is the dilemma of discernment: Am I in the role of abbot/prioress in this situation, called to provide care or the healing word of encouragement to friend, child, spouse, coworker? Am I ill and in need of care? Then who is to be abbot/prioress/*abba/amma* for me in this situation? Whom will I approach for help – physician, spiritual director, companion, counselor, oblate director, spouse? Perhaps a child speaks the wisdom that heals. At all times, in all places and circumstances of health or illness, the oblate seeks God in obedience to Christ, listening for the healing word, recognizing that health and sickness are both opportunities to live compassionately, humbly, and with the hope of ongoing transformation in Christ.

Health and Sickness

Notes

1 Citations from the Rule are taken from *RB 1980: The Rule of St. Benedict in Latin and English with Notes*, Liturgical Press, Collegeville MN, 1981.

35. Doors: One Man's Story of Retirement

FRANCIS BUXTON

Throughout my life there have been significant doors. Some, like National Service in the army, I was pushed through kicking and screaming, through some, like evacuation in September 1939, ushered with bewilderment, while through others, like retirement, eased with mingled relief and apprehension. I had realized that there would now be more time for doing all the things I loved – reading, gardening, listening to music, playing with my grand-children, going round the shops with my wife and foreign travel together – but among the retirement cards that I received there was one that said, 'Congratulations on your Retirement. I hope that you will be so busy that you will wonder how you ever found time to go to work'. This turned out to be quite true.

Why was I not surprised to discover that other new doors opened before me?

I had always wished to pray the divine office but had hesitated to do so because, as a layman, I had no wish to ape the clergy. Then at a study week on prayer some 40 years ago one of the speakers, a Benedictine monk, informed us that the office that St Benedict adapted from the Roman office of the day had been intended for laymen. I used a Christmas book token to buy my first book of daily prayer. My New Year resolution for 1 January 1997 had been that I would write down the words of scripture that had grabbed me each day, as well as my reply to them, as a sort of ongoing conversation between God and myself. As far as I know it is the only New Year's resolution I have ever kept. This, I was going to discover, I would know as *lectio divina*.

Thus, the opening of that major door marked 'Retirement' was only the first step to the opening of several others, each one offering its own type of fulfilment. I was led to join the Society of St Vincent de Paul, providing opportunities to meet those in need. Julian Meetings prayer groups encouraged active contemplative prayer and sharing. The parochial branch of the Lay Fraternity of Charles de Foucault, with its eucharistic adoration, gospel sharing and review of life was very formative.

However, the best was yet to come. In the autumn of the year 2000 I was returning from London to my home in Norfolk on a Sunday of pouring rain. I knew that a friend was giving a talk in Cromer that afternoon on Benedictine spirituality. I decided that I could not face the extra hour's drive and did not go, but afterwards I heard that the talk was a great success and that it had been decided to have further talks each month. After that, I did not miss a single one of these monthly meetings.

In January 2001 I became an oblate novice when the oblate director came to visit our group in Cromer, and established it as a chapter of the oblates of Douai Abbey, under the patronage of Julian of Norwich, the fourteenth-century mystic who wrote *The Revelations of Divine Love*, the first book written by an Englishwoman. Much of what I heard had the ring of familiarity. *Lectio divina* was by now an ingrained habit, as was the divine office, although Compline, which I had found the hardest office to say regularly up till then was the one urged on new novices. It seemed as if I had been quietly led to St Benedict's gentle Rule 'for beginners'. Prayer, study, work and service to the community all seemed to fit, too conveniently for it to be accidentally, into the framework of the office and the Rule.

By May 2002 when, with a group of 12 from the chapter, I made my oblation I had already visited the monastery at Douai several times. I was thrilled by the beauty of the abbey church and the peaceful rural setting with the ridge of Watership Down as the southern horizon, but what impressed me far more was the quiet hospitality of the community, their cheerful acceptance of strange oblates into their family and their invitation to join them in the daily praise of the divine office. I am tempted to say that sharing the office and conventual Mass are the things I love most about my visits to Douai, but the sense of peace that I find there, the ready opportunity for quiet prayer and reflection, the afternoon walk, the retreat sessions with sharing of ideas, the *lectio divina* are all clamouring for their place in my appreciation. I should add that the meals are pretty good as well and that the bookshop is a place of terrible temptation. I had already heard of Thomas Merton before becoming an oblate and had read his *Seeds of Contemplation*; however, since finding the abbey bookshop not only have I read more Merton, but I have discovered a host of other writers – Esther de Waal, Norvene Vest, Joan Chittister, Homan and Pratt – all were new names for me to cherish, while others, like Basil Pennington and Bede Griffiths, have been rediscovered.

I found that being an oblate began to impinge upon my life away from the monastery and the chapter. The Internet is a valuable way of keeping in daily touch with oblates scattered over Norfolk, the United Kingdom and the world. The sense of community, denied by being 'outside the walls', is maintained by the exchange of readings and *lectios*. I always wear my oblate medal back to front with the cross showing. This led to questions from several supermarket checkout clerks, shop assistants, and quite a long conversation with a salesman. I was even stopped in Norwich market and invited to join a lunch-time prayer meeting. As a member of the Society of St Vincent de Paul, I became a prison visitor. During a prison visit in Lent 2004 I came across a prisoner reading one of the series of articles by various Benedictine abbots in the *Catholic Herald*. This led Johann, from South Africa, to ask about the medal and eventually to enquire about the possibility of becoming an oblate. With the permission of the oblate director, Johann became a novice in prison and was guided by visiting order and letter. He understood that there would be no chance for him to make his oblation until he was released. Then he discovered, early in 2006, that he was to be repatriated and disappeared. I wrote this off as a quirk of officialdom, the whole situation unlikely to be repeated, then a few weeks ago I walked into the recreation room after Mass looking for anyone sitting by himself. A prisoner saw me and raised his hand in greeting. In the other hand he was holding *Benedictine Daily Prayer – a Short Breviary*. 'How do you find it,' I asked? 'Great,' he said. 'I want to become an oblate. The chaplain has promised to find a contact phone number.' 'Well,' I replied, 'if he gets it from the diocesan directory, you'll find you're talking to me.'

So many doors have opened in life and now, most importantly, the last great door must be close. Yet here, in time, I seem to hear the echo of a gentle chuckle as, in the paradox of God's eternal now, I stand with a portly gentleman (who dearly loves a paradox), looking down at my time-bound self, and join him in one of his brilliant final couplets:

For there is good news yet to hear, and fine things to be seen
Before we go to Paradise by way of Kensal Green.[1]

Note

1 G. K. Chesterton, 'The Rolling English Road'. Kensal Green is a well-known London cemetery.

36. Aging and Death

CHARLES PREBLE AND JANA PREBLE

While there is still time and we are still in this body, and there remains time to accomplish all in the light of this life, we must run and accomplish now what will profit us for eternity.[1]

Thus Benedict sets the parameters of our work on earth. It is a life-long work. In one sense there is not a time within this life or before death when oblates can say our work is done, for we do not retire from the work that God is doing within us. This is a work that will take our whole life.

In many cultures life is divided into three phases: growing up and education, a time of adult work, and a time of leisure and retirement. Along with this may come the practice of ageism when elders are discriminated against and the young are valued over the old, perhaps because the young seem to have more energy, will work for less, and may be less demanding. Youthfulness may be valued and pursued among those who as they age do whatever they can to preserve, enhance, or attempt to re-create their youth. Benedict presents us with a different model. Although lifespans are lengthened today beyond what they were normally in Benedict's time, the *Rule* does not acknowledge a time of retirement. The work goes on while there is the light of life. It is done in the context of scores and decades of years, but with the backdrop of eternity.

Presumably oblates use the Rule of Benedict as a guide to the life of transformation. The outward manifestation of our lives supports inner transformation. Aging and death are in support of and ultimately lead to arrival at complete transformation in everlasting life in Christ.

In this context aging is an integrated part of life. Aging is also part of a process that will lead up to our death. At each stage there will be a hint of the paschal mystery in which there is a type of death, a relinquishment, and a discovery of a new life. At each stage we have to 'let go' or surrender something. In doing so we come – we hope – to a new life, one in which there is a greater and deeper obedience to God and a greater and deeper resurrection of Christ within us.

Benedict continues (*RB* 50b): 'Then we will never depart from his teaching and will persevere in the monastery [in the oblate life] until death. Likewise we will participate in the passion of Christ through patience so as to deserve to be companions in his kingdom.' Our participation in Christ's passion may become more than a spiritual experience. It may be very real, with very real human suffering. A peaceful aging and death are to be desired but are not always a given. In the end our suffering is united with Christ's.

Benedict writes of juniors and seniors and how they are to relate to one another and to the life of the community. Within the monastery the seniors have a respected role, but Benedict says that the elders must give some deference to the junior members. The young may have insights that will help the entire community. As we age, Benedict would have us listen, even with the ear of the heart, to the young. As we age we learn that if we really listen to the young, God may be giving us a word of life.

The Rule of Benedict assumes that the young and the old will be within the same community and not separated. Even though there is a distinction made between seniors and juniors it is clear that they are all called to be one community in which each listens to the other, whether young or old. All are enriched in listening for Christ in one another. In this school of the Lord's service all know that 'they must bear one another's weaknesses of both body and character with the utmost patience' (*RB* 72.5). As oblates we can live so that the strong help the weak and do not take advantage of the weakness of others. Although this is particularly true with the sick, it is also true of the elderly. As we age we may learn that it can be very difficult to accept or ask for help. Having never learned to ask for help, the senior may now have no other option than to lose his or her life of self-sufficiency and realize her or his greater dependence on the community.

This is also a time that may call for new learning in how to accomplish tasks with less strength and greater patience. There is a practical lesson in Benedict's words from the Prologue (verse 50): 'we will participate in the passion of Christ through patience'. Each time we learn to let go, to relinquish, we have the opportunity to participate in the Passion of Christ. Each time we discover more our interdependence in the body of Christ.

Even as physical or cognitive limitations increase, some in the aging process claim new freedom. As choices become limited, the ability to choose what matters most often increases. Many take on a new commitment to truth and authenticity and to the priorities of people and prayer.

'Day by day remind yourself that you are going to die,' Benedict directs us (*RB* 4). In a world in which so much death is presented to us daily by the media there is nevertheless a kind of denial of death. It is almost as if death is something that happens to other people and it is hard for us to imagine our non-existence. Benedict would have this before us each day. The funeral bell tolls for us as well. Rather than being moribund, Benedict again is helping us to come alive. Benedict and the gospel see death not as the end but as the way through which we must pass to enter greater life. As we grow older, each step is a little death that has begun at birth. Yet this reminder of death is given to us so that we may realize even more the poignancy of living every moment rather than being in dread of the event that will take each of us one day.

Aging and the approach of death in our own lives or in the lives of others present an opportunity for oblates to evaluate our own lives, our priorities, even as part of our rule of life. It is a fact that when someone is dying, very often people who have been close to that person have a hard time. They avoid the dying person as if death were contagious. However, the experience of others is that when they do visit those at death's door they find the presence of Christ in a way never experienced before.

In thinking of the reality of our own death and knowing that now is the time to face it we are presented with the opportunity to get things in order for those who come after us. It is also one of the best ways for us to enter more fully into the present moment. It provides us with a far greater and more life-affirming way than the familiar 'eat, drink, and be merry, for tomorrow we may die'. It allows us more essentially to enter into the fullness of life in Christ.

'Let them prefer nothing whatever to Christ, and may Christ bring us all together to everlasting life' (*RB* 72). In the process of aging and death, the Christ we find ourselves preferring may be the suffering or dying Christ. When Benedict presents us with the question, 'Are you hastening toward your heavenly home?' and reminds us, 'then with Christ's help, keep this little rule that we have written for beginners', we may reply that even in aging and dying we would hasten toward our heavenly home though we move very slowly and may seem to die by inches. In the Lent of aging and impending death we 'look forward to holy Easter with joy and spiritual longing' (*RB* 49.7). With Christ we go through death into fullness of life. He is our guide, and we are in him.

Benedict knows the assurance, not unlike St Paul's:

No, in all these things we are more than conquerors through him who loved us. For I am convinced that neither death, nor life, nor angels, nor rulers, nor things present, nor things to come, nor powers, nor height, nor depth, nor anything else in all creation, will be able to separate us from the love of God in Christ Jesus, our Lord. (Rom. 8.37–39)

Benedict's focus is on life, on Easter. All, even death, is in the service of life. 'Never swerving from his instructions, then, but faithfully observing his teaching . . . until death we [as oblates] shall through patience share in the sufferings of Christ that we may deserve also to share in his kingdom' (*RB* 80, Prologue 50).

Note

1 Terrence G. Kardong (ed.), *Benedict's Rule: A Translation and Commentary*, Liturgical Press, Collegeville MN, 1996 (Hereafter *RB*), Prologue 43–44.

Afterword

We hope that you have found the chapters of this book both encouraging and challenging. Having read the book once, may we venture to suggest that you should keep it by you, and keep on returning to it. There is much here that will take time to assimilate and which, as oblates, you will find useful for *lectio* and to deepen your prayer, as well as your appreciation of the Rule of St Benedict and your daily Christian living according to its principles.

We would also suggest that selected chapters would be useful for reading and discussing at oblate chapter meetings, during retreats, and indeed whenever two or three oblates are gathered together. It is in listening to God's voice that we can discover his will for us. God speaks in many diverse ways and one of them is surely through the voices of our fellow oblates when we read and discuss in a prayerful manner. In discussing we should always remember and apply the teaching that St Benedict gives on calling the brethren to counsel: 'The brothers, for their part, are to express their opinions with all humility, and not presume to defend their own views obstinately' (*RB* 3.4). Thus we should always speak in such a way as to be open to listen to what the others have to say, rather than to assert our own views, or, even worse, attempt to score points.

May God's blessing and the prayers of St Benedict be with every oblate who, using this little book, seeks to progress in the 'school for the Lord's service' (*RB* Prologue 45).

Part Three Resources for Oblates

Appendix 1

Contributors to *The Oblate Life*

Robert Atwell is the Anglican Bishop of Stockport and an oblate of the Abbey of Le Bec Hellouin, France. He is the compiler of two volumes of daily readings for the liturgical year, *Celebrating the Saints* and *Celebrating the Seasons*, as well as three anthologies of readings on birth and parenthood, love and marriage, and death and bereavement, entitled respectively *Gift, Love* and *Remember*.

Maria Boulding is a Benedictine nun at Stanbrook Abbey in England. The joy of God's Word in scripture, discovered especially through monastic *lectio* and liturgy, is central to her life, and she has tried to spread love of the Word through her writings. These include *Marked for Life: Prayer in the Easter Christ*, and *The Coming of God*, and *Gateway to Hope*. She has also worked for the Augustinian Heritage Institute as a translator, especially of *The Confessions of St Augustine* and his *Expositions of the Psalms*.

Simon Bryden-Brook is a Catholic convert from Anglicanism and is an oblate of Douai Abbey. He was trained as a teacher of religion and music. He studied at Birmingham and Cambridge Universities and is currently working for a DMin. In 1998 SCM-Canterbury Press published his *Take, Bless, Break, Share*, a compilation of grass roots agapes and other para-liturgies. He remains active in the liturgical music ministry of his parish in Berkshire and is a member of the executive committees of *Catholics for a Changing Church, Church on the Move* and *The North Atlantic Federation for a Renewed Ministry*.

Lucy Brydon has been a member of the Turvey Abbey community for 20 years. During this time she has been involved with interreligious dialogue through work in the retreat and guest department of the community as well as for the Monastic Inter-religious Dialogue Commission of Britain and Ireland. (web site: www.mid-gbi.com). She has also helped with Oblate weekends and weekends on Benedictine spirituality.

Francis Buxton was born in London in 1933: he was head teacher of a primary school on the Isle of Dogs in London's East End dockland, is married with three children and now lives in Norfolk. He writes poetry and has been an oblate of Douai Abbey since January 2001.

Nicholas Buxton has visited and stayed in numerous monasteries around the world, he is an oblate of the Anglican Benedictine community of Elmore Abbey, and was one of the participants in BBC2's *The Monastery*. He has written widely on the practice and contemporary relevance of monastic spirituality.

Michael Casey is a Cistercian monk and is prior of Tarrawarra Abbey in Victoria, Australia. He is the author of *The Undivided Heart* as well as *Toward God* and its companion volume, *Sacred Reading*.

Janice Daurio and her husband Paul Ford are oblates of St Andrew's Abbey of Valyermo, California. She is a native of Brooklyn, New York, and professor of philosophy at Moorpark College, with degrees from Mount Saint Mary's College and Claremont Graduate University.

Esther de Waal is an Anglican lay woman who has written extensively on the monastic tradition. Her first book, *Seeking God: The Way of St Benedict*, has been widely used and translated world-wide. She lives on the Welsh Borders, where she grew up, combining gardening and family life with travel, lecturing and retreat giving.

Wil Derkse is an oblate of St Wilibrord's Abbey, Doetinchem, The Netherlands. At present he is leading the Soeterbeeck Program for Science, Society and Worldviews at Radboud Universiteit, a Catholic university in Nijmegen, The Netherlands. He is the author of *The Rule of Benedict for Beginners*, *Benedictine Spirituality for Daily Life*, and the forthcoming *A Blessed Life: Benedictine Guidelines for Those Who Long for Good Days*.

Luke Dysinger studied religion and medicine at the University of Southern California, receiving his MD in 1978. He joined the Benedictine community of St Andrew's Abbey in 1980, where he has served as novice master and prior. Dysinger received his doctorate in theology at the University of Oxford in 2000 and teaches at St John's Seminary in Camarillo, California.

Paul F. Ford is professor of systematic theology and liturgy at St John's Seminary in Camarillo, California. Along with his wife Janice Daurio, he is an oblate of St Andrew's Abbey of Valyermo, California. He is an internationally recognized authority on the life and writings of C. S. Lewis. His music publications are the books and CDs associated with *By Flowing Waters: Chant for the Liturgy*, and the *Psallite* program with Liturgical Press. He is a member of the Collegeville Composers Group.

Benedict Gaughan has been a nun at Minster, Kent, since 1975. She was born in North London and spent some time working with disabled people,

including a period at L'Arche. While she was guest sister, during the early
1980s, a local woman asked to become an oblate, so she organized an
oblate programme, and has been oblate director ever since. She has also
been novice mistress and is currently sub-prioress with responsibility for the
kitchen and maintenance. She is actively engaged in ecumenism, with a special concern for dialogue between Eastern and Western Christians.

Susie Hayward was a barrister and television producer and is now a human-
istic psychologist and psychotherapist. She also has a background in theology, spirituality and retreat-giving world-wide. She is a consultant to
Ampleforth Abbey in human development and is a Fellow of the Royal
Society of Arts.

Alan Hodgetts was born in Birmingham in the UK in 1954 and is married
with three children. He is a graduate in Mechanical Engineering and has an
MA in Pastoral Liturgy. He prepared for the ordained ministry at St
Stephen's House, Oxford, and was ordained priest in 1983 in the Church of
England. He is currently Anglican and Co-ordinating Chaplain at Her
Majesty's Prison, Woodhill, in Milton Keynes, Buckinghamshire, and is an
oblate of Alton Abbey, Hampshire.

Gervase Holdaway is a monk of Douai Abbey, Berkshire, England. He was
born in London and educated at the Cardinal Vaughan School, Kensington.
He studied theology at the University of Louvain, Belgium, and for some
years taught scripture at Douai Abbey, following which he was parish priest
in the monastery parish. He had a sabbatical at St Meinrad Archabbey,
Indiana, in 1995–6, since when he has been oblate director and director of
the abbey's programme of retreats. He teaches Scripture in the Continuing
Education School of the University of Reading.

Loretta Javra is an oblate of St Benedict's Monastery in St Joseph,
Minnesota. She lives in St Paul, Minnesota, and works at the Cathedral of
St Paul as the director of the Rite of Christian Initiation of Adults.

Maxwell E. Johnson is an ordained minister of the Evangelical Lutheran
Church in America and associate professor of liturgy at the University of
Notre Dame. He is an oblate of St John's Abbey in Collegeville, Minnesota.

Simon Jones is Chaplain and Fellow of Merton College, Oxford, and also
teaches liturgy in the Faculty of Theology in the University of Oxford and
at St Stephen's House, Oxford. An oblate of Elmore Abbey, an Anglican
Benedictine community near Newbury, he wrote the introduction to the
sixtieth anniversary edition of Gregory Dix's *The Shape of the Liturgy* published by Continuum, and has also edited *The Sacramental Life: Gregory
Dix and His Writings*, published by Canterbury Press.

Paul Kennedy is the Rector of East Winchester and an oblate of the Anglican Alton Abbey. He is married to a teacher, Paula, and they have three sons.

Carol Lewis was born in Crickhowell, Breconshire, Wales, and is an oblate of Douai Abbey in Berkshire, England. After qualifying as a solicitor she practiced for 33 years on her own account and in partnership. She has an MA in philosophy. Since retiring, she breeds and trains riding/dressage horses at her home in Berkshire.

Kathleen Norris is an oblate of Assumption Abbey in Richardton, North Dakota, and serves on the Board of Regents at St John's University, Collegeville, Minnesota. She is the author of *Dakota*, *The Cloister Walk*, and *Amazing Grace: A Vocabulary of Faith*. She is currently writing a book on acedia.

Simon O'Donnell has been a monk at St Andrew's Abbey in Valyermo, California, for 44 years. He has served his community mostly in administration and in formation as Novice Master. He currently devotes much of his time to oblates of the community and directing retreats. He is also a frequent contributor to the *Valyermo Chronicle*, a quarterly devoted to monastic topics.

Ron O'Toole was born at Devonport in 1930 of Irish parents. His father was in the Royal Navy, so he was educated in various places. At an early age he entered the Cistercians and was still young when he left. He is married to Inge, and has four children and seven grandchildren. He spent seven years working for the rehabilitation of ex-offenders, and at this time he was ordained deacon by Bishop Christopher Butler OSB. He spent 15 years caring for seafarers and the single homeless in the London docks. Since retirement to Cromer he has undertaken pastoral work in the parish and deanery. He and Inge are oblates of Douai Abbey and he has been elected leader of the Julian Chapter.

Charles Preble is an oblate of St Benedict's Monastery in St Joseph, Minnesota. He is an artisan in wood and an Episcopal priest. He lives with his wife, Jana, on an old farmstead a few miles from the monastery.

Jana Preble is an oblate of St Benedict's Monastery in St Joseph, Minnesota. She is a professor and spiritual director as well as a wife, mother, and grandmother. She and her husband Charles enjoy frequent contacts with the monks of St John's Abbey as well the sisters of the monastery of their oblate profession.

Susan Sink, an oblate of St John's Abbey in Collegeville, Minnesota, is a poet, writer, and an editor at Liturgical Press. She is the author of *The Way of All the Earth*, poems, and the series *The Art of the Saint John's Bible*.

Rachel M. Srubas is a Presbyterian clergywoman serving a congregation in Tucson, Arizona, where she is also affiliated with the Benedictine Sisters of Perpetual Adoration. She is the author of *Oblation: Meditations on St. Benedict's Rule* and *City of Prayer: Forty Days with Desert Christians*.

Judith Sutera is a member of the monastery of Mount St Scholastica in Atchison, Kansas. She has degrees in monastic theology and counselling and is editor of *Magistra*, a women's spirituality history journal, and *The American Monastic Newsletter*. Sutera is on the boards of the *American Benedictine Review*, the Conference on the History of Women Religious and Monastic Interreligious Dialogue, and has been an oblate director for many years.

Phyllis Tickle, a lay Benedictine, is the compiler of *The Divine Hours* series of prayer manuals for observing the offices. A popular lecturer and author, she speaks and writes frequently on prayer and, in particular, on fixed-hour prayer. She serves as a lector and lay eucharistic minister in the Episcopal Church.

Dermot Tredget, before becoming a monk of Douai Abbey worked in both the private and public sectors as a senior manager and was a lecturer at the University of Surrey in Guildford. He has an MBA from the University of Bath and an MA from the Graduate Theological Union, Berkeley, California. Currently he is involved in facilitating workshops and running seminars on a Benedictine spirituality of work, business ethics and corporate social responsibility at Douai for its Pastoral Programme, for the University of Wales at Lampeter, and further a field for businesses and other organizations. At present his main focus is on the way in which monastic spirituality can contribute to a deeper understanding of the meaning and purpose of leisure in the twenty-first century.

Derek Vidler was born in Central London in 1933 into a non-church going family. At sixteen he became a Catholic; he was drafted for National Service and also worked in accountancy. He was ordained priest for the archdiocese of Southwark in 1962 and served a number of South London parishes. From early on he had links with Quarr Abbey and Farnborough Abbey. For the last ten years he has been Judicial Vicar for the archdiocese of Southwark and has been an oblate of Douai Abbey since 2002.

Rowan Williams is the Archbishop of Canterbury and a distinguished theologian, writer and poet. After teaching theology in both Cambridge and Oxford Universities, he was ordained Bishop of Monmouth in 1991 and elected Archbishop of Wales in 1999, before taking up his present appointment in 2002.

Michael Woodward began his career as a primary school teacher. He then created Three Peaks Press, specializing in spirituality and poetry. He trained as a prayer companion and was part of an ecumenical retreat team in South Wales. At the inception of the Lay Community of Benedict in 2003, he was elected leader. He is a versatile retreat giver on *Lectio Divina*, St Benedict, Desert Spirituality, Thomas Merton, Bede Griffiths and scriptural themes. He is married to Nora and lives in Wales.

Ali Wrigley became an oblate of Douai Abbey in 2003 and is currently an Anglican. She considers becoming an oblate one of the most fulfilling steps she has undertaken in life, and attended the First World Congress of Benedictine Oblates. She used to teach English Literature at a local college, but gave this up to care for her disabled father, and now works part-time in the Exams Office. She lives with her husband and her father in South Manchester.

Appendix 2

List of Selected Monasteries with Oblate Programmes

Selected US and Canada Benedictine Monasteries

(Organized by location, January 2008)

House of Bread Monastery houseofbreadmonastery.com	Nanaimo	Canada, BC
St Benedict's Monastery mts.net/~stbens	Winnipeg	Canada, Manitoba
St Peter's Abbey stpeterscollege.ca	Muenster	Canada, SK
Sacred Heart Monastery shmon.org	Cullman	AL
Holy Angels Convent olivben.org	Jonesboro	AR
Subiaco Abbey subi.org/abbey.htm	Subiaco	AR
Holy Trinity Monastery holytrinitymonastery.org	Saint David	AZ
Benedictine Sisters of Perpetual Adoration tucsonmonastery.com	Tucson	AZ
New Camaldoli Hermitage and Incarnation Abbey camaldolese.com	Big Sur Berkeley	CA CA
Holy Spirit Monastery holyspiritmonastery.org	Grand Terrace	CA

Prince of Peace Abbey princeofpeaceabbey.org	Oceanside	CA
Monastery of the Risen Christ daily-word-of-life.com/Monastery.htm	San Luis Obispo	CA
St Andrew's Abbey valyermo.com	Valyermo	CA
Abbey of St Walburga walburga.org	Virginia Dale	CO
Benet Hill Monastery benethillmonastery.org	Colorado Springs	CO
St Anselm's Abbey stanselms.org	Washington	DC
St Leo Abbey saintleoabbey.org	St Leo	FL
St Gertrude's Monastery stgertrudes.org	Cottonwood	ID
Monastery of the Ascension idahomonks.org	Jerome	ID
Marmion Abbey marmion.org	Aurora	IL
Monastery of the Holy Cross chicagomonk.org	Chicago	IL
St Scholastica Monastery osbchicago.org	Chicago	IL
Benedictine Sisters of the Sacred Heart shmlisle.org	Lisle	IL
St Procopius Abbey Procopius.org	Lisle	IL
St Mary Monastery stmarymonastery.org	Rock Island	IL
Our Lady of Grace Monastery Benedictine.com	Beech Grove	IN
Monastery of the Immaculate Conception thedome.org	Ferdinand	IN

List of Selected Monasteries with Oblate Programmes

St Meinrad Archabbey saintmeinrad.edu	St Meinrad	IN
Mount St Scholastica mountosb.org	Atchison	KS
St Walburg Monastery stwalburg.org	Covington	KY
St Joseph Abbey saintjosephabbey.com	St Benedict	LA
Glastonbury Abbey glastonburyabbey.org	Hingham	MA
St Mary's Monastery stmarysmonastery.org	Petersham	MA
St Gertrude Monastery ridgelybenedictines.org	Ridgely	MD
St Benedict Monastery benedictinemonks.com	Oxford	MI
St John's Abbey saintjohnsabbey.org	Collegeville	MN
Mount St Benedict Monastery msb.net	Crookston	MN
St Scholastica Monastery duluthbenedictines.org	Duluth	MN
St Benedict's Monastery sbm.osb.org	St Joseph	MN
St Paul's Monastery stpaulsmonastery.org	St Paul	MN
St Scholastica (Sisters of Perpetual Adoration) benedictinesisters.org	Clyde	MO
Our Lady of Peace Monastery benedictinesister.squarespace.com	Columbia	MO
Conception Abbey conceptionabbey.org	Conception	MO
St Louis Abbey stlouisabbey.org	St Louis	MO

Annunciation Monastery annunciationmonastery.org	Bismarck	ND
Assumption Abbey assumptionabbey.com	Richardton	ND
Mount Michael Benedictine Abbey mountmichael.org	Elkhorn	NE
Christ the King Priory stbenedictenter.com	Schuyler	NE
Benedictine Sisters of Elizabeth, NJ catholic-forum.com/bensisnj/	Elizabeth	NJ
St Mary's Abbey at Delbarton osbmonks.org	Morristown	NJ
Newark Abbey newarkabbey.org	Newark	NJ
Our Lady of Guadalupe Abbey pecosmonastery.org	Pecos	NM
Mount Saviour Monastery msaviour.org	Elmira	NY
Queen of Heaven Monastery benedictinebyzantine.org	Warren	OH
St Andrew Abbey my.en.com/~brother/	Cleveland	OH
St Joseph Monastery stjosephmonastery.org	Tulsa	OK
St Gregory's Abbey monksok.org	Shawnee	OK
Red Plains Monastery redplainsmonastery.org	Piedmont	OK
Queen of Angels Monastery Benedictine-srs.org	Mt. Angel	OR
Mount Angel Abbey mtangel.edu	St Benedict	OR
Transfiguration Monastery emmausosb.org	Emmaus	PA

List of Selected Monasteries with Oblate Programmes

Mount St Benedict eriebenedictines.org	Erie	PA
St Vincent Archabbey monks.stvincent.edu osb.org/sva/obl	Latrobe	PA
Benedictine Sisters of Pittsburgh osbpgh.org	Pittsburgh	PA
Blue Cloud Abbey bluecloud.org	Marvin	SD
St Martin Monastery blackhillsbenedictine.com	Rapid City	SD
Mother of God Monastery watertownbenedictines.org	Watertown	SD
Sacred Heart Monastery yanktonbenedictines.org	Yankton	SD
St Benedict Monastery osbcanyontx.org	Canyon	TX
St Scholastica Monastery boernebenedictines.com	Boerne	TX
Benedictine Monastery of the Good Shepherd starrcountybenedictines.org	Rio Grande City	TX
Mount Benedict Monastery mbmutah.org	Ogden	UT
St Benedict Monastery osbva.org	Bristow	VA
St Martin's Abbey stmartin.edu/abbey/	Lacey	WA
St Placid Priory stplacid.org	Lacey	WA
Our Lady of the Rock Priory ourladyoftherock.com	Shaw Island	WA
St Bede Monastery saintbede.org	Eau Claire	WI

Holy Wisdom Monastery benedictinewomen.org	Madison	WI
Valley of Our Lady Monastery nonocist.org	Prairie du Sac	WI
San Benito Monastery sanbenitomonastery.org	Dayton	WY

Selected Great Britain and Ireland Benedictine Monasteries

(Organized by location, January 2008)

Priory of Our Lady of Peace turveyabbey.org.uk	Turvey Abbey	Bedfordshire
Douai Abbey douaiabbey.org.uk	Woolhampton	Berkshire
Elmore Abbey elmoreabbey.org	Speen, Newbury	Berkshire
Curzon Park Abbey curzonpark.org.uk	Chester	Cheshire
Buckfast Abbey buckfast.org.uk	Buckfastleigh	Devon
Holy Cross Monastery benedictinemonks.co.uk	Rostrevor	Co. Down N. Ireland
Alton Abbey starcourse.org/abbey	Alton	Hampshire
St Mary's Abbey orders.anglican.org/arcyb/ osbwmalling.html	West Malling	Kent
Priory of St Mildred minsterabbeynuns.org	Minster Abbey	Kent
Ramsgate Abbey ramsgatebenedictines.com	Ramsgate	Kent
More Hall Convent graceandcompassion benedictines.org	Stroud	Gloucestershire

List of Selected Monasteries with Oblate Programmes

Prinknash Abbey prinknashabbey.org.uk	Cranham	Gloucestershire
Belmont Abbey belmontabbey.org.uk	Hereford	Herefordshire
St Cecilia's Abbey stceciliasabbey.org.uk	Ryde	Isle of Wight
Quarr Abbey quarrabbey.co.uk	Ryde	Isle of Wight
Glenstal Abbey glenstal.org	Murroe	Co. Limerick Eire
Ealing Abbey members.aol.com/ealingmonk	Ealing	London
Edgware Abbey london.anglican.org/ religiouscommunities#abc	Edgware	London
Monastery of Christ the King church-of-christ-the-king.com	Cockfosters	London
Tyburn Convent tyburnconvent.org.uk	Marble Arch	London
Holy Cross Convent	Rempstone	Loughborough
Pluscarden Abbey pluscardenabbey.org	Elgin	Morayshire, Scotland
Burford Priory burfordosb.org.uk	Burford	Oxfordshire
Holy Trinity Monastery benedictinenuns.org.uk	East Hendred	Oxfordshire
Downside Abbey downside.co.uk	Stratton-on- the-Fosse	Somerset
Colwich Abbey colwichabbey.org.uk	Colwich	Staffordshire
Stanbrook Abbey stanbrookabbey.org.uk	Callow End	Worcestershire
Ampleforth Abbey ampleforth.org.uk	York	Yorkshire

Appendix 2

Selected Australia and New Zealand Benedictine Monasteries

(Organized by location, January 2008)

Jamberoo Abbey jamberooabbey.org.au	Jerberoo	NSW
St Benedict's Monastery goodsams.org.au	Glebe Point	NSW
Southern Star Abbey kopua-abbey.co.nz	Hawle's Bay	NZ
Holy Trinity Abbey newnorcia.wa.edu.au	New Norcia	WA

Appendix 3

Further Resources

Bibliography

Patrick Barry OSB et al., *Wisdom from the Monastery: The Rule of St Benedict for Everyday Life*, Canterbury Press, Norwich, 2005.

Jean-François Baudoz, *With Christ: The Gospel under the Guidance of St Benedict*, Liturgical Press, Collegeville MN.

Benedictine Daily Prayer: A Short Breviary, Columba Press, Dublin, 2005.

Benedictine Handbook, The, Canterbury Press, Norwich, 2003.

Robert A. Benson, *Good Life: Benedict's Guide to Everyday Joy*, Paraclete Press, Brewster MA, 2004.

Carol Bonomo, *Humble Pie: St Benedict's Ladder of Humility*, Morehouse Publishing, Harrisburg NY and London, 2004.

Marianne Burkhard Böckmann OSB and Matilda Handl, *Perspectives on the Rule of St Benedict: Expanding Our Hearts in Christ*, Liturgical Press, Collegeville MN, 2005.

Carmen Acevedo Butcher, *A Life of St Benedict: Man of Blessing*, Paraclete Press, Brewster MA, 2006.

Columba Cary-Elwes OSB and Catherine Wybourne OSB, *Work and Prayer: The Rule of St Benedict for Lay People*, Burns & Oates, Tunbridge Wells, 1992.

Michael Casey OCSO, *Truthful Living: St Benedict's Teaching on Humility*, Gracewing, Leominster, 1999.

Michael Casey OCSO, *Strangers to the City: A Voice from the Monastery*, Paraclete Press, Brewster MA, 2005.

Joan Chittister OSB, *The Rule of Benedict: Insights for the Ages*, Crossroad, New York, 1992.

Lonni Collins Pratt and Daniel Homan OSB, *Benedict's Way: An Ancient Monk's Insights for a Balanced Life*, Loyola Press, Chicago IL, 2000.

Elizabeth J. Cranham, *Heart Whispers: Benedictine Wisdom for Today*, Eagle, Guildford, and Upper Room Press, Nashville TN, 1999.

Guerric de Bona OSB, *Praying with the Benedictines: A Window on the Cloister*, Paulist Press, New York, 2007.

Adalbert de Vogüé, *The Rule of St Benedict: A Doctrinal and Spiritual*

Commentary, Cistercian Publications, Kalamazoo MI, 1983.

Adalbert de Vogüé, *Reading St Benedict: Reflections on the Rule*, Cistercian Publications, Kalamazoo MI, 1994.

Esther de Waal, Seeking God: *The Way of St Benedict*, Canterbury Press, Norwich, 1984.

Esther de Waal, *Living with Contradiction: Benedictine Wisdom for Everyday Living*, Canterbury Press, Norwich, 1989.

Esther de Waal, Seeking God: *A Commentary on the Rule of St Benedict*, Mowbray, London and New York, 1995.

Esther de Waal, *A Life-Giving Way: A Commentary on the Rule of St Benedict*, Continuum, London and New York, 1995.

Eric Dean, *St Benedict for the Laity*, Liturgical Press, Collegeville MN, 1989.

Wil Derkse, *The Rule of Benedict for Beginners: Spirituality for Daily Life*, Liturgical Press, Collegeville MN, 2003.

Wil Derkse, *A Blessed Life: Benedictine Guidelines for Those Who Long for Good Days*, Liturgical Press, Collegeville MN, 2009.

Demetrius Dumm OSB, *Cherish Christ above All: The Bible in the Rule of St Benedict*, Gracewing, Leominster, 1996.

Mary C. Earle, *Beginning Again: Benedictine Wisdom for Living with Illness*, Morehouse Publishing, Harrisburg NY and London, 2004.

Vena Eastwood, *Benedict Rules – OK: Daily Reading of the Rule of St Benedict for Young People*, Gracewing, Leominster, 2001.

David Hugh Farmer (ed.), *Benedict's Disciples*, Gracewing, Leominster, 1980.

Hugh Feiss OSB, *Essential Monastic Wisdom*, HarperCollins, 1999.

David Foster, *Reading with God: Lectio Divina*, Continuum, 2005.

The Glenstal Book of Prayers: A Benedictine Prayer Book, Columba Press, Dublin, 2001.

Anselm Grün OSB, *Benedict of Nursia: His Message for Today*, Liturgical Press, Collegeville MN, 2006.

Jeremy Hall, *Silence, Solitude, Simplicity: A Hermit's Love Affair with a Noisy, Crowded and Complicated World*, Liturgical Press, Collegeville MN, 2007.

Patrick Hart OCSO (ed.), *A Monastic Vision for the Twenty-First Century: Where Do We Go from Here?* Cistercian Publications, Kalamazoo MN, 2006.

Albert Holtz OSB, *Pilgrim Road: A Benedictine Journey through Lent*, Morehouse Publishing, Harrisburg NY and London, 2006.

Daniel Homan OSB and Lonni Collins Pratt, *Radical Hospitality: Benedict's Way of Love*, Paraclete Press, Brewster MA, 2002.

Katherine Howard, *Praying with Benedict*, Word Among Us Press, Jamsville MD, 1996.

Further Resources

Denis Huerre OSB, *Letters to My Brothers and Sisters: Living by the Rule of St Benedict*, Liturgical Press, Collegeville MN, 1994.

Basil Hume OSB, *In Praise of Benedict*, Gracewing, Leominster, 1995.

Christopher Jamison OSB, *Finding Sanctuary: Monastic Steps for Everyday Life*, Phoenix, London, 2007.

Laurentia Johns OSB (ed.), *Touched by God: Ten Monastic Journeys*, Continuum, London , 2008.

Terrence Kardong OSB, *The Benedictines*, Liturgical Press, Collegeville MN, 1992.

Terrence Kardong OSB, *Day by Day with St Benedict*, Liturgical Press, Collegeville MN, 2005.

Terrence Kardong OSB, *Benedict's Rule: A Translation and Commentary*, Liturgical Press, Collegeville MN, 1996.

Francis Klein OCSP, *Lovers of Place: Monasticism Loose in the World*, Liturgical Press, Collegeville MN, 1997.

Linda Kulzer and Roberta Bondi (eds), *Benedict in the World: Portraits of Monastic Oblates*, Liturgical Press, Collegeville MN, 2002.

Jean Leclercq OSB, *The Love of Learning and the Desire for God: A Study of Monastic Culture*, Fordham University Press, New York, 1961.

Dwight Longenecker, *Listen My Son : St Benedict for Fathers*, Gracewing, Leominster, 2000.

John McQuistin II, *Always We Begin Again: The Benedictine Way of Living*, Morehouse Publishing, Harrisburg PN, 1996.

Mariano Magrassi, *Praying with Bible: An Introduction to Lectio Divina*, Liturgical Press, Collegeville MN, 1998.

Thomas Merton, *Basic Principles of Monastic Spirituality*, Templegate, Springfield IL, 1996.

Augustine Morris OSB, *Oblates: Life with St Benedict*, Elmore Abbey, Newbury, 1992.

Kathleen Norris, *The Cloister Walk*, Riverhead, New York, 1996.

Kathleen Norris, *Amazing Grace: A Vocabulary of Faith*, Lion, Oxford, 1998.

Dennis Okham, *Monk Habits for Everyday People: Benedictine Spirituality for Protestants*, Brazos Press, Grand Rapids MI, 2007.

Guy-Marie Oury OSB, *A Monastic Pilgrimage: Following in the Steps of St Benedict*, St Bede Publications, Petersham MA, 1998.

David Parry OSB (trans.), *The Rule of St Benedict: Introduction and Commentary by Esther de Waal*, Gracewing, Leominster, 1990.

Basil M. Pennington OCSO, *Listen with Your Heart: Spiritual Living the Rule of St Benedict*, Paraclete Press, Brewster MA, 2007.

RB 1980: The Rule of St Benedict, Liturgical Press, Collegeville MN, 1982.

RB 1980: The Rule of St Benedict in Latin and English with Notes, Liturgical Press, Collegeville MN, 1981.

David Robinson, *The Family Cloister*, Crossroad, New York, 2000.

Appendix 3

Cyprian Smith OSB, *The Path of Life: Benedictine Spirituality for Monks and Lay People*, Ampleforth Abbey, York, 1995.

Rachel M. Srubas, *Oblation: Meditations on St Benedict's Rule*, Paraclete Press, Brewster MA, 2006.

Julian Stead OSB, *Saint Benedict: A Rule for Beginners*, New City Press, New York, 1994.

Columba Stewart OSB, *Prayer and Community: The Benedictine Tradition*, Darton, Longman & Todd, London, 1998.

Brian C. Taylor, *Spirituality for Everyday Living: An Adaptation of the Rule of St Benedict*, Liturgical Press, Collegeville MN, 1989.

Ambrose Tinsley OSB, *Carried by the Current: A Benedictine Perspective*, Columba Press, Dublin, 2004.

Jane Tomaine, *St Benedict's Toolbox: The Nuts and Bolts of Everyday Benedictine Living*, Morehouse Publishing, Harrisburg NY and London, 2005.

Benet Tvedten OSB, *The View from the Monastery: The Vowed Life and Its Cast of Many Characters*, Paraclete Press, Brewster MA, 1999.

Benet Tvedten OSB, *How to be a Monastic and Not Leave Your Day Job: An Invitation to Oblate Life*, Paraclete Press, Brewster MA, 2006.

Benet Tvedten OSB, *The Motley Crew: Monastic Lives*, Liturgical Press, Collegeville MN, 2007.

Korneel Vermeiren OCSO, *Praying with Benedict: Prayer in the Rule of St Benedict*, Cistercian Publications, Kalamazoo MI, 1999.

Norvene Vest, *Preferring Christ: A Devotional Commentary on the Rule of St Benedict*, Morehouse Publishing, Harrisburg NY and London, 1990.

Norvene Vest, *No Moment Too Small: Rhythms of Silent Prayer and Holy Reading*, Cowley Publications, Boston MA, 1994.

Norvene Vest, *Friend of the Soul: Benedictine Spirituality of Work*, Cowley Publications, Boston MA, 1997.

Norvene Vest, *Desiring Life: Benedict on Wisdom and the Good Life*, Cowley Publications, Cambridge MA, 2000.

Hannah Ward and Jennifer Wild (eds), *The Monastic Way – Ancient Wisdom for Contemporary Living: A Book of Daily Readings*, Canterbury Press, Norwich, 2006.

Work of God: Benedictine Prayer, Liturgical Press, Collegeville MN, 1997.

Websites

Some websites that oblates might find useful:

Oblates – general information
http://www.osb.org/obl/index.html

Oblates International Congress
http://www.benedictine-oblates.org

Benedictine Online Oblate Program
http://www.yanktonbenedictines.org/oblates_booc_intro.html

Oblate Forum
http://www.oblateforum.org

Oblate Group
http://groups.yahoo.com/group/monasticlife/

Benedictine Distance Learning
http://www.idahomonks.org/bdl.htm

British and Irish oblates
http://www.benedictine-oblates.net

North American Association of Oblate Directors
http://www.naabod.org

Daily liturgical texts
http://www.universalis.com

Lectio divina
http://www.valyermo.com/ld-art.html

MONOS – A Centre for the Study of Monastic Culture and Spirituality
http://www.monos.org.uk

Appendix 4

The Medal of St Benedict

Benedictine oblates are often presented with the medal of St Benedict at the ceremony where they are admitted to their oblate novitiate or candidacy. The medal may be worn on a chain around the neck, or pinned to one's clothing. Sometimes it is hung on the wall at home or at the workplace, or carried in the car; it is not unknown for it to be buried in the foundations of a house or barn.

The medal affirms our identity as followers of St Benedict in the school of the Lord's service. Its purpose is to call down God's blessing and protection upon us, wherever we are, and upon our homes, through the intercession of St Benedict. It is a prayer that the cross of Christ be our light and our guide, a prayer for strength in time of temptation and of firm rejection of all that is evil, a prayer for peace among ourselves and among the nations of the world, a prayer that we may courageously walk in God's ways, with the gospel as our guide, as St Benedict urges us.

We do not know just when the first medal of St Benedict was struck. For the early Christians, the cross was a favourite sign and badge of their faith in Christ. Devotion to the cross of Christ also gave rise to the striking of medals that bore the image of St Benedict holding a cross aloft in his right hand and his rule for monasteries in his left hand. The cross has always been closely associated with the medal of St Benedict, which is sometimes referred to as the medal-cross of St Benedict. In the course of time other additions were made, such as the Latin petition on its margin. At some point in history a series of capital letters was placed around the large figure of the cross on the reverse side of the medal. For a long time the meaning of these letters was unknown, but in 1647 a manuscript dating back to 1415 was found at the Abbey of Metten in Bavaria giving an explanation of the letters. They are the initial letters of a Latin prayer of exorcism against Satan.

These features were incorporated in a newly designed medal struck in 1880 under the supervision of the monks of Monte Cassino, Italy, to mark the fourteen-hundredth anniversary of the birth of St Benedict. The design of this medal was produced at St Martin's Archabbey, Beuron, Germany, at the request of the prior of Monte Cassino. Since that time, the Jubilee Medal of 1880 has proven to be more popular throughout the Christian world than any other medal struck to honour St Benedict.

Description of the Jubilee Medal

The cross of eternal salvation

On the face of the medal is the image of St Benedict. In his right hand he holds the cross, the Christian symbol of salvation. The cross reminds us of the zealous work of evangelizing and the building-up of England and Europe carried out mainly by Benedictine monks and nuns, especially from the sixth to the ninth and tenth centuries.

Rule and raven

In St Benedict's left hand is his Rule for monasteries that could well be summed up in the words of the Prologue exhorting us to 'set out on this [God's] way, with the Gospel for our guide'. On a pedestal to the right of St Benedict is the poisoned cup, shattered when he made the sign of the cross over it. On a pedestal to the left is a raven about to carry away the loaf of poisoned bread that a jealous enemy sent to St Benedict. (These legends are narrated in Book II of the *Dialogues* attributed to St Gregory the Great, a work which many scholars now consider to be inauthentic and a later composition.)[1]

CSPB

Above the cup and the raven are the Latin words, *Crux S. Patris Benedicti* (The cross of our holy father Benedict). On the margin of the medal, encircling the figure of Benedict, are the Latin words, *Eius in obitu nostro praesentia muniamur!* (May we be strengthened by his presence in the hour of our death!). Benedictines have always regarded St Benedict as a special patron of a happy death.

Monte Cassino

Below Benedict we read: ex SM Cassino MDCCCLXXX (from holy Monte Cassino, 1880). This is the medal struck to commemorate the fourteen-hundredth anniversary of the birth of St Benedict.

Crux mihi lux

On the reverse of the medal the cross is dominant. On the arms of the cross are the initial letters of a rhythmic Latin prayer: *Crux sacra sit mihi lux!*

Nunquam draco sit mihi dux! (May the holy cross be my light! May the dragon never be my guide!). In the angles of the cross, the letters C S P B stand for *Crux Sancti Patris Benedicti* (The cross of our holy father Benedict).

Peace

Above the cross is the word *pax* (peace) that has been a Benedictine motto for centuries. Around the margin of the back of the medal, the letters V R S N S M V — S M Q L I V B are the initial letters of a Latin prayer of exorcism against Satan: *Vade retro Satana! Nunquam suade mihi vana! Sunt mala quae libas. Ipse venena bibas!* (Be gone Satan! Never tempt me with your vanities! What you offer me is evil. Drink the poison yourself!).

It would be a valuable spiritual experience to study the array of inscriptions and representations found on the two sides of the medal. The lessons found there can be pondered over and over to bring true peace of mind and heart into our lives as we struggle to overcome the weaknesses of our human nature and realize that our human condition is not perfect, but that with the help of God and the intercession of St Benedict our lives can become better. The medal of St Benedict can serve as a constant reminder of the need for us to take up our cross daily and follow 'the true King, Christ the Lord', and thus learn to 'share in the sufferings of Christ that we may deserve also to share in his kingdom', as St Benedict urges us in the Prologue of his Rule.

Blessing prayer for medals of St Benedict

Let us pray.
Almighty God, the boundless source of all good things,
we humbly ask that, through the intercession of St Benedict,
you pour out your blessings upon these medals.
May those who use them devoutly
and who earnestly strive to perform good works
be blessed by you with health of soul and body,
the grace of a holy life,
and remission of the temporal punishment due to sin.
May they also, with the help of your merciful love,
resist the temptation of the evil one
and strive to exercise true charity and justice toward all,
so that one day they may appear sinless and holy in your sight.
This we ask through Christ our Lord.
Amen.

The medals are then sprinkled with holy water.

Notes

1 See Terrence Kardong, 'Who Wrote the *Dialogues* of St Gregory? A Report on a Controversy', in *Assumption* (Newsletter), Richardton ND, vol. 33, no. 1, January 2005.

Appendix 5

A Glossary of Benedictine Terms

Abbot/abbess goes back to the Aramaic *abba*, meaning 'father', as Jesus addressed God. Although he warned his disciples 'call no man your father on earth' (Matt. 23.9), that did not prevent the monks of the Egyptian desert from calling their elders *abba* or *amma*. The earliest monastic communities seem to have called their superior 'prior' (first), but by the time of Benedict, the leader is called abbot. The Rule (Chapter 2, first paragraph) explains that the superior is called *abba* because he represents Christ, who is our father. The monastic superior must strive to engender sons and daughters through Christ for the kingdom of God.

Cellarer comes from the Latin *cellarius* (storeroom). The qualities of the cellarer are outlined in the Rule (Chapter 31). The cellarer might be seen as the purchasing agent, or procurator, in charge of distributing the communal goods. In some circumstances this role could be likened to that of treasurer as well. Chapter 31, first paragraph, highlights the role as steward, 'regarding all utensils and goods of the monastery as sacred vessels of the altar'. The gentle, humble attitude one is to employ in this role is described clearly in Chapter 31, second paragraph.

Cenobite derives from the Greek *koinos bios* (common life) and ultimately from *koinonia*, which in Acts 2.42 means shared life in Christ. When Pachomius called his extended community in southern Egypt 'the holy koinonia', he intended the full Christian implications of the term. The Rule (Chapter 2, first paragraph) points to the same reality when it says that 'cenobites live in monasteries and serve under a rule and an abbot'. This is aimed at 'private monks', but in fact most monks before the time of Benedict, including anchorites, could be placed in that category.

Chapter. The Rule (Chapter 3), speaks of summoning the community for council. When all the professed members of a community are brought together, especially to vote, it is called a chapter. The purpose of such a meeting is to discern the spirit of God in whatever decision is being made. In his wisdom, St Benedict realized that God might reveal his will through any member of the community, regardless of the member's age.

Community of goods. St Benedict speaks out strongly against private ownership in the Rule (Chapter 33), and uses Acts 4.35 in Chapter 34 as a model for distributing goods according to need. All is to be held in common, but individuals should have the proper tools or supplies to do the job they are assigned to. This concept also appears in Chapters 54, 55 and 57. As with evangelical poverty, community of goods does not imply that the community as such is without possessions.

Compline comes from *completorium* (completion), the final office of the day. According to the Rule (Chapter 42), there was public reading before this service, with the monks gradually assembling after their day of work. Chapter 18, fourth paragraph, specifies that the same three psalms, namely 4, 90 and 133, are to be sung each night at Compline. These psalms were chosen because of their reference to evening, but also because they could be easily memorized and recited in the dark. The same custom prevails in many monasteries today. Chapter 42 demands the strictest silence after Compline.

Congregation. Benedict often calls his community *congregatio* (*con* + *grex* = gathered flock), but nowadays this term refers to a union of monasteries as mandated by the Fourth Lateran Council of 1215. According to that legislation, which was grudgingly implemented by the decentralized Benedictines, monasteries are to join together in regional associations for the purpose of mutual encouragement and discipline. The congregation must elect a president and council, who arrange for periodic chapter meetings and the visitation of individual monasteries. It is the general consensus of church historians that the congregational system has been helpful to the Benedictines.

Conversatio morum is one of three promises made at monastic profession (the Rule, Chapter 58, fourth paragraph). *Conversatio morum* means 'changing one's lifestyle'. Scholars have debated the meaning of this phrase for the last century, but the general consensus is that it refers to entering into monastic life and living it out as fully as possible.

Council. Although Benedict never uses this term, the Rule (Chapter 3, third paragraph) does speak of calling a few elders together for advice on minor matters. Modern councils, however, do a great deal of important business in the monastery. They are elected and appointed according to precise rules, and their function is governed by church and monastic law. Yet the basic dynamics of the council are still the same as laid down by Chapter 3: the abbot convenes the council and asks for its advice, which is to be given with honesty and modesty.

Appendix 5

Cowl or *Cuculla* is a formal choir robe, which may be worn over the habit or other clothes at liturgical solemnities. The Latin *cuculus* (hood) originally referred to a Roman hooded outer garment or cowl. Benedict mentions it in the Rule (Chapter 55, first paragraph). In recent tradition, it is black with 73 pleats (one for each chapter of the Rule). It is also the traditional death-shroud in many Benedictine communities. (Note that the garment monks use to cover their head is a hood, not a cowl.)

Customary. The Rule is the primary spiritual heritage of all Benedictine monasteries, but its great age makes it difficult to implement in detailed fashion. Since the early Middle Ages, monasteries have found it useful to draw up 'house rules' (*consuetudines*) to be literally observed. These customaries are less abstract and easier to amend than congregational constitutions. Customaries such as those published in *Corpus Consuetudinum Monasticarum* constitute one of our most important sources for monastic history, for they tell us how monastic life was actually lived in past ages.

Dean derives from the Latin *decanus* or *decani* (plural) and refers to one who is put in charge of a group of ten. The Rule (Chapter 21) offers the dean as an assistant to the abbot or abbess, especially in larger communities. These are to be people chosen for their skills and example, not by rank. Pachomius and John Cassian spoke of deans long before Benedict. In some larger Benedictine communities today (especially women's) the concept of living in small groups or deaneries still prevails.

Dialogues of Gregory. In AD 595, Pope Gregory I (the Great) wrote four books on Italian saints, meant to hearten the beleaguered Catholics of Italy. *Dialogue II* is entirely given over to the life of St Benedict. This account, which is full of miracles and portents, is the only written record we have of the saint. Gregory claims to have got its details from eye-witnesses, and from reading the Rule. Despite its charm and vivacity, *Dialogue II* has come in for increasing criticism by modern historians.

Divine office. The divine office, or liturgy of the hours, is the principal work of Benedictines. Early Christians prayed at morning and at evening. The concept of praying at the third, sixth and ninth hours (9 a.m., 12 p.m., 3 p.m.) was slowly added, and eventually there were seven hours of prayer in the cathedral tradition: Vigils, Lauds, Prime, Terce, Sext, None and Vespers. St Benedict introduced an eighth and final hour of Compline. Chapters 8–20 of the Rule all focus on this communal prayer, and suggest an arrangement of psalms to be used, but Benedict also recognizes (Chapter 18, sixth paragraph) that there might be a better arrangement of the psalms for different circumstances. Today some communities continue to pray the seven or eight hours, but many more communities have a modified format consisting of Morning Praise, Noon Prayer, Vespers and Compline.

Enclosure. From earliest monastic times (*Life of Pachomius*), parts of the house and grounds have been off-limits to visitors. Conversely, the Rule (Chapter 66) requires that all the necessities of life be contained in the same enclosure so that the monks need not go out, 'for that is certainly not beneficial to their souls'. Bishop Caesarius of Arles (*c.* 535) drew up strict rules of enclosure for a convent of nuns, to protect them from the increasingly turbulent public life of the Late Roman Empire. Historically, the church has required nuns to be more fully 'enclosed' than monks.

Fuga mundi literally means 'flight from the world' and was especially emphasized by the early hermits. In an effort to purify themselves from things of this world, these hermits largely shut out the world. This mentality carried into cenobitic monasticism for many years as well. But gradually, monks came to see that while they may be separated from the world by monastic enclosure, they can never be totally separate from the world, which must be embraced and prayed for.

General chapter. Every three or so years the president of a monastic congregation (with council) convenes a plenary meeting, which usually includes the superior of each member house, plus elected delegates. The general chapter is a decision-making body which alone can lay down the juridic constitution of the congregation. In addition to this, the general chapter deals with important questions involving the whole group as well as the individual houses.

Gregorian chant, or plainchant, is the name given to the homophonic music that is often associated with monasteries. Originally, these compositions were passed on aurally, but much of the music was collected, transcribed and placed in its final arrangement under the auspices of Pope St Gregory the Great (590–604). Most church music of the Middle Ages was written in this style, though some was lost in later years, and it fell out of use. In 1831, Dom Prosper Guéranger and the monks of Solesmes Abbey in France began a serious revival of plainchant. They clarified rules of performance, re-educated much of the monastic world in the manner of chant, and still constitute one of the world's great centres for chant. The importance of chant was reaffirmed in the 1967 Vatican II document, *Musicam Sacram*.

Habit. Monastic men and women have always worn a uniform of some kind to symbolize their status in the church. The ancient monks did not dress too differently from their fellow citizens, since the Rule (Chapter 55, second paragraph) directs that worn items be given to the poor. With the passing centuries, the monastic habit became more symbolic and less practical until in our own day it cannot be worn for many kinds of work. The great advantage of the habit is to increase the visibility and awareness of monastic values, both for the wearers and others.

Junior. After religious complete their novitiate, Canon Law decrees they must be temporarily professed for a period of at least three years. During this time they are usually referred to as junior members. Some women's houses use the term scholastic for this stage of formation.

Lectio divina. Literally 'godly reading', *lectio divina* meant biblical prayer for the early monks. According to the Rule (Chapter 48), *lectio* is to occupy about three hours of the day and usually the times when the mind would be most alert. Benedict says the monks should be 'free for' such pursuits, but to judge from Chapter 48 (fifth paragraph), many of them found it burdensome. *Lectio divina* requires a contemplative spirit, something difficult to maintain in activist cultures. *Lectio divina* lies at the very heart of Benedict's spirituality, and without it there is no meaningful monastic life.

Monk derives from the Greek *monachos*, and has had several different meanings in different times. In the very early church, monk may have referred to a religious hermit or anchorite; one who was alone (*monos* = one). But by the fourth century, the meaning had broadened, so that a monk might be a celibate religious, albeit living in community. While there is no exact feminine equivalent in English, nun is the closest term. Contemporary monastic writers sometimes use the term 'monastic' as an inclusive expression for monk or nun.

Novice. Before Benedict the formation of novices was intense but fairly brief; the Rule (Chapter 58) requires that it go on for a full year. Further, Benedict presents the novitiate as a well-developed institution, with a specially designated elder at its head. Throughout Benedictine history, novices were usually segregated from the rest of the community so as to inculcate monastic ideals while shielding them from some of the harsher aspects of reality. Today there is more concern to equip the novices with a spirituality that will nourish them in life as it is actually lived in the local community.

Nun. From the earliest days of desert monasticism, women have been seeking God in the same fashion as men. Pachomius built an enclosure for women, and Paula founded a women's monastery in Bethlehem. 'Nun' has obscure Egyptian roots, but may be found in second-century Greek *nonna* and fourth-century Latin *nonna* as a term of respect, meaning elder or grandmother. The Rule (Chapter 63, second paragraph) uses the male form *nonnus* in referring to the elders of the community as 'venerable father'. In strictest terms, 'nun' is a religious professing solemn vows and living within an enclosed monastery.

Obedience. From its very first lines (Prologue, first paragraph), the Rule insists that obedience is the way for sinners to return to God. For Benedict's monks, that largely means obedience to the abbot as interpreter of the Rule

A Glossary of Benedictine Terms

(Chapter 1, first paragraph). Following *The Rule of the Master*, Chapter 5 lays great emphasis on instant obedience as symbolic of a willing spirit. Yet Benedict goes beyond the Master in allowing a certain amount of dialogue in response to hard commands (Chapter 68). In addition, Chapters 71–72 speak of the 'mutual obedience' that cenobites owe one another, a thing that many monks find harder than 'vertical' obedience.

Oblate. People who believe that the Rule has value for them as they live out their daily lives become connected to a monastery as oblates, associates or third order members. They may reside at the monastery (tertiary or claustral oblates), or they may live out and work away from the monastery (lay oblates). Individuals make a temporary commitment to live out the Rule as their state in life permits. The only oblation Benedict refers to is that of children presented to the monastery in Chapter 59.

Ora et labora. 'Pray and work' is often put forward as the Benedictine motto, but this word combination is found nowhere in the Rule. Still, the three-word motto is useful as an expression of the Benedictine instinct for a balanced life that gives both the active and contemplative dimensions their proper place. If one were to base *ora et labora* loosely on Chapter 48, then it would have to be expanded to 'Pray, read and work', for Benedict's stress on *lectio divina* is more challenging to modern Western culture than his parallel emphasis on work.

Ordo. The Rule (Chapter 63), on community rank states, 'The monks keep their rank in the monastery according to the date of their entry, the virtue of their lives, and the decision of the abbot.' Using this system of rank, communal members ate in order, sat in order, communicated in order, so that they never lost sight of their rank. The Rule insists that the juniors pay respect and reverence to the elders. A second usage of ordo refers to a liturgical directory of all the daily readings for Mass and divine office.

Postulant is not an ancient term, but the reality is present in all the old Rules with people who first show up at the door. Invariably, they are to be tested for a few days in their resolve to endure the rigours of the monastic life (the Rule, Chapter 58, first paragraph) and then admitted to the novitiate. In our time, postulancy is more protracted but also gentler, with more stress on the discernment to be exercised by the individual as well as by the community.

Prior/prioress. One would think that prior and prioress would have parallel meanings, but this has not been the case throughout most of monastic history. In the Rule (Chapter 65), the prior is a monk appointed by the abbot to help him lead and govern the community. When Benedictine women came to the United States and formed new communities, they lost the right to be called abbeys, because they did not conform to the strict rules of enclosure enforced in Europe. Hence, the elected head of these communities is not called abbess but prioress. The second has become the first.

Profession. Benedict speaks of 'promises' in the Rule (Chapter 58), yet if a vow is an irrevocable promise made to God, then Chapter 58 (fourth paragraph) suggests that is what has taken place. Contemporary Benedictines actually make vows twice, the first time after the novitiate and in temporary form. After another period of formation (at least three years), monastics may petition the community for final profession as life-members of the community. The present-day profession ceremony still resembles that described in the fourth paragraph.

Promise is made by an oblate to follow the Rule of St Benedict in their private life as closely as their individual circumstances permit. The promise effects an oblate's spiritual association with a particular monastic community. (See also **Vows**.)

Rule of St Benedict is one of the two dozen or so monastic Rules that have come down to us from ancient times, and it is also the most famous and influential. Consisting of 73 chapters and in total length comparable to one of the Gospels, the Rule was probably written for Monte Cassino in about AD 540. We have no evidence of any other monastery following this Rule before about AD 700, but when Charlemagne wished to reform and standardize the monasteries of his empire in the early ninth century, he chose the Rule as the standard. He probably did so in order to capitalize on its Roman cachet, but subsequent monastic history has deemed it one of the best balanced and most evangelical of Christian monastic Rules.

Senior carries a multitude of meanings in the Rule. The title for one who has been a member of community and lived the monastic life for some time, and should be respected, is referred to in Chapter 63, Chapter 3 (third paragraph), Chapter 21 (first paragraph), Chapter 48 (fifth paragraph), Chapter 58 (second paragraph). It may also refer to the elderly and infirm members of the community, or to the wise *senpectae* (Chapter 27) who may be sent to help a troubled monk.

Sister. For most of their history, Benedictine women have been 'nuns', that is, enclosed religious living a contemplative life. With the coming of the Enlightenment in Europe, and especially in the pioneer church of the United States, some Benedictine nuns were virtually forced to engage in work outside the cloister. This prompted the Vatican to deny them the right to make solemn vows, and even to use the term 'nun'. In recent years, however, the Benedictine nuns and sisters have rediscovered their common vision, calling the terminology itself into question.

Stability is the first of three promises that a Benedictine makes at profession (the Rule, Chapter 58). It is a commitment to live out life as a Benedictine within a particular monastery. This is both a spiritual and geographical commitment, calling the monk to continue the daily living of monastic life (Prologue, eighth paragraph). This promise is very different from the lifestyle of a wandering monk of Benedict's day, or that of many contemporary religious congregations, where a person may be assigned to any number of religious houses throughout their lifetime. Stability is the 'till death do us part' aspect of monastic profession.

Statio. The place where monks or nuns line up in order before processing into choir. It allows for a few moments of reflection before beginning the Work of God.

Suscipe. Suscipe me domine is the Latin translation of Psalm 119.116, 'Uphold me according to your promise, that I may live, and let me not be put to shame in my hope.' After a monk reads and signs his or her monastic profession formula, this versicle is repeated three times by the individual making final vows, and the community echoes back in response. The procedure is described in the Rule (Chapter 58, fourth paragraph).

Table reading. Chapter 38 of the Rule is entirely devoted to table reading, a practice found in most monasteries throughout history. Table reading originally seems to have been an extension of the liturgy of the word at Mass, centred on the Bible. In *The Rule of the Master*, the brothers are encouraged to ask questions about the reading, and the abbot discourses freely on it. In contrast, Benedict wants general silence and laconic remarks at most from the abbot. Modern table reading often goes beyond scripture to secular works of interest to the community.

Vespers. This term for evening prayer derives from the Latin, *vespertina synaxis.* Morning prayer and Vespers are the two hours of prayer most commonly prayed within Benedictine houses as well as the broader church. In the cathedral style of office, Vespers used psalms with night images, but Benedict had another approach. He assigned the psalms in consecutive order, disregarding their content. The Rule (Chapter 18, fourth paragraph) suggests the use of Psalms 109–147 at this time of prayer. The proposed structure for vespers is given in Chapter 17 (third paragraph), consisting of four psalms, a lesson, response, hymn, Magnificat and a litany.

Visitation. Since Benedictine monasteries are largely autonomous, some form of outside reference seems necessary to prevent them from becoming decadent or myopic. The congregational system mandated by Lateran IV (1215) includes periodic inspection of monasteries by designated outside monastic observers to check on the quality of monastic life. Modern visitations include oversight of local finances. Special visitations are sometimes called for monasteries that find themselves in serious difficulties.

Vows. While the evangelical counsels of poverty, chastity and obedience are implied in monastic profession, in the Rule (Chapter 58, fourth paragraph) the monk actually promises stability, *conversatio morum* and obedience. Benedict uses 'promise', but the word most now commonly associated with profession is 'vow'. Currently American Benedictine women are re-examining the complex etymology of 'promise' and 'vow' to determine which will be used in their future. (See also **Promise**.)